Growing Up FISHER

Growing Up FISHER

Musings, Memories, and Misadventures

JOELY FISHER

wm
WILLIAM MORROW
An Imprint of HarperCollins*Publishers*

The names and identifying characteristics of some of the individuals featured throughout this book have been changed to protect their privacy.

Page 309 serves as a continuation of the copyright page.

HarperCollins books may be purchased for educational, business, or sales promotional use. For information, please email the Special Markets Department at SPsales@harpercollins.com.

A hardcover edition of this book was published in 2017 by William Morrow, an imprint of HarperCollins Publishers.

FIRST WILLIAM MORROW PAPERBACK EDITION PUBLISHED 2018.

Designed by Bonni Leon-Berman

Library of Congress Cataloging-in-Publication Data has been applied for.

ISBN 978-0-06-269556-7

18 19 20 21 22 LSC 10 9 8 7 6 5 4 3 2 1

This book is dedicated to my mother,
my daughters, and my sisters.

Carrie . . . my pavement

Tricia Leigh . . . my true mirror

and my "sistahs,"
my girlfriends and the women of the world,
for showing me what I can be and
for letting me show you who
I truly am.

ele

CONTENTS

Introduction 1

Chapter 1: The Road Is My Middle Name 7

Chapter 2: The Fishbowl 28

Chapter 3: Hail Connie Full of Grace 42

Chapter 4: Oh My Papa 71

Chapter 5: *Les Animaux:* It's a Zoo in Here 91

Chapter 6: Mother . . . Daughter . . . Sister . . . Fisher 98

Chapter 7: 243 Delfern 122

Chapter 8: Always a Soubrette, Never an Ingénue 143

Chapter 9: I'm Not a Lesbian . . . But I Play with One on TV 164

Chapter 10: The Courtship of Eddie's Daughter 185

Chapter 11: The Apple Doesn't Fall Apart Very Far from the Tree 213

Chapter 12: Leading Lady Plays House 231

Chapter 13: Blind Trust 253

Chapter 14: Come Fly with Me 275

Chapter 15: #CarrieOn 280

Chapter 16: Home 295

Chapter 17: After Thoughts 300

Acknowledgments 307

Credits 309

Growing Up FISHER

INTRODUCTION

Dear Ones,

My blood pressure is high, no, like legit . . . I've seen a cardiologist. A goddamned cardiologist . . . (no disrespect to doctors who take care of the literal drumbeats of life). You can imagine my dismay at my "numbers." I checked . . . just for shits and giggles. Or that's what I told myself. You know, Connie had a stroke last year and the Princess died at sixty. *We* have this "disease" in our hearts . . . the same one that makes fatherless children spend their lives replacing their nebulous patriarchal ideals with, thus far, a prescription of drugs, sex, shopping, fame, and people. As it turns out, the pharmacist has something for this (as opposed to the scripts I've written myself over the years). So, now, with lisinopril coursing through my veins . . . I've normalized my tempo and can rejoin the #Resistance.

Carrie died again today . . . and once again the world is off its axis. This time she was taken from us at the Fisher-Reynolds public memorial at Forest Lawn, and it was live-streamed for the world. I have spoken repeatedly about the fact that my sister—nothing half about her—was my mirror . . . When we look into reflective glass, we don't always like what we see. But we can't deny the truth it reveals to us, and that's the root of its power—or *her* power. What we're all now missing.

The sorrow is unparalleled, unimaginable, unenviable, undeniable . . . all the uns . . . without any of the fun. In this galaxy, not at all far away . . . I haven't even gotten started honoring my sister Carrie. And the story is so much bigger than just one Princess, brilliant and irreplaceable as she was.

Part of her I did idolize, and part of her I wanted to teach, to hold, and to save.

I keep telling myself I'm not gonna cry anymore . . . that's a lie . . . it doesn't stop. I've made screenshots of our final, cross-Atlantic text exchange, saving it to multiple backup hard drives, and I continue to cling to it as the last vestige of a connection with her. It's unfathomable—the idea that I can no longer reach her through the Twittersphere, or hear the dulcet tones we all shared on the other end, where she used to call me on the hell phone. That my not-so-smartphone serves me no longer in reaching the third member of our trio of Fish Girls. I am dying to—scratch that—I am living to report back on, well . . . *everything,* to the woman who spoke to so many. She made words dance. She made flawed a museum-quality art form. She made me feel triumphant and normal. No small feat.

Here's what I've decided. I cannot, nor would I ever attempt to, share intimate details of Carrie's life. First, there are so many who knew her far better than I did. And, let's face it, we have a lifetime of her own writings that are revelations. When you're feeling like you need to spend some time with her, you've got those.

But, since I've been given a whole book to air my filthy fluff-'n'-fold, I will tell the tale, not just of the ones who've left us, but of all the women in this unconventional un-family . . . tell how we all spent our lives living up to expectations, and living down the Fisher foibles and falls from grace . . . How about the man who gave us the Fisher moniker, the addicted playboy with the velvet voice, whom my mom still describes as "delicious" to this day? Let's talk about the legacy he bequeathed to us: the fucking voice, but also the genetic predisposition for addiction, infidelity, and financial idiosyncrasy. Lucky us! And lucky me, I was able to take these gifts and actually use them to ride the ups and downs of a career of my own—in television, in film, and on the Broadway stage. In the late nineties, it was super generous of Ellen DeGeneres—and her sitcom alter ego, Ellen Morgan—to let me and my more self-assured, self-centered, selfie self, Paige Clarke, be an integral part of her in-tandem coming-out soiree. One hundred thirteen episodes, sharing the screen with the world's most famous girl kisser . . . I mean, Medal of Freedom winner. I got to be the bestie!

There is that something in our DNA, a gift with purchase, that links us, and makes us better able to navigate, with incredible candor and wit, the experience of growing up in the "Fishbowl." Swimming through the constant deluge of questions, doing a full-time talk show, from the mall to the PTA:

What's it like to be the daughter of? What's it like to have a sister who's a Princess? What's it like to be a working actress? What's it like to balance marriage, career, parenting, and now, mothering your own mother?

And since I only speak in sound bites, it's incredibly—just as you would imagine—strenuous . . . lots of "heavy lifting." It's also much like your life, like anyone's life. Same issues, different square footage.

You can't "right" this shit, but you can "write" it. So that's what I'm going to do here. The loss of Sissy Fish and Mama Debs was the instigating factor for why I've invited you all in. But I've always written. All of us have. It's a fundamental Fisher tool for processing life's events.

And I'd already been thinking about the "family business" and searching for Joely Fisher in the past few years. My own mother, Connie Stevens, suffered a stroke in January 2016, just as we were in the process of selling our estate on Delfern Drive, the house that had symbolized, for her, a lifetime of hard work and spectacular achievement. For me, it was more than that—it symbolized home. I white-knuckled these experiences with my sister Tricia Leigh. Especially as they happened in the midst of my own financial forensic fiasco. During which I was forced to confront another Fisher trait: giving away the milk (money) for free; trusting husbands, business mismanagers, and shady Hollywood types, and literally paying the price. Something like this has happened to all the ladies in this family, so you'd think we'd all have a black belt in rock bottom. And yes, being stripped down to studs, I learned how to rebuild and reinvent, in part, by watching the fortitude and resilience of these divas from an era in which "diva" actually meant something.

But, still, I wake up in a perimenopausal sweat, in the middle of the night, thinking about my own mortality . . . and about legacy. And then, I was given the opportunity to express myself on the TED stage last year on my birthday. What an incredible honor. The whole idea of TED is ideas worth sharing. What ideas *do* I have worth sharing? With my daughters. With my sisters. With the women of the world—my sistahs.

A great deal, it turns out. My black belt in rock bottom is actually rainbow colored and comes with wisdom and a treasure chest of material.

Next up, the holiday season was upon us. I decided to shake my moneymaker and return to the stage after a sixteen-year absence. I was doing a play in Laguna. We were in celebration mode, and then, blindsided by unexpected tragedy and loss. I didn't have an understudy (that's not a metaphor, but it could be). So I wrestled with how to memorialize Carrie, a sister I'd treasured and turned to, on occasion, in times of my deepest personal doubt. Fittingly, in the wings of the stage on which I was performing. I acted like my heart wasn't broken during the moments I was in the spotlight, and then retreated to the shadows to attempt to express a fraction of what I was feeling, of what I knew we were all feeling. In my piece, which was published by *The Hollywood Reporter,* I proclaimed that my mission moving forward—which I've chosen to accept—is to press through grief, for myself, and my whole family. And especially, to make sure my niece Billie . . . my sister's self-proclaimed crowning achievement . . . is whole, which she's already on the way to being. Whole, and a whole lot more.

The piece went viral. And so, in a way, other members of my royal family, falling on their proverbial sword, presented me with the most cathartic gift—the opportunity to speak my truth. (I can hear, in that Fisher gravel that we all know so well, the words "You're welcome.")

So here we are. This is my story . . . well, my stories. A collection of musings, and memories, and misadventures, in a miraculous mash-up. See what I did there? I invite you to consume the selections on my menu. Take the journey through the delights, and the dark side, of Growing Up Fisher. Put together the puzzle that is formed from these pieces. The overall image is love.

If, perchance, I've ever made you laugh with my interpretation of a broad on TV . . . If I've caused a stir when speaking passionately on things I care about . . . If you've heard me belt out a Broadway ballad and recognized, in the timbre, a comfortable old friend . . . If you dig the fact that I've made a silk purse out of a sow's ear, while maintaining a two-decade marriage and creating a blended family with the precision of a *chef du Cordon Bleu* . . . If it impresses you that, as a family in a fishbowl, we Fishers manage to suffer through . . . I mean *spend* every holiday together . . . If you want to know the secret: I wanted to do it better, I wanted to give my children a present, caring father, and in turn, I got this great partnership (that's what you get when you don't marry Eddie Fisher). I had a baby on my bed, and then, being fortunate to have enough love to give, we added to the family by adopting our fifth child. (Oh, and did you know I am crafty, that I scrapbook, and make jewelry, and color-code my closet, and can cook a Thanksgiving turkey that would make Martha Stewart wet?) These all might be reasons for reading. I can tell you this, however. I am also desperately flawed (and desperately funny), and in the pages of this book I will show you that I am a cockeyed alchemist, with tense insensibility . . . and I'm forever straightening my crown. Welcome to the family.

Love, Joely

MARCH 2017

Chapter 1

The Road Is My Middle Name

THIS IS MY CHURCH. THE audience is filtering in . . . it's electric . . . Playbills in hand, we shuffle down the aisle and find our seats. Sliding into row F, folding down red velvet, pulling up a barstool, grabbing a folding chair, sinking into the crowd's rhythm. At once the strains of an overture, tonight's menu, the musical fare, or even just a universal A. We are in tune. I am already a mess. A spiritual hot mess. I know the lyrics to every song, much to the delight/dismay of my plus-one. "Sing it loud and there's music playing, soft, and it's almost like praying." It has always been like this for me. Captivating. Compelling. My life force. The music, it's thrilling from out here, from up there. My life has composition, a score, a soundtrack. Always.

ele

Inside the Music

When I was not yet three years old, I disappeared from backstage at Harrah's Casino in Reno, Nevada, while Connie was doing her thing onstage. This is among my earliest memories. As the story goes, my mom had taken her final bow after belting her guts out. She was wearing her sequined flame dress, and she was sexy and sweaty. These were the days of the Rat Pack, and headliners, and the showrooms, and she had a full orchestra onstage with her back then.

Our Scottish governess, Christine, approached my mom right away.

"I don't want you to get alarmed, but we can't find Joely," she said.

Of course my mom was alarmed. Very.

"What?!" Mom said. "Oh my God."

Musicians and stagehands, backup singers and dancers, everyone was enlisted in the search for Joely. And soon enough, the police were there, too, but there was no sign of me. By this point, my mom was fully freaking out. And then, the concertmistress, who was the first-chair violin and was wearing a long black gown, emerged amid the melee. She was carrying me as I slumbered.

"Shhhh," she said, hushing all those around her. "She fell asleep."

I opened my eyes, and I saw this vision before me—this sparkly, beautiful creature with tears in her eyes. My mother.

"Joely, where were you? You can't disappear like that. You made everybody worry. You have to let someone know if you go somewhere. You're just a little girl."

My response: "I wanted to hear the music from the inside."

In my quest to do just that, I had climbed into the orchestra and fallen asleep in the violin section, where the concertmistress had covered me with her dress until the end of the show.

I got a minor scolding for disappearing, but also, the admiration of a mother who saw that I would have the confidence to be led by my curiosity and to take chances. She knew she didn't have to worry about me. She realized in that moment: My path was clear. I was a seeker. And I would be that kind of artist, and human, for the rest of my life, like her. But that's when the real worry began—this career, and this life, that all of us in our family were destined for was a mixed bag—for every time you come offstage triumphant, there's a show that gets canceled. There's always someone younger—with better tits—waiting to push you down the stairs. Oh, but that's *Showgirls*. Back to me. Of course she was worried—I would be a risk taker, and sometimes I wouldn't see the danger because I would be too focused on what I was trying to accomplish. 'Cause this wouldn't be the last orchestra pit I'd climb into.

That's Entertainment

There she was. Mom. Connie. Singing "Music and the Mirror." She was wearing a black-and-white sequined gown with white marabou trim everywhere. And what she was doing onstage was as close to magic as a mere mortal could get.

I wanted that.

The faces of the audience members at their tables—men and women who were experiencing the delight of being brought inside, taken on a journey, teased. This was an intimate thing. Back then it was different. The venues where you got this kind of entertainment gave you dinner and a show, and you got to be up close. With all the spectacle today, there's a distance between the performer and the crowd. Back then you didn't wear shorts to go see the headline act in the ballrooms of these casinos. People got dressed up, had their dinner, and their two-drink-minimum Tom Collinses, and settled in for an evening of raucous entertainment, close up to the stage. And Connie made them all a part of it all. She was a wizard at this. The audience knew what they were coming for, and she always delivered.

Now listen, I also saw what it did for her—to her. And I was like: *I gotta get me some of that.* 'Cause it was almost a sexual thing. It was definitely sensual. The song choices she made, which were very contemporary for that time. She always said: "I'm not nostalgic." She was ahead of her time in her eclectic choices, which were sometimes met with criticism, because everyone wanted to hear her sing "Sixteen Reasons." But she had sixteen reasons why she should sing songs by Billy Joel, the Eagles, the Doobie Brothers instead. She was a fan, and she wanted to curate a show filled with music that inspired and moved *her.* It wasn't always what the audience thought they wanted, but she wooed them, won them over with her set list, her sensibility, her sexual, sensual performance. It was electric.

There was also the way she communicated with her band; the way she flirted . . . with everyone. I was enamored, immediately. And I definitely wanted to emulate her. That's what I was after in my life, too. There was nothing else I wanted to do, ever. Well, I did want to be the cruise director for the Love Boat, like Julie McCoy, but come on, *that's* show business.

Even before I'd ever been onstage myself, I had the bug. It was partly a desire for what my mom created out there. And partly a desire just to be near her. On multiple occasions, I could be heard wailing through the halls of LAX as my mom boarded planes. It didn't help that our governess for most of my childhood—nine years in all—was a Scottish woman named Helena. She was Mary Poppins meets Nurse Ratched. Let's just say she had a heavy hand when it came to disciplining me, whether because she was jealous, or she thought I was getting away with more than I should have, or she was just a person with issues, or she preferred my sister. It may have been all of these things. It definitely didn't make me eager to be left alone with her when Connie was on the road. And to this day, I still get PTSD flashbacks whenever I hear Sean Connery.

As was our family ritual, Helena had brought Tricia and me to the airport so we could say our good-byes to Connie. You remember—people actually used to do that. When it was time for my mother to leave me behind, I couldn't bear it. Distraught, I cried, hysterically. It worked. She crouched down and pulled me into her arms.

"Come on," she said. "You don't have any stuff, but we'll get you stuff there. Tricia, how do you feel about staying home? Are you going to be okay if Joely goes?"

And the tiny little independent Capricorn soul that she was shrugged and nodded, and said, "It's okay. I'll be fine."

Thinking back, I'm sure she wasn't always . . . fine.

Relieved to be temporarily free of my nemesis, my breathing returned to normal, I happily boarded planes alongside my mother, without confessing to the real cause of my meltdown. I was afraid to tell my mother, as many kids are in situations like this, thinking it would only get worse. And having heard so many times that it was "for my own good." And perhaps the overzealous discipline, in some small way, did shape my resilience and strength of character. Many years later, Helena and I have repaired our relationship. I'm the one who always remembers her birthday.

FOR ALL THE times I remember leaving, and Tricia not going with us, we did "Three Musketeer" it for a long time. Tricia and I were definitely partners in crime. When we traveled with Connie, we sometimes sat in our reserved seats down front. But we could be found most nights backstage, in the wings. On some nights, I happily sat in Connie's dressing room and listened to my mom on the monitors as she did her whole show. I put all the makeup she had used back for her, cleaning the brushes, replacing the caps, creating an elaborate mosaic of powders and creams on her dressing table.

My sister and I could have done every song, every joke, every nuance. On the rare occasion when Connie didn't do her act verbatim, Tricia and I gave each other a knowing glance. Year after year, every night, there was a bit in my mom's act where she would invite two guys from the audience up onstage to sing with her. They were *never* "plants." These were real, unsuspecting Connie Stevens fans, who had hit the jackpot.

"Come on up here, come on up here," she said, inviting two gentlemen up.

Some bounded up to the stage, and others she had to convince or drag. She always checked in with their "dates" for permission, reading them, too. From this first interaction, she could already tell how the bit would go.

Making it, all the while, seem spontaneous and fresh, she'd ask for their names, get them to talk into the mic. She'd introduce them to the room. To the band. To each other.

"I have an idea," she said, as if it really had just dawned on her. "Wanna hear Bill and Joe sing?"

The audience enthusiastically responded.

Playing with the guys, she drew them into the plan.

"Let's do an easy one," she said. "'Close to You.' Everybody knows that one."

"Guys, 'Close to You,'" she said, cuing the band.

Connie took Bill and Joe by the hand, and the three of them swayed onstage to the music.

"First thing I gotta teach you is how to get loose . . . next you learn how to take a little bow, in case you gotta get off fast," she said, demonstrating for them, to much laughter from the audience.

Then she led the first guy through the first verse. Turned to the second.

"If you get nervous, give my hand a little squeeze," she said. "Ow."

Sometimes, the man hadn't even squeezed.

Most times.

Drawing a raucous laugh from the audience and beaming, as if she'd just thought of the joke in that moment and was thrilled it had landed so well. No matter what happened, she could turn it around and bring it back to life, like she did with everything. In forty years of Bills and Joes, she had the ability to size people up, to make everyone feel comfortable, and she knew everyone could sing. She knew that, in everyone's heart, they wanted to entertain, and for most, this was as close to their fifteen minutes as they would ever get. She was happy to give it to them.

"Big finish," she exclaimed. "They long to be close to you," they all sang as she gave them their final lesson. She took each of them by the hand, raising up their arms with a triumphant flourish, before a deep final bow, as they enjoyed their ovation.

One whole summer, Cory Wells of Three Dog Night was the show's "surprise" guest performer. He came out in the second act, and they did *The Love Medley*. It was a complete love story, told over the course of ten different songs. Connie, always ahead of her time. Each night, Tricia and I decided who would be Connie and who would be Cory. Then Tricia and I would do said love medley, from wherever we were watching the show, lick for lick.

Fantaseye. Yep, Connie's space-age show at the Aladdin Hotel in Las Vegas. Mind you, this was before *Star Wars.* Once again her thumb on the very pulse. Using a galaxy's worth of music for its theme, from the Alan Parsons Project and Earth, Wind & Fire to Gustav Holst's *The Planets,* Connie did some interstellar travel, from the planet of decadence to the planet of love—in search of the meaning of life. She communicated through song and dance with everyone she encountered—an exquisite company of twenty-five dancers. The depth of her creativity and storytelling, however kooky and odd it seemed to some, inspired me, a daughter and future entertainer.

On her visit to the planet of decadence, she encountered "The Money Machine." In her search for greater purpose, the lesson was not to get encumbered by material things.

On occasion I would say, "I want to be the money machine tonight."

In this role, I had to spit fake money—fast, fast, fast, fast—out of this little slot. One night, just as I was about to go onstage, I realized I didn't have any money. So I improvised. I pulled out a single, crumpled-up five-dollar bill from my jeans pocket, and in order to make it through the number, I slid it out *very, very slowly.* Showbiz, folks.

No direct relationship to my performance that night, but the show was met with mixed reviews. I think the prevalent reaction was: *What is Connie Stevens smoking?*

Probably the most accurate answer, around that time, would have been:

The good shit.

Before my star turn as the money machine, I'd actually already done my first number onstage with my mom. Helena had taught Tricia and me a patter song to sing for our mom. And since we were the clan we were, of course that didn't mean singing it to her at the breakfast table, or before lights-out. It meant belting it out in our natural familial habitat: onstage.

Connie beamed as she introduced us with pride. Tricia and I exchanged a quick glance and launched into the first verse.

And the second verse.

And the third verse.

Jump to the punch line—we sang all *nine* verses of that song, proudly, for our mom. She pantomimed asking forgiveness from the less-than-captivated—however captive—audience.

I'm not even going to play at the cute, innocent version of this story, either. It wasn't like I sang all nine verses because I was young and naïve and I didn't know any better. I sang all nine verses because, once I was onstage, I never wanted to leave.

My mom saw it, too.

I couldn't stop her with a train, Connie has often said of my desire to enter into the family trade. Historically, it's been said to all the Fisher girls: *I had no idea you sang. Where have you been? Under a rock?* There was no escaping. The pipes. The throaty, low timbre. The range. Both our father's velvet, golden power and the blue-eyed soulfulness of the blondes. And from this early age, I was hooked. We all saw it. We all knew this was what I was going to do. We just had to work on my material a little bit.

Not long after that, Tricia and I became a part of the act. We had charts in the orchestra book and everything. We did a duet of Barry Manilow's "Daybreak." And then, as a trio, we sang "Through the Eyes of Love," the love theme from *Ice Castles*, and "Not While I'm Around," from *Sweeney Todd*.

We've all seen the footage of my sister Carrie having the same experience in her mother Debbie's show. And now I realize, this was the standard Fisher family coming-of-age, and not without its complexities. They felt like we were good enough to be in the show. As single women, it was a way to have their family with them as they worked. We sang for our supper, quite literally.

The Gypsy

I've always had insomnia. These days, I'm up at 4:21 . . . every morning. You know, those nights when you feel like you're watching yourself *not* sleep, hovering above yourself. I see the clock. It's 2:00 A.M. It's 3:00 A.M. Now it's 4:21.

I'll just stay up.

My cell phone is down at the side of my bed, still tethered to its charger. I create a pillow barrier between my husband and me, so the light doesn't wake him. I pore over Facebook, and Twitter, and Instagram, to distract me from the pain of sleeplessness. Oh look, there's Russell's giant cat, and Spike's finished another marathon. I know my children will need me, two hours from now, to fashion a lunch and get them off to school, to be a mom.

Even when I was a little girl, I used to get up in the middle of the night. We had a lovely little place in Malibu at the time. It wasn't glamorous, really, at all. Salty and sandy, it was a beach house, period. It was right up against the ocean. The sound of the waves was constant. We got used to it, so it was like a meditation, but it was lonely to me, especially in the middle of the night. The house was shaped like a U, and I would go from one end of the U to the other and back again. And back again. I didn't need anything. I didn't know what I was looking for. I was just wandering.

My mom found me one night, when I was about ten. We sat down on the deck, with the waves crashing in front of us, the chilly night air sticky with spray from the ocean.

"What's going on, Joely?" she asked. "What's happening?"

"I don't know, I guess I just miss all the people. I want all the people."

"Maybe that's a little bit my fault that you guys have been on the road so much . . . but I gotta go to work, and I know those people are like family. I feel the same way. You know I love my band."

I smiled at her, with my freckles and crinkled-up nose.

She got it. I got it.

That was it, exactly. I missed the crowds and the chaos. And being at home meant going back to school, and it meant being a child, which I didn't feel like I was, after about the age of eight. I'd gotten my first passport at six days old, and I was much happier living out of suitcases; the frenetic pace of going from place to place. And of course, dressing rooms, and backstages, and film sets, and new cities. My mom always called me the Gypsy. Being brought into this world as an observer, as a person who wanted to know about people, and learn their stories, and eat their foods, and hear their music. Not just read about it all in books, as I would have done in the classroom.

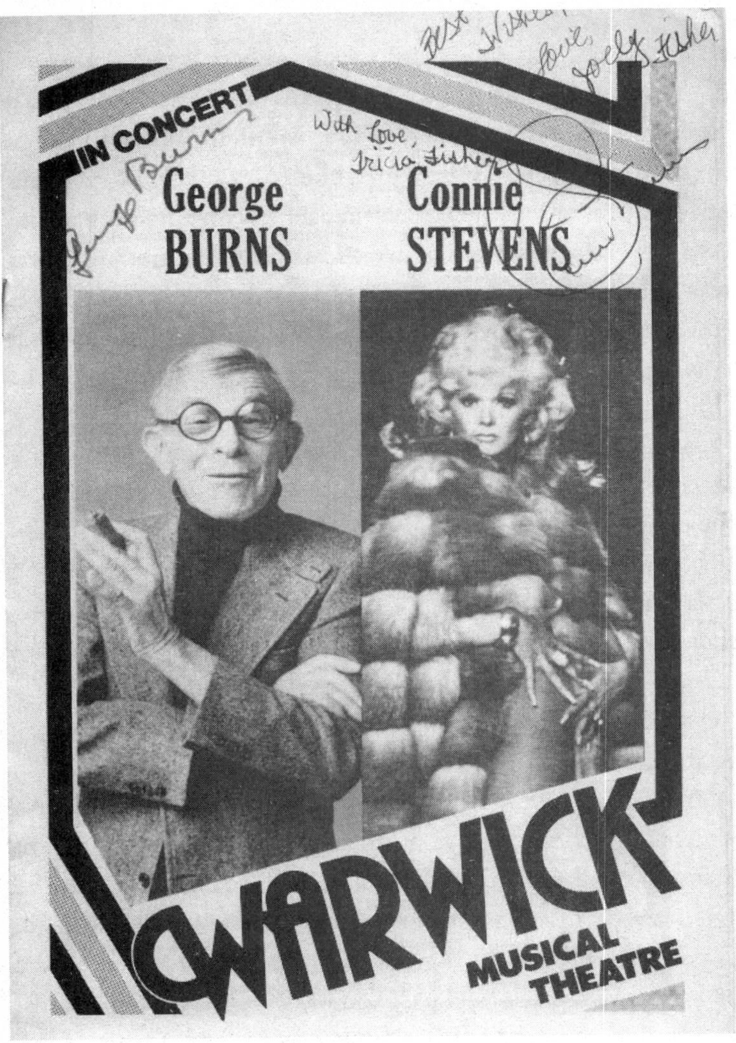

NOW THERE'S *AMERICAN IDOL* and a slew of other musical talent contests, and the prize is a fast track to stardom. I paid my dues in music tents and theaters-in-the-round along the eastern seaboard. It was the summer of 1980 when Tricia and I became an official part of my mother's act. She was on a double bill with George Burns. We spent seven weeks touring New England with him. Adventurous but not totally glamorous.

When we were driving through the night, between gigs, my sister and I slept in the luggage racks, which were like little bunks for us. We would try with all our might to stay awake to hear it all, but would fall asleep to the sound of the adults talking. We arrived at the next town—Warwick, Rhode Island; Cohasset, Massachusetts; Wallingford, Connecticut—in the wee small hours and finished out the night's sleep in the motel that would be our home for the next week. Go to the new theater, do the sound check, and then a week of shows. In the afternoons, George Burns would sit there in his skivvies and his socks with the little suspenders, no hair, having an afternoon cigar and martini out by the motel pool.

It was on those stages, singing "Through the Eyes of Love" as a trio, that I realized I was beginning to develop my own relationship with the audience. As I sang, I could feel a glimmer of the same reaction from the crowd that I'd seen my mom drawing out in people since my earliest memories. Our eyes met across the stage. She was beaming with pride. For a moment, we recognized the radiance in each other. Or was it just the sparkle of her Swarovski-encrusted strapless gown? Nah, she was proud. And I knew, someday, I was Broadway bound.

Connie's Contraband

In addition to featuring us in her show, Mom eventually figured why not enlist the girls as her background singers?

Nobody blended like the three of us. On one occasion, the planets aligned, and we all spontaneously showed up in the foyer of our Delfern house, singing the same Eagles song, "I Can't Tell You Why," in perfect three-part harmony. I always took the top.

My whole life I'd been staying up until seven o'clock in the morning and listening to the likes of Tom Jones, Phyllis Diller, and a bevy of hilarious musicians and comedians unwind after their shows, when most little girls were tucked in their beds. It certainly grew me up. But I was inherently mature and observing, and so my showbiz education only made me more so. By the time I was a teenager, I was Connie's de facto road manager. Not only did I hang with the band now, but also, I was often given the duty of handing out paychecks and holding passports.

We went everywhere. We sang for kings and queens—mostly queens. Just a smattering of my performances for heads of state included the king and queen of Sweden, the premier of Taiwan—just after my turn at the Golden Horse Awards, where at age sixteen, I proceeded to get drunk in order to avoid being disrespectful. I'm just a girl who can't say "no"—especially to the premier of Taiwan. Then there was that trip to the Philippines, where Connie was due to sing for President Ferdinand Marcos and his wife, Imelda, on New Year's Eve. We stayed at this beautiful resort, and the owners were lovely. They had two sons, and it was set up so that Tricia and I got to hang out with them by the pool. We were essentially ordered to do a little pubescent flirting. Equally as charming as getting on the bus and going to Wallingford, Connecticut.

When we accompanied Connie to do her show, it became apparent how many fans she had in the Philippines. She had filled an entire arena.

As an honored guest of the country, my mother received a gift of the most sacred animal in Filipino culture—a water buffalo. I can still see my mom, standing off to the shoulder of this tropical country lane. She's glamorous—very thin and very twinkly, in a frilly, off-the-shoulder blouse, with her chocolate-brown lip liner and her frosted malt lipstick, lots of lashes, and a flower in her hair—holding her water buffalo on a rope. Only problem was—how do we get a gift of this magnitude into our luggage?

Connie spent the rest of our time there surveying everyone she met.

"Do you have a water buffalo?" she'd ask. "I have a water buffalo."

Finally, she found a guard who didn't have one. Now he would.

Connie had a big group of singers and dancers with her on that trip, as usual. It was New Year's Eve, and they had a fabulous after-party back at our suite. This was the late seventies, and a holiday fete meant lots of "party favors." I could hear the elation from the next room as, one at a time, they exclaimed, "Happy New Year!"

I was curious, as I was about all adult matters. I peeked around the half-open door and saw the source of their excitement: glimmering white powder, in plentiful amounts, fashioned into tiny lines on the coffee table. It was love at first sight, and not many years later, I'd be having celebrations of this sort on my own, and I'd know how to expertly roll a hundred-dollar bill.

We toured Southeast Asia many times during those years. On one occasion, we arrived at the airport in Indonesia, where there is zero tolerance for drugs, and we were reminded of this fact by a huge sign:

Death Penalty for Drug Traffickers!

Now, my mother wasn't trafficking, per se, only just "holding" for personal consumption. She looked at the sign. She handed me the passports. There were twenty-one of us on that trip, and now I had all twenty-one passports in my hand. She approached the next available local immigration officer. And she started talking very loudly, in her brightest, most blond-haired, blue-eyed American movie star voice.

"Hi, I'm Connie Stevens," she said. "We're entertainers. We're so happy to be in your beautiful country."

She grabbed my hand and indicated the stack of passports.

"Here's everybody's passports," she said, helpful as could be.

Turning to all of her dancers, singers, and crew, she yanked them all through, introducing them with exaggerated animation as they passed by.

We could always find fans in these countries, and we were in the habit of sussing out the most helpful person wherever we were. Just then, one of the customs officers shouted her name.

"Miss Stevens, oh Miss Stevens!"

Now, I was holding my mom's bag.

We both turned to look at the woman who was addressing her.

"Come through here," she said, gesturing us in her direction.

As they talked, the customs officer opened Connie's bag, took out a makeup bag and held it in her hand. My mom distracted her with more bright chatter, trying to remember whether she had anything besides makeup in the makeup bag or not, and keeping the woman's eyes on her face.

"Let me help you zip that up," Connie said, as the woman lifted her hand from Connie's contraband.

As if it was nothing, Connie returned her makeup bag to her carry-on, took it back from the woman, and we entered the country. Penalty of death avoided.

ele

Summer Stock

The summer I was sixteen, my mom got the lead in *The Unsinkable Molly Brown,* for the nationally recognized summer stock company the Kenley Players. (The role was made famous in the film version by Debbie Reynolds.) They offered her the sheer joy of traveling city to city, throughout Ohio. And if I'm being completely honest, which I always try to be, Connie made a phone call and asked if the company's founder, John Kenley, would audition me for a role in the chorus.

When we arrived in Ohio, I was sent to audition for John. I did a number, read a scene, did a few turns and a high kick, and was sent straight to costumes. This was my first exposure to the LGBT community of the theater world, as my first boss was known within his inner circle to be self-proclaimed intersexual, and to live as "Joan" during the off-season. But what left a real impression on me was my first gay "love affair" with a fellow hoofer in the chorus, Larry Lane. I was completely enamored with him. When Connie flew ahead to the next city between appearances, I was perfectly happy to ride on the bus with Larry, reading aloud to each other from a single copy of *Lady Chatterley's Lover.* And I got my Actor's Equity card out of it.

ele

Around the World . . . in Eight Days

My mother comes from a generation of women stars who were enlisted by Bob Hope, starting during World War II, for morale-boosting missions to provide the troops with a diversion and a little love from home. So I've listened to the stories from men she's encountered her entire career, who recount how seeing her and hearing her sing got them through several wars. Her impact on them was profound.

She raised Tricia and me with a reverence for this tradition and the men and women who serve our country. It could have been that many men in her family had served in the military, or perhaps it was her own philosophical devotion to the idea of service. A devotion that took her away from her newborn children several times to return to Vietnam, where one of her brothers had served and come home suffering from PTSD. Even decades later, her memories of her trips with the USO are among the most vivid and reverent of her entire career. She says to this day: "I served in four wars."

When Bob Hope planned his final USO tour, to be televised as a Christmas special in 1987, and Connie told him she couldn't be away from her children at the holidays, we were enlisted to join the troops. This wasn't during a time of conflict for our country, so she agreed we could go. It was an honor and one of my most iconic family holiday memories. At Andrews Air Force Base, we boarded a C-141 cargo plane, made into the temporary home of Bob Hope, Connie Stevens, Barbara Eden, Lee Greenwood, all the singers, dancers, and crew members . . . and Connie's kids.

We circumnavigated the globe in just over a week, and rang in Christmas Eve with a multidenominational celebration in the anchor room of the aircraft carrier, the USS *Midway,* near an anchor chain the size of a Buick. It didn't go unnoticed that these people, who were the same age as me, had chosen a life of service. I understood for the first time why my mom felt so strongly that we should be there.

We were gifted with flight suits. We each had our own escort officers. Mine was the air crew chief. And later that night, they smuggled my sister and me down to the lower decks for an innocent dance with some of the boys. One of the young men had just found out that his wife back stateside had delivered their son, and he was feeling melancholy but trying to celebrate anyhow. We climbed down eight decks, feeling more and more closed in with each level, and arrived at a tiny little room that slept four, decorated with one strand of Christmas lights. We toasted with diet soda and shared a laugh. It was truly, in a more intimate way, what the USO brings to servicepeople who are far from home. We're bringing them a little peace from home (not "a little piece"—let me just assure you that everyone kept their clothes on). It was an emotional moment. A real connection was made.

The day after Christmas, we found ourselves on the USS *Iowa,* known as "The Big Stick," an important battleship in our fleet. Another day, another show. But we had literally flown thousands of miles in a matter of days, and we didn't think we had it in us. Tricia and I were lying in our bunks, with our feet hanging over the edge, when Mom came in.

"Girls, get up," she said, again reminding us of her devotion . . . and her position in the family. "We've got a show to do."

We shook off our jet lag and did what we had to do.

But all these years later, whenever Tricia or I have reason to say, "I'm tired," the other one replies: "Are you USO Persian Gulf tired?" We never are.

As we boarded to leave the Persian Gulf for the then-top-secret military base in Diego Garcia, Connie and Barbara were so exhausted, they took measures into their own hands. We all had to sleep sitting up in our seats. Only Bob had his own bedroom with a bunk. 'Cause he's Bob. While Mr. Hope lay sleeping, they snuck in and commandeered the top bunk, managing only a little shut-eye as they giggled and imagined the headlines: CRICKET AND JEANNIE CRUSH BOB HOPE TO DEATH IN HIS SLEEP.

Every show ended with Lee Greenwood's famous song "God Bless the USA," and when I hear that song today, it still brings tears to my eyes. More than anything else, the experience gave me a sense of what it felt like to serve the people who serve our country, something I would continue to do later in life.

There Are Worse Things I Could Do

Years later, I did find myself as the headliner. In 1995, I went to Broadway as Rizzo in *Grease* at the Eugene O'Neill Theatre in Tommy Tune's revival of the musical. Before my first performance on opening night, with Connie, Eddie, and Tricia in the audience to see my debut, I was sitting in front of the mirror in my dressing room. I started putting out my makeup, lining up the lipsticks, cleaning the brushes, and then setting them up in their special places. And then all the little bottles, I put just so . . . and it dawned on me: *I've done this my whole life. Literally.* During backstage moments, I'd been watching. Learning. I had been exposed to so much over the course of my life. I knew how to manage a rowdy crowd. I knew how to handle the microphones going out. I knew what to do when the sheet music flies across the stage and you have to make up the words, as the top of the tent is being ripped off by a tornado. No, really. It had all taught me that when I was ready, I could handle anything that was thrown at me. I had learned from the consummate entertainer. Through osmosis I had absorbed the rules of the road.

Chapter 2

The Fishbowl

GROWING UP . . . IMPLIES GETTING BIGGER? Getting older? Ascension, to where? Away from Fisher? That there are restraints, or boundaries, or rules that apply—given the moniker? Or does it mean *the sky's the limit*? Someone just told me—a new friend—I met him on Instagram (insert eye roll—I know)—that he thinks "Growing Up Fisher" implies winning, so yeah, I'll take that. I'll buy that for a buck! What it does come with is: scrutiny—rising under the watchful eye of the world, swimming in the "Fishbowl," onlookers tapping on the glass to check our vitals, to see if we respond; to get our attention, or just to watch. Look how pretty they swim! Well, not that one—she's awkward. Not nearly as agile as the bigger one. The dark one there, that one's the most interesting. I can't take my eyes off that one. It makes us want to either hide under the coral—camouflaged, hidden—or try to impress you with our stroke. *Watch how deftly I navigate the water. Watch me do the butterfly.*

Wait . . . hold on . . . I'm going to mix imagery and metaphor. Get ready. Did you know that most butterflies live only a few short weeks? It's cruel and unjust. And strange, and mysterious, how something wildly unremarkable bundles up and later emerges as a creature that is that stunning. In every language, a lovely word—*butterfly, farfalla, papillon, mariposa*—as if we had to name it to fit its glory. All good words. The best words.

As I am writing, I have moved into a new home. The day I "landed," I heard a flapping and fluttering sound. From where I sat, I could see her. She was dancing around the foyer. Showing off, or perhaps just trapped against the glass, imagining the freedom of the outdoors. In any case, she landed for brief interludes, allowing me to catch glimpses of her chromatics and the intricacies of her wings. Glorious. I was reminded of the short time she has to exist, so, I ushered her out into the world—vast and filled with others who may want to gaze upon her. I would not mourn her. Just knowing we shared this intimate moment, I chose to bask in it for just a moment.

Carrie was like this—fluttering around—dancing, showing off—trapped—and landing, briefly, every so often, so we could revel in the intricacies of her wings. She had also found a way to flip off those who tapped against the glass. It's a raw and painful experience to have your "flight" or your "swim" judged.

I looked to Carrie—and everyone, frankly—who came before me to learn how to handle the scrutiny, the judgment. I carefully crafted my stroke by observing my predecessors. Advantage Fisher? Sometimes. The way we are perceived is oftentimes more important than the way we actually feel when our privacy is compromised. And then we went and chose the career we did. I am a glutton for punishment—however, in an effort to charm you, to entertain you, I "executive produce" the "show." I reveal the good bits and try to keep it together for my audience. Suck it all in, conceal, hide flaws—work diligently on my craft. Mother wants me to only show the good bits. But that felt—feels—like a lie to me. I want to show it all.

I think I looked to Carrie because she found a way to make her flaws Louvre caliber. It wasn't easy, I imagine. We're all just hurt, frightened, unfathered little girls inside, and then we were all made part of the act. Our mothers tapped back when the onlookers came to the glass. The aquarium was the stage, the camera, the red carpet. We were carefully taught that the angle we were seen at was important. When I once asked, "Aren't these fantastic shoes?" my mother replied, "If they're looking at your shoes, you aren't doing your job." Still, Debbie and Connie were impeccably groomed for onlookers at all times (well, most times). And we girls in the next generation were schooled to be the same. But it's exhausting, impossible, to keep it up at all times. We are human and have moments of vulnerability. On occasion we all let our guard—and our hair—down. That's when they get ya! (Insert faux pas or wardrobe malfunction here.)

No mea culpa piece here about the burden, the cost, the agony of fame. Just an attempt to be real about how complicated—and surreal—it is to grow up this way, especially when life must inevitably ebb and flow. We age. We change. We grieve. All in the public eye. And people are bound to have opinions about it.

AS ANDERSON COOPER wrote in the book he coauthored with this mother, *The Rainbow Comes and Goes,* "the name Vanderbilt was cumbersome." That's so how I felt as a kid, carrying the weight of it. Looking back, maybe it's because the Fisher name came with so much to live down—the marriages, the scandals, the gambling, the drugs, the flops—and so much to live up to—the voice, the talent, the charisma, the success. And yet. When I told my mom that my book was called *Growing Up Fisher,* she paused the perfect beat and said: "Well . . . you didn't." Her assessment may be more accurate. But it didn't matter if Eddie was around or not . . . thy name is Fisher.

The idea that anyone would consider a friendship, a relationship, hiring me, not knowing my last name—this was the safer, the truer barometer of whether I had value, on my own merits, OR NOT. The satisfaction came from personally meeting people and developing a friendship with them before they saw where I lived or knew who my mom was. Or getting hired for something, and only having it come up after the fact that I was "Connie Stevens's daughter." Or "Eddie Fisher's daughter." I'd gotten the job because . . . *I* got the job.

Because it wasn't just the Fisher side of it. When people knew I was Connie's daughter, they always said, "Ooh, you look just like her." Five foot two, eyes of blue, I would never measure up . . . then, I towered over her. And, well, that was its own pressure, she was so beautiful, everybody loved her so much. As I was growing up, my lineage was like my own personal game of Truth or Dare. Sometimes I hid it. And then, in certain circles, when I didn't feel like I was enough: "My mom had an affair with Elvis"—"Do you know my sister's Princess Leia?" As I got older and had my own identity, nepotism no more, I etched out my own place in the world. But still, there were all those loaded projections and those pitiful looks. The ones I've been getting again since the loss of Carrie and Debbie. Like the whole world wants to give me an unsolicited hug I'm not sure I want, as if their arms around me can help to ease the pain. On occasion, it does. Everybody has a bad day . . .

ele

Snapshots and Scaffolding

Last year, they began construction on the new Waldorf Astoria Beverly Hills, and as I was driving by one day, I couldn't believe my eyes: to trumpet the arrival of the iconic, glamorous Waldorf Astoria franchise to Beverly Hills, they'd draped its exterior in ENORMOUS photographs that took up one whole side of the building. Not just any pictures, but family pictures—my family pictures.

I glanced to my right . . . to see the soulful sparkling eyes of Connie Stevens and Eddie Fisher smiling back at me. *Hey, Mom. What's up, Dad?*

My daughter, True, was in the backseat.

"True, look . . . there's Nana *and* Popsie," I said.

I went on to muse about the phenomenon—how Auntie Tricia and I are the only two people—wait, as I kept driving, the next photo was revealed to us.

"There's Mama Debs," I said.

Scratch that . . . make it four people—in the world—who could relate to the experience of having these particular entertainment icons as parents, let alone currently plastered on the side of this building in our hometown.

With the loss of Carrie, now it's only three people on the planet who are in the rarefied inner circle of Fisher offspring. And the loss of all the hilarious, realer-than-real commentary she gave us—her siblings and the world—about the experience. So I'm trying to wrap my head around it on my own, for my own sanity, and as a way to explain it to my kids, who will grow up into their own Fisher-Duddy version of it.

ele

Enter Center Stage

I exploded into this life. (I don't know, perhaps the last one didn't go so well.) This time I chose my arrival, and my parents, wisely. I came barreling in on October 29, the late sixties, while my father, Eddie Fisher, addicted playboy with a velvet voice, was onstage at the Frontier Hotel in Las Vegas, Nevada. Natch. Meanwhile, my mother, Connie Stevens, iconic sixties sex kitten, was in twilight sleep in Burbank, California. Dr. B. J. Gregorius was at the ready, and when I was due to make my debut, the doctor rang backstage to the Frontier, in order to include Eddie in the delivery of his new offspring onto the planet.

To hear then-busboy Steve Wynn tell it, as he was in the showroom at the time, clearing away vodka gimlets: a stagehand brought the phone onstage for my father. Oh, my Papa held the receiver up to the microphone . . . so the audience could hear the smack on my ass that produced my first wail. "Papa, can you hear me?" Already demanding the spotlight.

Not that it was my first time onstage, mind you—just my first speaking line. Connie had performed on Broadway in Neil Simon's *The Star-Spangled Girl* until just three months before I was born. (There were even a few tabloid suggestions that when she delivered, perhaps the baby might look more like Neil Simon than Eddie Fisher.)

All of this played out in the public eye. As did everything my parents—and now I—did. Imagine the early seventies, in that fishbowl, their very big, very public split. Think Brexit. All of it covered, breathlessly, in the press. So now, before I was five, my birth had been covered, my parents' romantic lives had been covered, their split had been *very much* covered.

HOW CONNIE AND EDDIE WILL RAISE THE BABY!

DAILY NEWS

NEW YORK'S PICTURE NEWSPAPER

10¢

CONNIE'S A MOM & EDDIE'S A DAD

Fisher: 'Yes Sir, That's My Baby'

And I was already learning that even the most intimate, or sad, or embarrassing, or hard, or weird things in my life were public knowledge, fodder for the gossip mill. So of course I chose show business!

You're groomed for it. And I was. Connie was a star. And she showed Tricia and me how it was done. It was very clear to us, her daughters, that she was to be shared. She was, in part, public possession—it went with the business—and we would have to adapt. Of course, we always came first. But when we were out and about, we were expected to be mini-ambassadors for Connie Stevens. I took my training to heart, and I could, from a young age, recognize when people *recognized* my mom. My whole life, I've had bionic hearing. I could hear the whispers, the thoughts. That's how intense the experience has always been for me. It came from moving through a space—whether it was at a theater, or an airport, or a restaurant—and catching the whispers and the looks. Everybody's eyes lit up and sparkled when Connie came into a room. Everybody put aside what they were doing and fawned over her . . . and us, Tricia and me.

"Are these the girls?" they asked, beyond excited.

"Oh, Connie, I've always loved you!" they gushed.

"I'm such a fan!"

Which, of course, was flattering and rewarding and incredible—I've always thought my mom sparkled. So I loved to see people basking in it, and I wanted to protect her when she didn't.

And, of course, then there's the phenomenon of growing up alongside this.

"Connie, over here," the cameramen yelled when we were on the red carpet . . . at the airport . . . on the set . . . everywhere. I lived for being next to my mom, and being in the spotlight, so I was right there.

"Joely! Connie! Joely!"

"Tricia, come here, Tricia Leigh," Connie would say, pulling Tricia closer to her. "Get one with the baby."

We took our rightful positions alongside Mom—and the flashbulbs popped.

I loved it.

A onetime manager, who was among the earliest people who really believed in me, summed it up perfectly.

"There's something really interesting that happens to you, cellularly," he said. "You touch down on a red carpet and it's as if there's a vibration that happens to you."

Yeah, there was something that happened to me on a cellular level—Eddie and Connie. And it does feel perfectly natural for me to be on a red carpet, on a stage, or honing my craft. Not only that, but my work thrills me.

But for me, much of making peace with fame has been making peace with having a beautiful mother, who was always photographed looking beautiful. And how I felt about myself, and photographs of myself, because of that.

Byron Griffiths, my very first manager, who'd once represented my mother, took me to lunch on Santa Monica Boulevard when he was courting me. Fondly, he described the way my mother smiled with her eyes closed. She smiled a lot, and he said he had to teach her to open her eyes when she did. Good advice for someone who wanted—no, expected—to make a living telling tales with her eyes.

"Do I do it, too?" I asked.

"Slightly, but we'll work on it," he said.

He had a class for all his clients—once every two weeks—scene work, and tips, and stories. It was during this time that I started going on my first auditions and getting feedback. Byron told me that I was a better actress than my mother, and that I would eventually outshine her. I never told anyone that.

It thrilled and scared me.

I put on twenty pounds.

ALONG WITH THE fanfare, the pomp and circumstance of living life in the public eye, the stage is also set for the unwanted attention, the weird, and the beautifully bizarre, and the sometimes frightening . . . or potentially dangerous situation.

For Connie's fiftieth birthday . . . 8/8/88 . . . the sheer numerological symmetry and harmony of it provided the perfect milieu for an outrageous celebration. We boarded the USS *Norway,* a giant cruise ship bound for the Bahamas and a few Virgin Islands. There were fifty of us—ya know, 'cause fifty—caveat was we had two shows to do—easy, peasy. The rest was a solid week of swimming, gambling, and shenanigans with the band. This time our band of merry players included the gang from South Philly, and by that I mean the Mafia. No, really. Because she was a Sicilian, her friends and family included some "bosses" of the day. Our friends on this trip were stunning stallions, low-level henchmen. This provided Tricia and me with extra entertainment and food for thought. Did this culture still exist? Racketeering, extortion, hit men? Rough . . . but they sure were cute. Tricia's "friend" is in prison. Mine is dead. Crime doesn't pay. And this was pre-*Sopranos.* It was thrilling and a little dangerous, but it also felt surprisingly acceptable to have low friends in high places. This was just how life was when you're the darling of the Sicilians.

And then there are the times we are caught being human, in moments of weakness, or fragility, exercising our lack of discretion or discipline . . . or we might just not have had our makeup on. I came across an article about my mom, at the Moustache Café, with her then-boyfriend, Charlie, throwing a drink across the bar. The headline read: CONNIE STEVENS GETS OUT OF HAND, THREATENS YOUNG BARTENDER. Charlie, apparently, was looking at someone. Connie had one too many drinks, threw a glass across the bar, and it hit the wall. There's always a grain of truth in those articles. Authorities may or may not have had to "drag" her out. She probably left going, "I can go myself. Don't touch me." Not the end of the world, but doesn't feel great either.

And of course, my sister Carrie was the poster child for tabloids and social media postings. Drugs. Dalliances. Dealers. All dirty words. It's easy to imagine why she chose to turn the pen on herself—to write funnier, more raw, meaner shit than any tabloid scribe could. Self-deprecation before self-destruction. It's an old technique of beating them to the punch, and then, you can at least give the impression that the scrutiny hasn't cut you to your core. So up out of the fetal position we go, and write it out. Of course it fucking hurts.

And then there's the darkest, most hazardous facet of what we do—the evils of obsession. One year, we arrived home from Jackson Hole, Wyoming, where we had all attended Connie's Celebrity Ski Extravaganza. We stopped to pick up some fresh flowers and foliage to decorate our house, which had been empty during our absence. While replenishing the pantry for the week to come, Connie got a call from Cosentino's on Pacific Coast Highway:

"We tried to make your delivery, but your guest was very rude."

Not wanting to encounter our uninvited "guest," we had the Malibu sheriff accompany us home. There was writing on the walls . . . in shit . . . like Helter Skelter kind of shit. Every glass and pot was used. He had cooked and left dishes and food out. Then he had taken my mom's eight-by-tens. He was an artist. He had drawn penises coming out of her mouth. It was lewd and disgusting. All the pictures were completely covered with pornographic threats. It looked like death.

Apparently, the young man, a crazed, obsessed fan, had merely walked along Carbon Beach and asked: "Hey, is that where Connie Stevens lives? She's my cousin . . ."

The crazy dude just walked in . . . broke in.

He went to jail. And we put the house on the market.

ee

The Fifth Wall

It's hard to face the effects of aging, when you catch a glimpse . . . or sometimes desperately stare in the mirror, pulling back the sides of your face, just enough for a natural-looking adjustment, which you scrutinize from all angles. Maybe all I need is to pull this up a teensy bit . . . are we talking surgery? No . . . never . . . well, maybe? Especially when you've chosen a career that doesn't allow women to age. Unless you've been a character actress from the start, women are obligated to uphold the fantasy and the ideal standard—and you're trying to do the impossible. It just can't be done.

So what happens when you can't hold your arms up long enough to blow-dry your hair? Or the prescriptions you're on make you bloated beyond? Or any kind of serious medical condition, or life-threatening medical event, causes your decline? For a trio of women—for any woman—who has been known and loved for physical prowess and beauty, this is devastating. And then to have it happen publicly, and to have this process be recorded, and cataloged, and broadcast, and chronicled . . . it's eviscerating.

My mother, she doesn't look like herself anymore. You'd have to really be a connoisseur of all things sixties to recognize her. I wonder if that's because she had a stroke? Or just her natural evolution? A year ago, I think her appearance bothered her. Now she isolates herself and doesn't really want to be out.

Reality television, in a way, has changed how we look at

people. Some people are really good at it—the Kardashians and the Osbournes of it all—they broke through the fifth wall, the sixth wall . . . they broke through all the walls . . . and artfully let us see what we wanted to see. They allowed it, so now it's expected of all of us.

When Carrie and Debbie decided to draw the curtain back in their joint documentary, *Bright Lights,* the world got to see a candid, but curated, picture of their relationship and their life together. How courageous of them. It's difficult to watch your own story unfolding, however carefully choreographed and lit. Is it too much? Have I revealed more than I intended to? Even when you're a lifelong master of the private/public pas de deux, it can leave you feeling not so fresh.

When a person is grieving, that's when we should have the most respect for her right to be unpolished. And yet the conundrum we're in, here in the fishbowl, means it's also the time when others might be the most curious about us. *Never mind how fast I got back into my bikini body . . . watch and learn how I get my grief on.* This is the thing I understand least about human nature—that in the most tragic of times, along with the outpouring of support, comes judgment. The downright detailed critique of how a person chooses to mourn a famous family member is outrageous and mystifying. When I experienced it firsthand, it threw me for a loop.

Nothing illustrated this for me more vividly than when I went on an audition in the first month after Carrie and Debbie's passing. One particular casting director had sent me a condolence e-mail, but I didn't mention it when I walked into the room. I read my part, thanked them, and turned to go. The casting director followed me out.

"Did you get my e-mail?" she asked.

"Yeah, I didn't want to lead with the dead Princess."

We embraced. As I knew, she had lost her mother and her father. And because my loss was so public, there was immediately that shared commiseration. But in my raw state, I couldn't possibly do my job, and therefore, I didn't get the job.

Double Dare

Here's where I'm edging toward the highest degree of difficulty. I now have subjected the next generation—my offspring—to the same kind of exposure and scrutiny I survived. How dare I? How dare I not? In order to ensure the little bit of their happiness I can control, I feel it's my obligation to show them all of it, perhaps even in the pages of a book . . . or in those historic YouTube videos we gather around to watch together . . . the life and times of Nana, and Mama Debs, and Popsie, and Big Auntie Carrie . . . and all of our lives. Through this introduction, I want to give them the tools to make their own choices about where they're headed, based on history . . . and the fact that there are seven minutes of my life that are undocumented. They can choose their own elaborate swim strokes, and whether or not to let the world see the intricacies of their wings, and they can take their rightful place alongside me . . . as we've got a few red carpets still to hit.

Chapter 3

Hail Connie Full of Grace

MY MOTHER ALWAYS MAINTAINS, "SOMETHING wonderful is going to happen . . ." I'm not so sure I am always convinced. But she is. Whether it is naïveté, or genuine faith . . . she *believes*. So when I observe her standing in that truth, I can't help but wonder where that hopefulness comes from, considering her start.

Connie Stevens was born Concetta Rosalie Ann Ingolia at Coney Island Hospital on August 8, 1938, to Eleanor McGinley and Pietro Ingolia, whose stage name was Teddy Stevens. (His family hailed from Messina, in Sicily, née Ingoglia, the second *g* got dropped at Ellis Island.) Eleanor was a band singer, and Teddy played bass in big bands and jazz bands, playing with the likes of Stan Getz. He was a stud—charismatic, handsome (and he was a bass player, and they're all crazy). He was often away on tour. During one of these absences, Eleanor, who was of Irish and Iroquois descent, took up with another Italian guy, a pharmacist named Ralph Megna, basically orphaning Connie and big brother Chuck, who by that time had enlisted in the army.

At a young age, following her parents' divorce, Connie went to live with her paternal grandparents, who were awarded custody. She called her grandmother "Mama," and her time with them left a deep impression on her. When Tricia and I were little, Connie forever reminded us that her Italian grandma, in their four-story walkup—a multigenerational home of the era—in the roughest of neighborhoods, would cook for everyone. She somehow managed to stretch a single meal across a week. Connie still wondrously recounts the tale of how her grandfather grew a tree in Brooklyn, near their apartment building, amid the asphalt jungle, and how he hybridized an apple and a pear tree and used his amazing green thumb to produce an all-new breed. To this day, fruit trees and gardens make her happier than almost anything else.

On an infrequent visit to where her mother lived with her new family, in Rockaway Beach, eight-year-old Connie got off the train and walked to her mom's apartment building. Through the window, she observed her newly married mother, who'd recently had a baby. As she recalls it, she saw "a mother deeply in love with a new child that wasn't me." Connie came to adore the baby, her younger half brother, Ralph, as well as the two other children Eleanor would go on to have—Ava and John. John, her "kid brother," as she called him, grew up to be actor John Megna, who tragically died of AIDS in 1995 at age forty-two. When she had a family of her own, Connie felt a responsibility to gather everyone together for big dinners and holiday celebrations, something missing from her own childhood. And my sister and I were very close to our aunt, uncles, and slew of cousins.

Connie and her older brother, Charlie, were enamored of each other growing up. My uncle Charlie was not unlike his father, in that people in the neighborhood respected him, maybe were even a little scared of him. Nobody dared fuck with Connie, because that was "Chuck's" kid sister. They'd grown up poor in an apartment on Gates Avenue in the Bushwick section of Brooklyn, which was very territorial, very Italian, back then. So her big brother even mapped out Connie's routes home from places for her, telling her which streets to take when she was passing through the Irish neighborhood, the black neighborhood. He kept her safe by telling her when she could walk and when she'd better run. I'd like to think times have changed, but all evidence, unfortunately, suggests otherwise. There are still neighborhoods through which we are told to run.

When she was nine, she was briefly sent to a Catholic boarding school run by Dominican nuns (the same order that ran the school that Christina Crawford describes attending in her memoir, *Mommie Dearest*).

Even after she settled in Los Angeles and became a star, Connie remained a true New Yorker. Eventually she would keep an apartment in NYC, but even before then, we made regular trips back that included ritualistic laps of the city, starting with her bull shot (a vodka with a bouillon cube in it—soup on ice that'll put hair on your nips) at the Oyster Bar in the Plaza Hotel. Splurgey shopping trips to Bloomie's and Bergdorf's, because now she could afford that. And then a pilgrimage back to the old neighborhood. She took us to the front door of her former home, regaling us with tales of hanging on the stoop and playing stickball in the street. And she showed us the little metal mailbox out front, where, scratched in the bottom, were the words CONNIE LOVES ANDREW. I'm not sure if Andrew ever returned the feeling, but her affections for Andrew were forever immortalized. Our trip always culminated with a visit to the cemetery, where her beloved father was buried.

Connie adored her father, and she was the apple of his eye. With her mother fully engrossed in her new life and family, and Connie finally at an age to go to him, she chose to be wherever he was. As Connie tells it, when she was around fifteen, in 1953, she followed her father out to Los Angeles. And by "followed," I mean he came and whisked her away. While they were making this cross-country trip, Connie was tuning the radio dial one day when a local station came through. She heard an unfamiliar type of music, full of twangy guitar, banjo, and plaintive vocals. It sounded funny—strange and new—but it was also thrilling and wonderful—she really loved that sound.

"Daddy, what is that?" she asked.

"It's country music," he told her.

"I like it." She was hooked.

Upon their arrival in Los Angeles, they lived in a little bungalow in Eagle Rock, a community with a cute, small-town feel on the east side of the city, near Pasadena. She finished up her education at Hollywood Professional School. While she was attending classes there, she began singing with several different vocal groups—one of them included the gentlemen who later became famous as the Lettermen. Their group featuring Connie was called the Foremost. And then she joined the Three Debs, which was her first group to make a splash, taking her to perform in Hawaii for the first time.

During these years, Connie attempted to break into Hollywood by getting cast as an extra in films, and she did appear in a few teen dramas with names like *Eighteen and Anxious* and *Dragstrip Riot*. She was gaining experience and building her resumé, but nothing really rose to the top. And then Jerry Lewis cast her in Frank Tashlin's 1958 comedy *Rock-a-Bye Baby.*

In the midst of a scene together for Connie's screen test, she sat in a chair while Jerry Lewis paced around her. He suddenly leaned over right into her face, and with his broad, comedic delivery blared, "Do you like VEAL cut-LET?!" It frightened her and made her laugh hysterically. She got the job.

My mom has always remembered Jerry Lewis as being very kind to her. She could make him laugh, too. He adored her. And I cherish a souvenir from that time, a beautiful gold number *3* brooch he gave her to commemorate their three films together. His telegraph was the first to arrive for my Broadway debut.

Connie had been discovered. Warner Bros. put her under contract and gave her a starring role as singer-photographer Cricket Blake in the television show *Hawaiian Eye*. The show became a hit and Connie was an instant teen idol. She made the ponytail and crinoline petticoat skirt all the rage. You know you've made it when someone shows up trick-or-treating at your front door, dressed as you.

The next few years featured a flurry of parts on screens big and small—movies starring opposite her good friend Troy Donahue and a guest spot on the TV show *77 Sunset Strip*. She played opposite Edd Byrnes, whose character's name was Kookie. In the episode, they sang a duet called "Kookie, Kookie, Lend Me Your Comb." Released as a single in 1959, it went to number 4 on the *Billboard* Hot 100 and sold a million copies, resulting in her first gold record. From then on, in addition to her acting career, she became a beloved singer with several hits, including her biggest, "Sixteen Reasons," and "Too Young to Go Steady." They don't write songs like they used to—nor should they. After that, she was never not working—singing, acting, and performing live.

This was the era when movie stars were covered ad nauseam in the tabloids, and much of the "news" was manufactured. Come to think of it . . . nothing's changed in this department. I still have big plastic bins full of these magazines, like *Screen Stars* and *Movie People*. The studio would send my mother out with Troy Donahue, to make it look like they were a couple.

They were friends, but they never got it on. Troy ended up marrying Connie's best friend, Suzanne "Suzie" Pleshette. So then the studio had her go out with Glenn Ford, or whomever, just to keep her in the headlines. (Soon, she'd meet her two future ex-husbands, and they'd generate plenty of headlines on their own, without needing help from anybody.)

As I remember it, when Connie became a star, my grandmother showed up. However she may have felt inside, my mom forgave her mother's abandonment and betrayal. Connie always opened her home to her mother and her whole family, and would continue to do so from then on. My grandmother was a character. Not super warm, and not maternal, especially for someone who had given birth to five children. But imposing and very funny. Because of her two Italian husbands, she made great sauce, and she used to joke she was "Italian by injection." True story.

In 1963, Connie married her first husband, actor James Stacy, whose real name was Maurice Elias. She was a big star, and he was a handsome young actor primed on the verge of success. They had a lavish wedding at a church in North Hollywood that was covered in the screen magazines of the day. When it was time for them to exchange their vows, he slid her wedding ring on her finger and said, "With this wing, I thee wed."

The way Connie tells the story, they all laughed. But looking back, it didn't bode well for their life together when the wedding vows were a joke from the beginning. I have their wedding album and pictures from their marriage, and they look as if they couldn't have been happier. He was part Lebanese and stunning. Her father adored him, which was a major plus for Connie.

But he was broken. I've witnessed over the course of my lifetime how Connie gravitated toward broken men. Given her home life growing up, it's perfectly fitting that she would have trouble in this area. Not that her dad was "broken," but if this were Therapy 101, I'd say that the early breakup of her family, and her mom's choice to throw herself into a new family, left Connie feeling abandoned. And with that kind of low self-esteem, she didn't feel she deserved someone who was going to stick around and truly adore her. (I told you this was Therapy 101.)

Connie's first husband soon revealed his true nature. He was vengeful and full of rage. He burned her baby pictures. He cut off her hair while she was sleeping. He got physical with her. Within three years, their marriage was over. Seven years after they divorced, he was in a terrible motorcycle accident, in which he lost an arm and a leg, and the girl on the back of his bike was killed. But because of Connie's sense of always being inclusive, and in turn, teaching us the importance of family, Jim Stacy's father, "Grandpa Zeke," remained a part of our lives for many years.

Connie and I were together in 2016 when we heard about the passing of her first husband, James Stacy. We had already experienced so much loss that year, and of course, a death is always affecting . . . and she had been married to this guy. But my feelings were ambivalent. Sure, loss is loss. But this man had continued to randomly, and bizarrely, show up in the periphery throughout my life. When I was a teenager, he had tried to force himself on me by pushing me into a hotel bathroom, and although I was able to defuse that situation, I wasn't surprised when he was convicted of child molestation roughly a decade later. For many years, he showed up to hear me sing. My mom defended him: "He's just a fan." Which was difficult for me to process, but I ultimately made peace with the fact that my mom sees good in everyone.

Delicious Eddie

Tricia and I have joked that Connie and Eddie met at the airport lounge at JFK. They weren't really quite so transitory when they encountered each other at the Plaza Hotel, but they were definitely both on the rebound. Connie was coming off the disappointment and heartbreak of the end of her first marriage. She was popping pills, partying, and trying to stay one step ahead of the sadness (and working, of course—Connie was always working, no matter what was going on in her personal life).

Eddie had been fired by Liz, so he was in a state as well. They were both very much on the prowl. I'm not sure what, beyond that, attracted them to each other, or why they stayed together. I do know my mom still gets wistful when she tells the story of going to hear Eddie sing in a temple and being brought to sobs by the sound of his voice singing the "Kol Nidre." Obviously, he was charismatic—he had something about him. And as I've said, she would describe him, even years later, as "delicious." For his part, Eddie said: "We couldn't put two days together, but we sure could put two nights together." Enter Joely and Tricia.

Beyond that, I think maybe it was a case of how people who lead chaotic lives do occasionally try to pull it together, either because they feel like they should, or because they get tired of the chaos. A well-timed pregnancy and birth was how Connie achieved greater stability in her own life. And I think that's why motherhood was so important to her. It also seems clear to me that, with Eddie, Connie was looking for *her* idea of family. And while his track record was well known, and maybe it should have been a warning to her *not* to marry him, she plunged right in.

Connie and Eddie were America's New Sweethearts, for real. Liz had shacked up with Dick. And the first ex–Mrs. Fisher, Debbie, was married to Harry Karl, and they were raising Carrie and Todd. But a dazzling Connie had cast a spell on the press. And so, even though (as I later found out by reading my father's first memoir, *My Life, My Loves)* Eddie and Connie weren't actually married when she got pregnant with me, the press looked the other way when a newly pregnant Connie and Eddie had an engagement party and went public with their relationship. Many pictures from this party linger on the Internet. She's in a little black-and-white minidress, with this little platinum pixie cut, and there's a big, magnificent cake, and she looks happy, happy, happy. The press loved Connie and wanted her to be victorious, so they protected her. When I was born in October 1967, it wasn't really known, publicly, that she'd delivered a baby out of wedlock. Rather than attempting to dig up dirt, the press just assumed Connie and Eddie had run off together somewhere and gotten hitched, as they eventually did.

When I was about six months old, syndicated Hollywood columnist Marilyn Beck interviewed Connie:

> She held Joely at arm's length a moment, as if still unable to fully believe the miracle that had been bestowed upon her, and she whispered, "And now that she's here, and it's more marvelous and more wonderful than I ever dreamed it would be." Connie smiled as only a mother smiles.

Joely placed her tiny rose petal lips against her mother's cheek, as Connie laughed and said, "And you know something? She's got the best mother in the whole world. I mean, really she does.

"I was worried at first that she might like the nurse better than me! Oh, I know that's silly now, but I did.

"I take her with me everywhere, tip-toe into her room at night to pick her up and hold her close.

"And when I'm working I can't wait to rush home to my little Joely Girl, to my baby.

"I give the nurse extra time off just so I can care for Joely Girl alone. But I love being with her so much, bathing her, feeding her. She's my pal, my delight." . . .

(Connie calls the baby "Gorgeous" so much that the milkman was surprised to hear Connie call the baby "Joely." "I thought her name was Gorgeous," he said. This is Connie's favorite story.)

Not long after that, Connie found herself pregnant again. She and Eddie had gotten engaged, but were working on different coasts, and I don't think they were ever together very much. This is when a longtime friend to both Connie and Eddie, Frank Sinatra, apparently got involved. He pulled Eddie aside and told him, "You have a second child on the way with this woman. You should marry her. Borrow my plane to take her to Puerto Rico to get married."

So they did, tying the knot soon after, although the public record would always state they'd already married in '67. The turbulent, terrifying flight that made them both sick might have turned someone else around, but they persevered. "We could have died in that little plane," Connie has always said. "But instead, we landed and got married."

Tricia Leigh was born fourteen months after me. Now, Connie was really in a position to put together what her picture of a family looked like, everything she didn't have as a child. But her marriage was tumultuous and always fraught with uncertainty and sheer self-doubt—the covers of all those same magazines talked about Eddie as a cheater, Eddie as a drug addict. A picture of Connie ran with the headline: DRUGS RUINED MY MARRIAGE. And, POOR CONNIE, WHAT IS SHE DOING? At that time, she wondered the same thing herself.

Not long after Tricia was born, Connie came home one day and found Eddie in bed with two Swedish girls. As she tells it, she left—in her sequined gown—with a baby on each hip and a diaper bag slung over her shoulder. The scene might not have been quite that literal, or quite that dramatic. There were Swedes. And it was the last, coke-filled straw. Connie did leave Eddie. She took us to a motel on Sepulveda, just down the hill from where they lived. Every time I drive by the place, I think how that's when our life started. She left Eddie Fisher behind and started to create what would be our family. She'd gotten what she wanted (Tricia and me). That doesn't mean it was easy, though.

Eddie never gave her any alimony or child support (I believe he may have asked her for some, though). And she was now raising two children on her own, in a fickle industry. She wanted to have a career that was rewarding and meaningful to her, and even before we were born, she'd had the strength of character to begin moving in this direction. I've already said that she's the great exaggerator, but I don't believe this story is an exaggeration. Apparently after a few years on the Warner Bros. hamster wheel of album, TV show, movie, repeat, she was fed up with feeling like the studio's property.

She walked into Jack Warner's office, dumped a pile of cash on his desk, and broke it down for him:

"I can't do this anymore," she said.

Without a studio behind her, now she had to find her own way. My mom said "yes" to pretty much everything she got—whether as a means of financial survival, or because she thrived on working, I'm not really sure. Lucky for her (and us), plenty of work came her way. As a child, I don't remember my mom ever auditioning for anything. She was a star, and was in demand and flush with roles as the perky, wide-eyed blonde. By the time I was old enough to really be aware of my mom's career, she was doing her nightclub act, in Vegas, Reno, Atlantic City, and cities around the world. And her name was landing her guest spots on movies of the week and shows like *The Love Boat, Fantasy Island,* and *Murder, She Wrote.* Television goes in and out of vogue as something actors want to do, and that was at a time when it was hot to be on TV.

All of her characters are Connie. I've seen her be really solid, and really good, and she's moved me, and she's made me laugh. Of course, when I was little and saw her films, it didn't take much to convince me she could embody a character. I remember seeing her in the movie *Two on a Guillotine* when I was very young. There was a scene where her head got chopped off. Even though I could see my mother sitting there next to me in the living room, I was also watching her have this terrible thing happen to her on-screen. I burst into tears.

"Oh, I didn't really realize that would be scary for you," she said. "You know it's not real."

I knew, but I didn't know. I mean, she was right there in the room, but she moved me as the character.

My mom was really good at what she did, and obviously she

had that special something. That's why it pissed me off so much when, years later, I read my dad's book and found a passage where he described my mom as "something light," which totally diminished her talent. I didn't like it any more when I went to see Carrie perform *Wishful Drinking* and Carrie put up a picture of Connie and Debbie next to each other and basically said: Clearly Eddie had a type, but this one (Connie)—"Debbie-light"—was less of an actress . . . woman . . . human being . . .

Wow, I thought, because there was really no need to draw a comparison between the two women (and certainly not a negative one). Other than the fact that they were both blond actresses and singers, who were incredibly ambitious and hardworking, and they'd both survived Eddie, nothing else was the same—not their personalities, and not their personas. I spoke to Carrie about that. I think she toned it down in the next version. That's the thing with blended families—everyone will always see some aspects of the clan differently. That's just how it is.

AS I'VE ALREADY described, Connie worked hard after she and Eddie split up. My most formative years were spent in Malibu. During our first year, in a leased house, Connie began to write a book, *You Had to Be There.* I hear lifelong echoes of Connie in moments that clearly should've been recorded for posterity: "That'll be in my book," which I thought should be titled *Ballbusters I Have Known.* A female writer, not my mom's style of woman, as I recall, was to stay with us for three weeks, following Connie around and listening to her stories. She lasted three days. I think it overwhelmed her to be shadowed in this way, and so she decided to write the book herself. But the prospect of actually doing so was equally daunting, and she eventually abandoned the project. Recently, she's gotten the bug again, so maybe she just needed a few decades to percolate.

After our first year in Malibu, Connie bought a house on Carbon Beach. This was at a time when Carbon Beach wasn't filled with movie stars and CEOs, pools and tennis courts, but the house next door to the one we were looking to buy did have a swimming pool. When my mom walked out onto the deck with the Realtor, Connie laughed and said: "Who's the asshole who has a swimming pool on the beach?" The Realtor tried to stifle a giggle and said, ". . . Debbie Reynolds." My mom bought the house. For five of the seven years we lived there, we would have daily interactions with Debbie—coming out onto the deck and waving to each other. My brother, Todd, awkwardly including us (his much younger half sisters whom he was just getting to know) in his daily routine. He never took to us, really, not the way Carrie did.

I think one idea was that it would make it easier for Eddie to visit his brood. I almost never saw Eddie by then. Most of the time, I didn't even get calls on my birthday. Sometimes I would hear my mom in the other room, on the phone with Eddie, saying, "It's Joely's birthday. You get on the phone with her *right now*."

A much-anticipated paternal pilgrimage happened once in all the years we lived there. When Eddie finally materialized, it was anticlimactic, to say the least. He arrived at our house, and en masse, we all went over to Debbie's house to visit. She'd apparently thought this was a good idea, but then at the last minute, she seemed to have some reservations. I remember she was upstairs, getting ready, for a long time before she came downstairs to join the rest of us. Then it seemed awkward for her, which made the teenage me wonder if she still carried a torch for him. A photo was taken of Eddie with his two exes and his four children, but it was a Polaroid, and it's since been disappeared by the sands of time.

Debbie and Connie did far more to help each other co-parent than Eddie ever did for either of them. (I remember my mom giving Eddie money a few times when I was a teenager, but never the other way around.) When Tricia and I were teens we had what's called an El Niño year, when several winter storms crash into each other and gain force. The waves were bashing up against our house, smashing against our windows. The beach had been swallowed up completely. It was terrifying, almost like we were on a ship in the middle of a raging sea. Connie was on the road, working, and we'd been left home alone.

Not that we were really alone—we always had someone living at the house with us, taking us to school and doing all the day-to-day stuff. But this was the kind of scary situation where we needed something a little closer to "Mom." Apparently, we were told to evacuate the beach and go to a hotel. Connie called to make sure we were okay, and she told us to go to Debbie's house and that she would take us to a hotel. I don't remember it being that big a deal. But there's another version of the story, which Debbie told, with the addition of "So, of course, again, your mother had left you alone." Looking back now, I find the whole thing hilarious. They were both great moms, but they each wanted to make sure they were the one who did it better.

While we were living in Malibu, we were enrolled in Catholic school. Connie was Italian Catholic, and our governess was an extremely devout Catholic, too. But Connie wanted us to choose our own religion for ourselves. We were learning about Jesus Christ and his teachings at school, but we knew that our father was Jewish and that Jews didn't believe in Jesus. We weren't sure who was right, or whom to believe.

"Okay," Connie said. "Well, then, why don't we study all religions? Make sure you know that everyone believes something different. Let's give you a choice."

And she actually kind of did. We went to all different kinds of temples, mosques, and churches around Los Angeles. Ultimately, we chose to be baptized as Catholics. I guess we were swayed by our governess, and even more than that, by Connie. Of course, she was thrilled, especially when we got done up in our little white dresses for our baptism and communion, and when I sang in the church choir and had solos on Sundays. I definitely wasn't a convert through and through, but even as a little girl, I could tell my mother's faith helped her to get through certain difficult times, and so I saw the value of it.

CONNIE ALWAYS HAD this wide-eyed childlike nature. When I was a child myself, it was incredible to have a mother who could get down on my level and see the world with the same immediacy and wonder that I did.

Connie weaves a fantastic web. When I was little, she would turn to me with the most excited expression on her face—as if we were about to experience one of the Seven Wonders of the World.

"How 'bout you go downstairs and get me a big tall glass, with lots and lots and lots of ice, with a sparkly Diet Coke—cold, cold, cold?" she said in a revelatory voice, making it sound like it was an adventure on which I just *had* to embark.

I've got to go do that! I thought.

And I literally got excited about dashing downstairs and fetching her a Diet Coke—all of the sensory details of it, the icy coolness of the glass in my hand, the hiss and pop of the bubbles as I carried it back upstairs to her. And all this because she was thirsty and didn't feel like going downstairs and getting herself a soda. It really is a fantastic talent. And she did this with so many areas of life—she created drama out of the mundane. In my childhood, this quality often elevated our life together into a rollicking adventure. When I stop and look at it now, really examining the quality in my mother and where it came from, I realize that I don't know anyone else who raises this art to quite the same level. But then . . . she would actually take us to see the Seven Wonders of the World.

Maybe this instinct, other than talent, is the root of why we choose acting as a profession. When asked in interviews why I love acting, I insist that it really comes down to the experience of getting to live in someone else's skin for a moment in time. And as I witnessed, my mom wasn't always really comfortable in her skin. She was the woman who, if Tricia and I barged into her bathroom when she was getting out of her bath, as kids will do, would respond with a panicked, "Oh, just a second!" And she'd already be covering herself with a towel, or whatever was available, not wanting even her daughters, who had different versions of the same body, to see her naked form. And, for a time, I was just as uncomfortable in my own skin. So acting called us both.

However, it did get frustrating later on, especially when it came to Connie's boyfriends. When I was impressionable, I realized Connie had a thing for broken men. Maybe she was afraid of losing control of the situation again, like she had when she was little, like she had when she was married, no matter how worldly and successful she became. And so she preferred to be in relationships where she felt like she could maintain the upper hand by fixing men, and even controlling them. The problem is that you can't really control anyone, and people who are broken tend to be extremely unreliable, so as much as she'd tried to avoid it, Connie ended up getting hurt.

I also think that the people she chose to partner with early in her life (i.e., her husbands) sort of broke her spirit by making her doubt that love and marriage could ever really work out. She would never marry again. And she would hold back, even when she dated someone really wonderful, as she did in the case of Bill Medley of the Righteous Brothers. He was stable, and they were devoted to each other—I think she would even go so far as to say he was a soul mate, one of the great loves of her life—but she was put off by his dedication to routine. He ate the same thing every day (Grape-Nuts for breakfast, and steak and a baked potato for dinner). Every day. There was no real spontaneity there. Who knows, maybe she could have gotten used to his more docile nature. But during the moments when they could have come together, in marriage or as a real couple, they were always married to other people. (I, however, did see the value and stability in the Medley name, and I "married" his son, Darrin, when we were around eleven.)

In her mind, there were the ones that got away—the sparkly ones, like Elvis Presley and Neil Armstrong. Again, both married. But my mom never ended up with greatness. The serious relationships she had after my dad, well, none of the men were ever as successful, or even just as realized, as my mother. As I said, she didn't want to lose that upper hand.

All of this was hard to witness, even at a young age. Obviously, I was devoted to my mom. I didn't particularly like sharing her attention (not that any of her boyfriends really competed for her affection with Tricia and me), and many of her broken men had substance abuse issues. This caused some dramatic moments around the house throughout the years. And on several occasions, I even went toe-to-toe with these men. Maybe that was a questionable thing for a child to do to her mother, but it was an honest expression of how I felt. I wanted better for her—and for all of us.

Drum roll, please.

First, there was Ralph. He was from Las Vegas, and he was in Connie's band. He was a monster drummer (that means a really good one). He was also a raging alcoholic (that's bad). I don't remember if I was aware of him when he was just a musician in her band, but suddenly, he was in our lives. He lived with us, and I could never be sure when he was going to be drunk or high. One day, the school bus dropped Tricia and me off outside our Malibu house, wearing school uniforms and saddle shoes. When I opened the door, there he was passed out on the ground in the entryway, with a shotgun. I know this sounds crazy, but even with scenes like this, I was never afraid for my safety. But I was glad to have Tricia, as we often huddled together in the wake of such behavior. Mostly, I was sad and disappointed for my mother's choice, which was heavy for a daughter to take on for her mom.

On many occasions, I came home from school to broken glass, food overcooking on the stove, and Ralph passed out on the couch. Or him slumped at the kitchen table, having what he called a "tuna party," eating a tuna sandwich, which I could smell from the moment I crossed the threshold.

"Come here, give us a kiss," he'd say to Connie, lurching over to where she was. I even remember him climbing over his drum kit while Connie was midsong onstage, drunk out of his mind, in search of a kiss.

He was never inappropriate with me. He even took me to my father-daughter dance in middle school. But I immediately recognized that such behavior wasn't attractive or appropriate—it was disgusting. I also knew that he wasn't my mom's equal—he was living in her house, working in her band, and he had nothing to contribute to her life. I don't mean he had to have money to be worth her time. I mean he had to have something.

I had a strong pull over my mom, and I was finally driven to wield my influence regarding Ralph. That same year of El Niño, we had a dramatic rockslide in Malibu, and part of the Pacific Coast Highway near our house was closed for almost a year. To leave the neighborhood, we had to park our car on one side of the rockslide, then walk down the PCH and get into another car we'd left parked on the other side—and vice versa to get home. So for the first two years I went to Marymount Junior School, we took a bus, walked, and then got on another bus. One day, we were in my mom's little Mercedes, with WILDFL on the license plate. Ralph was driving. For some reason, I was in the front seat, and my mom was in the backseat. He was a drummer, so he was always tap-tap-tapping out a beat on whatever was at hand—this time, the steering wheel. We were waiting at the slide, where they were actually letting cars through by now. I watched him drumming. It was erratic and unsettling. And then, just like that, I couldn't take it anymore. I jumped out of the car, and I went running down Pacific Coast Highway. My mom came after me, obviously concerned.

"I can't live with him anymore," I said.

He moved out.

I don't think we were the only family where something like this ever went down. Connie wanted Tricia and me to be happy, so we were given the liberty to make our own decisions about what we thought. And she wanted our opinion (until she didn't want our opinion anymore).

When I went away to college, and I wasn't there to supervise, my mom hooked up with another one, a onetime actor who brought up the same feelings for me. I came home on break to find that she'd bought a house on Cherokee Lane and was now living there with him.

"I have big plans for this house," she said.

The house was strange and dated, a fixer-upper, and I'd never lived there before. There was a little front house, over a garage, where Tricia was living, but there was no place for me. I felt out of sorts. But more than that, I didn't like how my mom seemed to be changing for this guy. Not just the house, either. He drove a Corvette. So my mom got a Corvette.

Really, Mom, again? I thought.

This relationship also changed my connection with Connie dramatically. That probably would have happened naturally, because I was an adult now, and I didn't have the same influence on her that I'd had when I was a child. But if I'd been around, I would have spotted this guy a mile away and never let him get his hold on Connie. He and I used to get into terrible fights. He thought I was a bitch. I thought he was a loser. We were both right. Even after they stopped being romantically or sexually involved, she let him live at Delfern . . . for decades . . . and gave him a job in the shipping department and kept him on the payroll of her skin-care company, Forever Spring. He was still living in the lap of luxury when we sold Delfern in 2016. Before then, though, I had my own life to lead. My girl was grown up, and I had to let her fly. But when she became vulnerable and needed me most, I felt I couldn't stand by and watch this strange relationship drain her anymore.

It was never that she didn't care about her children or what we thought. It was more that she was at max capacity of how to parent. Now, I look back and wonder, at what point do you abandon your needs and your dreams for your children, and when do you put your children first, in terms of what job you take or which man you bring home? And at what point do you choose something because it fulfills *you* and makes *you* happy, even if your kids don't agree?

"I did the best I could," my mom has always said.

And I absolutely know she did . . . her best.

The Hole

During all these years, my mom always seemed to be giving to everyone—her boyfriends, her kids, her extended family, and her many philanthropic causes. In the early nineties, she was invited to an event in Jackson Hole. She fell in love with the place and the people. And because she does have a big heart, and she is generous with her time and her money, she decided to hold an annual event there, with the proceeds going to a community-run charity. It was a great excuse to show off her new town, and I really felt that she was delivering something to them by creating an atmosphere of love and generosity, almost always at her own expense. I'm not sure if the charity ever made a lot of money, but in the twenty years we went up there, we enjoyed bringing together a group of familiar faces, and the town seemed to enjoy it.

From the old Hollywood guard to hot young stars, a who's who of talent was in attendance over the years. The events included a celebrity hockey match, a ski race, and in the evening, the Extravaganza, as Connie always called it. There are twenty years' worth of great stories of artists from all walks of life gathering in the Snow King ski resort lobby to sing until four in the morning. Connie ordered up breakfast, which arrived in dozens of styrofoam containers and was passed around by local cowboys.

One year, Debbie came. After she and Connie both performed at the Gala, we all reconvened at our beautiful Jackson Hole home. After a little wine, everyone overshared about family and career. The consummate pro, Debbie knew that I had a video camera. (If only we could show video in this book.) Clearly visible on the video was the mix of affection and everlasting competitiveness between the matriarchs of the Fisher brood, as they compared notes on their careers and their children's.

Connie had become an accidental mogul. In the place of romantic relationships, she turned to work, where she revealed her business acumen. When she started her skin-care line, Forever Spring, she found something that she loved and was good at. She got her groove on and made millions of dollars, which afforded us the luxury of real estate, and family trips, and security. She was absolutely in her prime.

But, personally, the nineties were a hard decade for my mom. In 1992, she and Tricia were in Las Vegas for the annual industry-wide cosmetics show, where Forever Spring had a booth and business was booming. Out of nowhere, my sister called me.

"Mom's in the hospital," she said.

"What?!?"

"Yeah, she collapsed," Tricia said. "I don't know. I'm freaking out. Can you come here right now?"

I went right to the airport. As I was walking through the airport, I saw pockets of people raptly watching the wall-mounted televisions. They were looking at fires, and big plumes of smoke, and riots in the streets of Los Angeles in the wake of the Rodney King verdict. I was concerned, but I was very consumed with getting to Las Vegas, so I just glanced at the televised inferno and got on the plane.

When I landed, which was only forty-five minutes later, and approached a bank of televisions, Los Angeles was still aflame. I didn't have time to really think about it, though. I just wanted to get to my mom. The doctors reassured us it was "just a little scare." Okay, but what was happening? Stress because she was working too hard? Or the fact that she didn't eat well, and she never had? She didn't exercise? She didn't even drink water? Was she still taking diet pills? The warning signs were glaring, if only to Tricia and me. And this wouldn't be the last time we would find ourselves agonizing over Connie's heart. The doctors got her back on her feet, and she was ready to go. By now, though, I was fully aware of the L.A. riots, and we had a new concern—getting home.

A concerned business associate, hearing of our plight, offered us a private plane, which would fly us to a little airstrip north of Malibu. Once there, we were taken to a friend's house, where we'd be safe and Connie could rest. But it was only a temporary solution. The city was crazy, Connie was in a weakened state, and we didn't know how bad the conditions would get.

So we got into a car with a couple of our friends and went to our little house in Palm Springs. The whole incident was terrifying. It was the first time I saw my mom as anything less than invincible. I saw the beginning of deterioration, and it was horrible. I was scared by the possibility of losing her, and what that would mean for Tricia and me. All this with the backdrop of civil unrest and violence in the streets of Los Angeles.

Just a few years after that, juxtaposed with a career that brought her great success she didn't really expect, she was brought down once again. This time, with the loss of her mother, her three brothers, and her favorite uncle . . . in rapid succession over the next few years. First Ralphie; then her mother; then John; then her favorite uncle—who was my godfather, my great-uncle Joe; and then big brother Charlie. Connie felt tremendous loss. Her only surviving family is her sister, Ava. Not a day goes by that Connie doesn't mourn the loss of these loved ones who meant so much to her.

Then, it should have been a time of celebration and accolades, leading up to a milestone birthday. She was rejoicing over the birth of her first grandchildren and enjoying great success, including the sheer accomplishment of writing and directing her first movie, *Saving Grace B. Jones,* when she was seventy years old. As she always likes to say, the film is a true story . . . or at least "inspired by true events," as the movie includes murder and a child drowning. Although not quite as dramatic, Connie's own story was just as terrifying for her.

When she was around eleven years old, Connie did witness a violent fight that ended in a stabbing in Brooklyn. There was obvious concern for the impact this might have on a girl, and the family sent her to live with a friend of her father's in Boonville, Missouri, for the summer. While there, the family patriarch's sister came home from the mental hospital she'd been invited to, and Connie developed a remarkable connection with her. Although their interaction was relatively brief, they truly connected. The impression their rapport made on Connie was so profound that she would dramatize the woman as the title character in the film she made nearly sixty years later.

I was incredibly proud of my mom for embarking on such an intense artistic endeavor and for finally bringing it to fruition at seventy, an age when plenty of people are content to go on cruises and paint watercolors. Because I was so inspired by Mom's determination, I was excited to attend several screenings of the film with her. I can't tell you how many times someone approached her after the movie.

"Connie, I can't believe you went through all that!" the person would say, radiating concern.

Connie would nod intently, as if reliving the trauma all over again right there.

When the person walked away, I'd lean in to Connie. "Mom, you can't do that! That's not what really happened." But I've come to accept that this aspect of my mom's personality is best viewed as one of her charms. My mom leans toward exaggeration, even just exuberance. She's a storyteller. The truth is that many aspects of her childhood were difficult and upsetting. And as any human being might do, she chose to costume the pain of her childhood abandonment as something dramatic and romantic. Not a bad trait for someone who gravitated toward the business of make-believe.

Connie had long wanted to helm her own film, and so she was rightfully proud of her accomplishment when she released *Saving Grace B. Jones* into the world. But what should have been a time of revelry was marred by her poor health. She continued to not take care of herself and ignored the warning signs she'd been given.

In the days approaching her seventieth birthday, while attending to another health concern, her doctors told us they needed to insert stents immediately into her arteries, which were 99 percent blocked. These days, this is a routine operation for somebody who's in fantastic shape, and even though Connie radiated light wherever she went, she wasn't. It would be the second time the threat of possibly losing my mother became very real. Tricia and I debated whether to cancel all our plans, alert all of Connie's friends. We knew how she would feel, and what a prideful person she was, so that was out of the question. She would recover. And she did soon find herself recovering quickly.

Up until then, I'd always believed there was nothing this broad couldn't do and nothing that was going to take her down. Now I wasn't so sure. We had entered into an era of vigilance over her health. We paused for a moment to take this in and adjust to our new normal. And then we did as Connie always had—helped her to put on her makeup and high heels, and celebrated her milestone birthday with family and friends. We ended up throwing her a beautiful party. She felt healthy and looked gorgeous . . . but behind the scenes, within our family, everyone was a little shaken up.

The resilience of the lioness, the matriarch, the self-proclaimed Italian street fighter who did everything better than everyone else and wasn't going to go down without a fight was still there. She picked herself up by her bootstraps. No matter what was thrown at her, she persevered. Still having many responsibilities, and being a master in the art of saving face, she continued to act, to further the development of new projects, and to perform in Vegas at the Riviera for the last time.

A few years ago, we even acted together. I was starring in a movie, *Search Engines,* with another actress set to play my character's mother. She fell out, and the director suggested that my mom do it. I wasn't so sure. Not that she wouldn't be great—the part was very much in her wheelhouse. But I knew what it was like to have Connie for a mom. I wanted to work with someone else, so I could explore another type of mother-daughter relationship. Suggestions were made for

Lainie Kazan, who'd played my mother on TV, and Valerie Harper, who'd also played my mom on TV. So why not give a girl a break?—Mama needed a new pair of shoes.

On the set, Connie was a little sluggish (we didn't know it then, but her stroke was imminent). It was indie filmmaking at its finest. In the heat of summer, we had to use a porta-potty. Until the woman across the street poked her head out the door, realized she was in the presence of greatness, and offered Connie Stevens her AC and her bathroom. Mom was a trouper. I *hate* that word, but she really was. She was there because she wanted to play this part. She was great. And the film has been well received and even won awards at a bunch of film festivals.

Not long after that, and not knowing she was on the verge of a major health crisis, Connie was cast in another movie. They had just started shooting when I got a call from the director and producer, whom I had worked with before. I was alarmed when I got a message from them, saying they needed to talk with me right away. My first thought was: *Oh no, something happened to my mother on set.* But they wanted to know if I would come in and do these couple of scenes with her. *Really?!* As much as I love to work, and as much as I'd love to work with her again, I wasn't sure. But it was a different role for me—it was the part of the villain, my mother's antagonist. It was a fun part to play, but it was a hard shoot. My mom had a medical emergency on that set. And right after that: her stroke.

Unfortunately this stroke was not one of genius. Or insight. It was an actual cutting off of blood to my mother's brain.

Softly, she screams uncle. She has a faraway look, as if trying to figure out who we are all the time—she can't hear us at all these days and has refused hearing aids, blocking us all out.

It's not as if she's had enough. She's just stopped attempting to join the conversation. The struggle is real. She has screamed uncle, only softly, in the language and tone of an elderly woman. Exactly like my grandmother Eleanor, who stopped speaking—in the sparkling blue pools of light I could see flashes like those I see from my own mother now. Tiny flashes of the warrior—the street fighter we all knew: "Ooh . . . your mother, I loved her!" Everyone loved her . . . I loved her. I love her. How dare she leave me at a time like this? I mean, she hasn't left per se, but she has turned right, away from the light.

It's different now than it used to be. A vintage journal entry of mine from my twenties captures perfectly how Connie was in her full power: *"I can see the lion from where I sleep. Where I wake. When Leo yawns it's threatening. She has this hold, an assuming way of looking at me that makes me feel held. She wants to hold me—to keep me. To spit her pearls at me. With her rant: been there, done that, done it all, nothing I ain't seen or done. Nothing I can learn. Nothing you can teach me—'cause I'm the teacher. You're the student."*

But she's still the lioness. Then, and now, she occasionally roars: "My God took care of me. My God let me live." And often she finds the fight within her to argue with me about politics.

And so she maintains: "I believe that something wonderful is going to happen." The word "wonderful," every time I hear it, I hear her saying it, because wonderful implies full of wonder. And she is . . . full of wonder most of the time. Even now. She is full of enthusiasm and optimism. She's the cockeyed optimist, through and through. She's my mother.

Chapter 4

Oh My Papa

IT WAS A REGULAR SCHOOL night in May. We were perched as a family around the island in the kitchen of our home, watching YouTube videos on my laptop. A regular scene in millions of homes, only these also happened to be home movies of sorts—performances by my father, Eddie Fisher. My three daughters exploded in unison:

"Popsie is just like Mommy."

"Mommy, you sing just like that," said Luna, my youngest.

"That's your face . . . that's my face," said Skylar, my oldest.

"Was Popsie famous, like you?" asked True, in the middle.

Yes, Virginia, there is a Santa Claus.

"Yes, girls, Eddie was an icon," I said. "Incredibly famous . . . the most number-one hits till the Beatles and Elvis."

"Who are they?" Luna asked. HA!!!

How to explain my father to my children? How to understand him myself? The tabloids captured the incredible, one-in-a-million triumphs . . . and the addiction, gambling, womanizing . . . and the wreckage it caused two families . . . including my own. All true, of course. And also, of course, only part of the story. I find Eddie harder to pin down than Connie. It makes sense. He wasn't around in the beginning—for many years. And then, when he was, he wasn't the kind to sit down and pore over old memories—he was always in action, making more memories in every moment. He could be maddening, and absolutely lovely. A contradiction. He was my dad.

Sonny Boy

Eddie Fisher was a South Philly boy. He was born on August 10, 1928—yes, ten years minus two days before my mom. Leos!!! His parents were Russian Jewish immigrants, but I don't really know anything about them, other than the fact that his mom gave him the nickname "Sonny Boy," which stuck. I didn't even realize until recently that he was one of seven children—I'd always thought there were only five of them. His baby sister, Eileen, was his only sister I ever met. My mom says I met his favorite brother, Bunny, but as a baby, so I don't remember him. I think the story I've put together of my father is based on images I've seen, from which I made up my own tale.

Eddie was cute but not in the traditional sense. He had big ears. And he was tiny. As I've heard it, he first sang on the radio when he was twelve or thirteen, after having won some local amateur talent contests and been discovered and introduced by Eddie Cantor. After he was discovered, his star was born immediately. He was a touring singer from the age of eighteen, and he signed his first record contract at twenty-one. All of this can be verified on his Wikipedia page.

But the part of the story I made up, because I wanted to make sense of who he was, has to do with his real story—what shaped him and in turn what shaped me. I think his father was controlling, and the attention he got when he sang was different (i.e., better) than any other interactions he had with anybody. I do believe his mother adored him. Maybe, quite possibly, he was the favorite child. And, naturally, he was even more the favorite when he became famous and started supporting his family. But I wasn't there, so I can't be sure.

I do know that South Philly still claims him as its own. That he served in Korea, but mostly as a morale booster—he didn't actually see any action. That he got all the ladies' panties in a twist, very early on. Apparently, a few pairs of those panties were, from time to time, thrown onto the stage when he was singing. I'm not really sure what he was supposed to do with them when they landed at his feet, but it meant there were girls without panties in the audience, and that made him happy.

My father had thirty-five songs in the Top 40 between 1950 and 1956. He was the Coca-Cola Kid. His million-dollar contract with the soda company was all the talk in 1954. As was the scandal when he married Elizabeth Taylor three and a half hours after getting a divorce from her best friend, Debbie Reynolds.

Both of these tabloid toppers were pure Eddie. He had the voice, sure, but more than that, he had the charisma, the personality. Beautiful women, many of them with a great deal of substance, gravitated toward him, so there must have been something. He himself didn't have a type—female, that was his type.

Bashing Eddie Fisher is old news—to talk about what a cad he was . . . or that he fucked Debbie Reynolds and left two children behind (as Carrie put it in *Wishful Drinking*). As a woman entering the middle of my life, it's hard for me to whine about something that's old hat—the fact that he wasn't around when I was a child.

But let's do it anyway . . . for old times' sake.

He has two memoirs for you to cuddle up with if you care to hear his two different versions of the truth. He spelled Tricia's name wrong in one of them, *My Life, My Loves*. Was it an instance of ego gone awry, or were there no fact-checkers back then? Like, really, how could that happen? Did he think that's how her name was spelled? Did he insist that was how to spell her name, and did they check it and tell him no, and still, he insisted?

We'll never know. But it's very Eddie. Unfortunately.

I'VE ALWAYS DESCRIBED the feeling of growing up as Eddie's daughter, with his famous Fisher name as my own, as having a comma after your name. Which we all did—Joely Fisher, comma, daughter of . . . Carrie Fisher, comma, daughter of . . . the perception was that we all had the same things, were treated the same way, had greater access to showbiz jobs . . . and showbiz money. When the reality of Eddie's legacy was much more complicated.

"I see you in my face," he said to me, years after we'd reconciled.

"I see my mother," I half-truthed.

I see them both. I hear them both.

THERE'S ALSO A lot of Eddie that has to be set aside to get to the good stuff. That's just the truth. Earlier this year, I was at a family dinner when my brother, Todd, reminded me of an interview we'd done—Eddie, Todd, Tricia Leigh, and me—with Larry King when Eddie's second book, *Been There, Done That,* was published. In an attempt to "get it right" this time he'd hired a ghostwriter, David Fisher (no relation), to collaborate, and Eddie was sober.

Todd recounted Eddie saying, "Connie stopped putting out. Of course I left her."

I remember the interview. All of us, *almost* the whole family, in this little CNN satellite studio on Sunset Boulevard in Hollywood. It was very cold and we were speaking in front of a tiny live audience of five people. There was a feeling like Eddie was showing us off. It felt good to be shown off by Eddie, until we were once again blindsided by his obliviousness.

He was cool and charismatic. Mysterious, but funny, and made you feel interesting and beautiful for a moment. Like Connie, he never really cared if we were smart. It didn't matter . . . as long as you were pretty. And he always said I was beautiful. When Tricia and I were a part of Connie's stage show as teenagers, when she would bring us out onstage to sing, she used to always introduce us with the same joke: "Bodies by Fisher." I think for Mom, it was almost like: *Eddie was good for something.*

He loved my singing. He was proud and impressed by my talent—I think he was even humbled by it. He loved to sing with me. And he told me I was a better singer than he ever was. He used to say: "I'm a singer, but you're a zinger."

Depending on which one of his kids was in the audience on a given night, he used to repurpose his material when he was onstage. If Carrie was in attendance, it was:

"I used to be Eddie Fisher . . . now I'm Carrie Fisher's father."

Or, if I was catching his show:

"I used to be Eddie Fisher . . . now I'm Joely Fisher's father."

ele

Bridging the Gap

I only saw Eddie a handful of times as a child. I once told my mom that I had a vision of my father in the house, before they were divorced.

"Oh, Joely, that's ridiculous," she said. "You were nine months old when we started to diverge."

I knew what I remembered was true. It looked—and felt—so real in my memory.

"I can see you guys at the edge of a pool," I said, demonstrating how they were reaching toward me. "And I'm on an army green raft . . ."

"Ahh," she said, because now she could remember it, too.

"How could you remember that?" she asked.

"I don't know," I said. "I wasn't old enough to even really see it."

I'd been less than a year old, but I had a vision of my father and mother together. According to Connie, somewhere there were photos that were taken when Eddie was in fact living at our house with us. It left an impression. I always had a keen sense of people coming in and out of Connie's life . . . and that was probably the last time I ever saw my dad in that particular house.

After that, the promise of time with Eddie meant the promise of a visit from him. Me and Tricia waiting by the front door, with our Snoopy suitcases, for a visit that would never happen. There were the handful of visits—the attempt at the Dodgers game that ended in a car crash (literal), the joint visit to Debbie's and Connie's Malibu homes. In these years, Connie did attempt to connect us with our father, to get him on the phone with us for our birthdays. She was usually unsuccessful, but she never said a negative word about him to us. And when we were old enough to be capable of reaching out to him ourselves, she was maybe cautious . . . but always encouraging of the burgeoning relationship.

When I was sixteen, I decided to do a semester of college, early, and in Paris. I told my mom that I was going to stay with Eddie in New York City for two weeks on my way to France. I think she knew this was something I needed to do, and if she had her reservations (imagine the reservations?), she kept them to herself. She suggested I call him first. Arrangements were made. And I arrived on his doorstep, for the first time going to him, instead of waiting in vain for his arrival.

At the time, he was living with his girlfriend, Lyn Davis, who is now Lyn Lear, as she's been married to Norman Lear for decades. I arrived, with my suitcases, at his beautiful brownstone on Seventy-Fourth Street. I had the whole bottom floor to myself, while they were upstairs. I'm not sure what was really going on up there, 24/7, but the windows were blacked out and covered in heavy drapes. One day, Lyn asked me if I wanted to go for a run. So I went for a run with her. Which was weird, because I don't run, and she'd probably been up all night.

Eddie may not have been anything like a traditional father figure. He did make sure I had money, giving me a few hundred-dollar bills here and there—Dad always loved a pocket full of Benjamins. I was free to come and go as I pleased—and I did do some underage clubbing. But he was keeping an eye on me, in his own way. When I came home at three o'clock in the morning, he came out of his room, in his underwear, and leaned over the balcony to make sure it was me.

"Oh, good," he said. "You're home."

And he went back to bed—or at least back to his bedroom.

I didn't see a whole lot of him during the two weeks I was there, but I appreciated having the time with him. We visited from time to time after that. A year or two later, he was living on Ninety-Second and Second, and he had a girlfriend, Jeannie. She worked in PR and had gone to Emerson College, and she ended up influencing my decision to go there. While I was staying on his couch for a few days, I was coming out of the bathroom one morning, after I'd taken a shower. I was wrapped in a bath towel, and so when I saw my dad standing there, I decided to make a joke.

"Hey!" I said, and (cheekily) showed him my ass—on purpose. Just as a goof.

"Oh!" he said. "Do that again."

He always brought it up after that, and he'd say: "Show me your tits." Not just to me, but also to Tricia. And . . . Carrie. And, sadly . . . Carrie's daughter, Billie. He often spoke inappropriately about all of his daughters. He never, ever, ever would have touched us in any way. But he didn't know how to communicate with a woman, other than sexually. And his charms had gotten him so far in all other areas of his life that it was the only device he had. He thought it was a funny, clever, sexy way to be. And a way to express that we were beautiful and desired, which I know . . . is a very weird thing to say about your father, and to let him off the hook. But I don't think he was actually objectifying us sexually. I really think it was the only thing he knew. It was just who he was. He thought of women—all women—as beautiful creatures, including his daughters. He revered them and was in awe of them, and he admired women who had brains and talent, and, yes . . . tits.

When I began attending Emerson College in Boston in 1985, I was on the same coast as Eddie. He even came to parents' weekend my first year at Emerson. That was the first time Eddie and Connie had been in the same room in more than a decade. To be thrust into the same space with long-time divorced parents would have rocked any nervous, nubile daughter. Astonishingly, they showed up wearing the same sweater. Swear to God. The photo of the three of us from that weekend has always been one of my favorites. Seeing them flanking me, in crazy, brightly colored eighties print sweaters from French Connection, and the deer-in-headlights look on this normally cool, mature college freshman. These polar opposites at least had an equally distinct sense of fashion.

I used to love to go to New York City for the weekend, and now I had a key to Eddie's apartment in Battery Park. This was a huge leap, from having only seen this man maybe three, or five, times in my childhood to getting to know him when he was there—and now I had the key. Even just being around his stuff was a novelty. And, just like that, without any discussion or fanfare, we had a relationship. During one winter stay, I didn't have a coat. Like any Fisher (the first in a long line of enthusiastic givers), he ran to the hallway closet to give me one of his. This one was a floor-length beaver coat—floor length on him. His initials monogrammed on the inside pocket, EJF, actually, two-thirds of which are my initials. It's fur . . . so I don't wear it anymore, but I still have it. Years later, I wore it onstage in *Cabaret*. It was Sally Bowles's prized possession—the one she had to sell at the end to get an abortion. It had an enormous significance, personally, which infused my character's relationship to it and the letting go of it onstage night after night. My father came to see me in that show nine times—he was so proud of me. He was quoted in the *Toronto Sun* as saying, "I was one of the worst fathers in the world. And there's no way I can change any of that. I can't make up for it by seeing Joely every night in *Cabaret*." What he said to me was, "Is that my coat?" LOL. He felt like a part of the act. Truth be told . . . having either of my parents in the audience, ever, made me reach for the notes.

From there, I started to have a relationship with Eddie that I don't think my other siblings did . . . I don't really know why . . . yes, I do. I pushed myself on him. I demanded of him more than anyone else, so I got more. Because he wasn't going to volunteer anything, but if you demanded it, he wasn't going to say no. I mean, if you show up on someone's doorstep (literally) they have to deal with you. Carrie has, famously, said that Eddie liked her better after she was famous . . . he liked famous. It got his attention. But that wasn't the only thing that did.

Enter the Dragon

Around this time, he met his fifth wife, Betty Lin. She was a wealthy Chinese businesswoman who lived in San Francisco. I've heard some people be dismissive of Betty Lin and sort of roll their eyes when they refer to her. But I have nothing but admiration and respect for this woman who adored my father. She made his final years so much better than they otherwise would have been. She didn't love him because he was Eddie Fisher. She liked Eddie offstage. And she improved his relationships with all his children. She really did. She wanted him to be a father, and she would remind him to call his kids, to show up for us.

They had a really great, normal relationship (especially compared to Eddie's track record). They traveled. They cooked dinners together. She monitored his diet. Yes, she admired his talent and helped him to release a final album, but that wasn't where most of their focus was. She kept on top of his medication and made sure he was eating right. She took care of him when he wasn't well. And most notably, Betty Lin sent Eddie Fisher to Betty Ford.

During the early years of their relationship, they traveled all around the world together. I made several trips with them to the South of France, beginning when I was twenty-one. We stayed with a family who were very well connected in Iran. They were Betty Lin's friends from San Francisco, and this was their summer home. The patriarch had died, but in his lifetime, he had been the architect of the Shah of Iran's summerhouse. It was through them that we met the exiled Iranian queen, Farah, as they all summered in the South of France.

The lifestyle was something to be seen, really—lavish parties, yachts, sprawling coastal palaces, and racing along the Haute Corniche in Monaco (where Princess Grace lost her life in a fatal crash). Sure, I'd grown up in the world of show business, but we were like carny folk compared to the wealthy, cultured people I encountered in Europe. Fortunately, I was well versed in the language of derbies, and Grand Prix, and having an audience with royalty, thanks to my mother.

One of the nights we were there, Eddie and I were asked to sing for Queen Farah, who is still the queen of Iran, although she has been in exile since 1979. It wasn't a show, per se. Our hosts had set up chairs in their living room, where a small, well-heeled audience sat. There was this reverent feeling of singing for royalty, but I was struck by the sensation of singing *with* royalty—my father. Once again, my father kvelled when I unleashed my voice, respect and admiration radiating out of him.

Eddie gave to me, in a few summers of familial vacations, something I hadn't experienced with him until then—the broadening of horizons, which I'd previously only had with my mother. It brought us closer together, so naturally, I would be his best man when he married Betty Lin on July 14, 1993, in Laguna Beach. It felt special, to be there with him for the launching of this new chapter in the Eddie Fisher story, now my story.

Eddie may have been tamed enough to survive, but he was always larger than life.

He always wore these, literally, rose-colored lenses (much like Carrie with her purple progressives—the Fisher family penchant for enhancing the color of reality . . . another family trait). He would wisp into the room, put me in his sights, and . . . I was pink.

The nineties were a great time for our relationship. I'd just pick up the phone and call him, talk about nothing, talk about everything. When Eddie was in L.A., I loved to share one of my favorite hot spots with him, Fred Segal on Melrose (especially knowing that, as the original King Fisher, he loved to shop). Perhaps it's silly to hold this moment so close, us bonding as we shopped for velvet loafers, but having grown up without him, I grabbed at anything I could. And so, yes, I was thrilled to take him shopping—and for the two of us to get matching pairs of shoes. Betty Lin, always by his side, was a great documenter and curator of our time together. She always had a camera and always made sure I got a copy of our moments together, photographs of Eddie and me, souvenirs . . . proof.

After having had almost no connection for so many years, it's strange and wonderful to look back on this period of time when I saw Eddie with frequency. For my mom's sixtieth birthday, in 1998, we had a big party in San Francisco. And because Eddie's seventieth birthday was two days later, it became a joint celebration.

Before the evening's festivities, Tricia and I joined Eddie in his hotel room. He came out of the bathroom in his underwear, jumped up onto a chair, and posed.

"Shazam!" he yelled, arms up, dramatically.

He was kooky, and charming, and inclusive. He loved working the room, even if his daughters were the only people in it. But of course, maybe, he would have preferred a big crowd. He loved the fame, the feeling of being Eddie Fisher. Performing came naturally to him, always.

That party was a knockout. Food and drinks and . . . of course . . . music. We all sang as a family—Connie and Eddie and Tricia and me. In the photos you see a shared love of showbiz . . . the symmetry, the circumference of the mouth in full belt, and the joy of being together. The takeaway . . . it's hard not to wonder what could have been.

The setting for the party was a nightclub, DV8, which was owned by Betty Lin's son. His name was Lawrence, but he called himself Dr. Winkie.

If someone asked, "What sort of doctor?"

He responded: "A doctor of the night."

'Nough said.

I spent a bit of time, here and there, with Lawrence and his then-wife, Este. They had been among the few guests at my dad's wedding to Betty Lin. They were always quite pleasant.

All of this would have been fine—more than fine. I mean, my family is certainly no stranger to eccentricity. But. When Betty Lin died in 2001, she created a trust that would have left my father more than comfortable until he died. That's what her orders were. He'd have a home and caregivers and all that he needed. And Winkie got the many buildings the family owned in San Francisco. But if anybody contested the will, everything went into a trust controlled by Betty Lin's brother. Naturally, Winkie contested the will. A man his mother had loved for more than a decade was to get nothing.

My father ended up destitute, basically. It was awful. And when he reached a point where he couldn't sing anymore—devastation. Years of addiction had taken a toll on his voice, and then age and loss did the rest. For somebody like that—Eddie, Connie, Debbie—when you're no longer able to do the thing you love the most, that brought you the most joy—quite literally produce sound—how can you feel like you have a place? From there, it's a downward spiral.

Before *Wishful Drinking* went to Broadway, Carrie toured across the states with her show. This included a long engagement in Berkeley, California, in early 2008. What a great idea to move my father from San Francisco—where he'd lived in an apartment on top of Ghirardelli Square, with views of Alcatraz, with Betty Lin—to this cute little house in Berkeley. It was charming and had a view, and he would be near her. But it isolated him. Prior to that, he'd had a social life, a few remaining friends, and his caregivers, whom of course he fondled inappropriately. Adorable. They loved him and took care of him. Now he remained in his new house, which wasn't as easy to get to as his centrally located San Francisco condo.

In mid-2010, I went up to San Francisco for an AIDS benefit in which I'd often sung. It seemed like a good excuse to bring all the kids, and to get Tricia and her family in on it, too. We went to see Eddie the morning after my show. Tricia was there with her husband and her three sons. And I was there with my two older girls, Skylar and True, and newly adopted Olivia Luna. So my father got to meet all the grandchildren.

The visit was bittersweet. He had been diagnosed with prostate cancer, degenerative arthritis in his spine, and Parkinson's. He was bedridden. He was obviously weak and had moments of confusion. At one point, he saw Tricia standing in the doorway of his room.

"Tell Carrie to come in," he said.

Tricia and I exchanged a loaded look.

Perhaps understandably, when he saw Luna, he wanted to know:

"Where did the black baby come from?"

"She's mine, Dad," I said. "That's Baby Luna."

After that, he didn't seem to give it another thought.

True went out and picked some flowers and brought them in for him.

"Here, Popsie," she said, putting them onto his bed.

"One of the little blond girls brought me flowers," he said.

A little heartbreaking, but a tender moment. Tricia's husband, Byron, at the piano, all of us singing, and then, piling onto Eddie's bed for a photograph to capture the memory.

I TALKED TO Eddie quite frequently that summer, but I didn't get back up to see him. Several months later, one late afternoon in September, I received a call from one of the women who cared for him. She was upset, and she told me that he wasn't well—we should come. It wasn't going to be long. I got on the phone with him right away.

"Okay, Dad, you're going to be okay," I said, trying to make light of the situation—for him, for me. "We're going to come see you. We're all going to come."

"Okay," he said.

"I love you, Dad," I said, and I could tell he heard me.

"Love you," he said, his voice weak, but I could just barely make out the words.

I conferred with Tricia and Carrie—who would be flying in from somewhere other than L.A.—about whether or not we should get on a plane immediately. We all had the urge, the need, to be there with him. But we also had families, schedules to organize. *Could we get there?* The last flights to the Bay Area were approaching fast. We agreed to all get on the first flight out in the morning.

His caregiver called an hour later, crying. "He's gone."

Damn it, couldn't he have held out till morning? Could we have made it? Could I have saved him? Could we have saved each other? Perhaps in some way we did. I know, at least, he heard my voice as he departed. And although I wouldn't be there to send him off, we all knew forgiveness in that moment.

When we arrived the next morning, Tricia and I met Carrie and Billie at the hotel in Berkeley where Carrie had stayed when she did her show there. Carrie had already made phone calls and organized the removal of Eddie's body from his house. Eddie's dog, Minnie, was there in the corner. We spent the day in the room, not really knowing how to feel, but huddling together, awkwardly laughing and telling Dad stories. We wrestled with the decision that had been made to move him to Berkeley, where he was isolated. We all were just trying to wrap our minds around the loss. And then, the next day, we were going to take care of business.

Betty Lin had made all the arrangements in advance, and as she had passed years before . . . everything was already set up. So we drove to just outside of San Francisco, near the airport, passing the Italian burial grounds, the Greek, the Irish Catholics, the Temple Sinai, one after the other. In this area, there are more bodies laid to rest, per square foot, than anywhere else in the world. All those headstones and mausoleums. Finally, we arrived at Cypress Hill. This cemetery is for the remains and burial of Chinese people. And Hells Angels. And now, Eddie Fisher.

The man who took us around, and showed us where the urn would rest, seemed from central casting. He was six foot six. He was, literally, an undertaker. We all snickered about his resemblance to Lurch . . . his embalming fluid nightcaps . . . hopped up as we were on exhaustion and grief. I'm sure Carrie's remarks were funnier than any of ours, but we were all rattling them off like we were on the "Borscht Belt."

We washed up in front of the shelf where Betty Lin's urn rested.

"Is that where Eddie's is going to be?" we asked, our voices hushed, taking it in.

And then we were brought to a room where he rested in a simple wooden box.

Carrie had gotten there before us and had already seen what he looked like, so she was prepared. And she also, naturally, fell into her role as the eldest. She grabbed Tricia and me by the hands.

"Come on . . . come on," she said. "We're going to do this."

The three of us stood there, arm in arm, looking down over our father . . . our father who art in heaven. He looked nothing like himself. Nothing at all. He was a tiny guy, but his stomach was distended. We all have these full Fisher lips, a flat one on the bottom . . . all of us. I looked for any resemblance . . . to myself . . . to Eddie.

But he was not in there.

I heard it said once in a movie that people look smaller without their spirits . . . and that's exactly how it was with Eddie. He looked like something was missing—his spirit. He was dressed in the same hospital gown he'd been wearing in the end. It still breaks my little-girl heart that he didn't get to be made up and decked out in a purple velvet tuxedo jacket, which he probably should have been, even though he was being cremated. Still, we dug deep and managed to wring the humor out of a heartbreaking situation, talking about how he would have probably been pissed at what he looked like.

We three Fisher girls stood over our father's body, clinging to each other, in such a crazy, unfathomable moment. We held our arms around each other and, of course . . . we sang.

"So if you're worried and you can't sleep . . . count your blessings instead of sheep . . . and you'll fall asleep counting your blessings."

We tucked joints into the box around him, so he'd go out on a "high" note.

That was Eddie's funeral.

And then, we collapsed into this trio of Fisher girls and sobbed . . . and sobbed.

Carrie was the one who didn't allow the tears to go on for too long. I appreciated that, because the moment was like a good-bye kiss, or when you're on the phone with someone you love who's far away, and neither of you wants to hang up, severing the connection. It was impossible to accept that we were going to walk out of that room without him, and we would never see him again, never hear his deep tenor voice, never make him laugh. Thank God for my sisters.

"Okay, that's it," Carrie said, scooping us up once again. "We love you, Oh My Papa."

And then there was nothing more to do, so we left.

Carrie, who was still on the road with *Wishful Drinking,* had to fly out right away. Not quite ready to break up the trio, we stood in the courtyard of our friends' San Francisco home and let them salve us in laughter. And then the moment came when we had no choice but to say our good-byes. Carrie left.

Tricia and I continued on to Eddie's house, daunted by the task ahead of us. We had only been there once before, so the property was strange to us, and even more so because of what had just happened there, and the fact that our father was now gone. We went through his remaining possessions, trying to work as quickly as we could, but it still took a full day. It wasn't like we were digging through his things for items of value. We were looking for things that were valuable to us—pieces of him. By the end of his life, he was destitute, and there was nothing left of his wealth or his finery. But there were still many items that had major sentimental value for us—his records, his glasses, even his dry cleaning.

We rented a car to drive back to Los Angeles, and we packed it with what we saw as his treasures. I have a beautiful bright purple silk shirt; another silk shirt, pink with pinstripes, that I can just see him wearing, which was still in the dry cleaning bag, stapled, with EDDIE FISHER written on the receipt; this perforated leather beige jacket that he always had on; a pair of his glasses; a box of bow ties; a pair of velvet shoes, which I gave to a dear friend, making her very happy; Eddie's dog, Minnie.

It's striking what captures your heart in moments like this. I came across these Chinese soup bowls that were Betty's. As long as he was with her, I'd seen him eating out of these bowls. I smile now, if I see my daughters eating cereal, or if I enjoy a scoop of ice cream, out of these silly, sentimental bowls.

That was the bulk of what we took, along with photos and a giant bag of empty prescription bottles that we needed to dispose of. Tricia wanted his piano, which we were all in agreement about. Then we called Todd to tell him we had some things for him. He was at his ranch, so he was closer to Dad's house in Berkeley than we were in L.A.

"What do you want us to do?" we asked. "Do you want any of his clothes or anything? There's probably not really anything you want here."

"Let me try to arrange to get you the piano," he said, trying to be helpful. "I don't want any of his clothes. I don't want anything of his."

Tricia and I drove back to L.A. together, just the two of us (plus Minnie), trying to get used to the fact that Eddie was gone. Because he'd been interred in San Francisco, there was no big service for him. But we did organize a small memorial here at Factor's Famous Deli in Los Angeles. Connie paid for it.

"Invite friends," she said. "We have to celebrate Eddie. You've got to celebrate your father."

A few of the old guard were there. Carrie and some of her friends attended. I put together a slide show, in memoriam. My mom was surprised. She hadn't realized how much time I'd spent with Eddie over the years.

"Wow, you have a lot of memories with your father," she said, simply, without judgment. Happy that he hadn't completely failed as a father—that he had come around in the end.

It was true—I had spent a lot of time with Eddie in the last twenty-five years of his life. I had many incredible images of us, celebrating birthdays, traveling around the world—I love me a photo. Although he'd missed the early years, he'd made up for it.

I wrote something to read at the memorial. Tricia wrote something. Carrie wrote something. We all got up and said we were his favorite. There was probably a moment in time when he made each one of us feel like we were his favorite. So it was all true.

Chapter 5

Les Animaux: It's a Zoo in Here

ANOTHER MEMBER OF THE FAMILY died today—Minnie. I first met Minnie when I went to visit my dad in the little Berkeley house Carrie had found for him. Minnie was a sweet little Cavalier King Charles spaniel with the saddest eyes ever. She lay with Eddie, who was bedridden, and they talked—Minnie barking at the TV anytime anything piqued her interest. When he died, she was there. When we arrived at the hotel to meet up with Carrie and Billie, there she was. She had been handed over on a thin blue-and-white rope. She had a chew toy and a burgundy cashmere throw that had belonged to my father, which she would never part with because it still smelled like Daddy. I texted a pic home to the family: "Can we keep her?" Naturally, I took the animal, as she felt like an extension of my recently departed father. And we love our dogs in this family. We love animals—well.

My mother and father and Carrie and Debbie and Tricia and Todd and Billie. All of us. Animal people.

Fisher/Stevens/Reynolds/Lourd—all animal people.

Connie with her husky packs and her Malti-Peki-Bichi-Poos (little whitish terrier mutts, the yappers). Eddie had Jack Russells—Jazz, that peed on my head—the Papillons, Butterfly—ya know, the Chinese dogs when Betty Lin came along. Then Minnie—named for a plaything he met in San

Francisco, or the small fridge filled with tiny bottles in hotel rooms. Minibar.

When you grow up on the beach in Malibu—there's that giant stretch of ocean and sand, a dog's paradise—the huskies would bring offerings to my mom—Catch of the Day—seagulls dropped at her bedside with pride. On the other side, the Pacific Coast Highway was a forbidden zone. I can hear my mother now: "The door's wide open!" she'd yell. "Where's Aja [or Kanon or Caine]?"

We lost seven dogs to the treacherous PCH. One survived only because my mother was an animal healer. She nursed him back to health, which she did again on Delfern—where Sunset Boulevard was the culprit. She would lay on hands—carry the dogs around, hand-feed them, and stay up all night, if need be.

She had a dog named Shane (a chow-spitz combo) for seventeen years. When she was pregnant with Tricia, Shane kissed her good-bye and went off to die on the hillside next to the house. Connie cried so long and hard, she induced labor. Tricia was a preemie.

Then of course there was the time that Connie bred huskies—no, really—a litter of ten puppies that I saw delivered at Delfern in the pantry. Naturally, we kept four. Caleb was one of those. Caleb and his father, Gammon, would notoriously get into it. One fateful morning, they scrapped. We were all leaving for a cruise, and it seemed as though they'd have fought till the death without intervention. Connie loved to intervene.

"Stop it! Stop it!"

Not get a hose, or throw a can full of pennies. She would get right in between them, and this time, the fight would end in a giant bite to Connie's right calf. Warrior that she was, we quickly dressed the gaping wound and got aboard a flight . . . and a ship. She started feeling sick—high fever, vomiting. Now we were at sea. She had to be airlifted to Mercy Hospital in Miami.

"I'm gonna be fine," she said. "You all stay. Have a good time. I'll meet the ship in St. Thomas. They just want to be sure I'm okay."

The crowd was expecting my mom, but Phyllis Diller flew in to do the shows.

After a promising ship-to-shore phone call with Connie, we assumed the prognosis would be good, and we kept vigil with shuffleboard and piña coladas. Connie was then flown to UCLA and given astronomical amounts of penicillin. As it turns out, Caleb had killed a possum and carried a disease only found in them—and jungle felines. The infection could have killed Connie at sea.

There were my first-memory dogs, Eppie and Pasha. When I was very young, Tricia and I had our first dogs to call our own. Fidji—after my mom's perfume—and Sascha. One day, after the groomers, I came home from school and named a very fluffy Sascha "Sascha Gabor," after Mom's longtime friend Zsa Zsa. There was Tricia's longtime companion, Roxanne. Cooper, Xander, Gracie, and Gary, Rosie, Aja, Caleb, and Oliver and Cossette and Mack.

We still have Lucky the Chihuahua, whom I bought from two crackheads at a farmers' market. He is pocket-size and travels with us. And Roadie, the rescue, with whom I have developed an intense friendship unlike any of the other dogs I've had. For a time I had two Yorkies, who came to the Eugene O'Neill Theatre every night. Remi and Jezebel got into their bag and went clubbing with me often. I remember sitting in the VIP section at the bar at the W Hotel, post–Broadway performance, with my two designer dogs—enjoying a beverage with Princess Diana—very Paris Hilton.

One night at Carrie's house at Oak Pass, many years ago, we brought over Mom's new skin-care line. The group was the usual suspects, including Albert Brooks, whom I would shortly after get to work with. We were excited to share and tell everyone about the natural ingredients and lack of preservatives and "no animal testing."

"Oh, really?" Albert said. "Rosie!"

Then proceeded to cover Rosie the dog in bright green Baby Soft facial clay.

Then of course, rather famously, Carrie had Gary. I remember sitting on her bed, talking about dogs' names. For her, they had to have people names, and preferably, plain sort of old-fashioned ones—Phil and Ralph made us particularly laugh (with apologies to the Phils and Ralphs out there). Gary was a beloved pet, and as you know, went everywhere with his Momby—nonexclusively, airplanes, talk shows, and conventions. We tend to pick our animals, or they pick us, to save us—I don't trust anyone who doesn't like animals.

Some people like animals more than people. Some people call their dogs their "fur babies" or "four-legged children."

MY LOVE FOR animals extends to the ones out in the world. The ones that are endangered, or even near extinction. Many years ago, when I was just a tiny, fledgling starlet in training, I witnessed elephants in their unnatural habitat. Chained up backstage in a basement, awaiting their next appearance, feathers, rhinestones, et al., in full regalia. Bertha and Tina were the cornerstones of the show at the Golden Nugget. There is even a photo of Connie atop Bertha, as she would join them on the bill the following week. At the other end of the strip was the MGM Grand—the old one that housed a shopping arcade, an old-fashioned candy store, and a movie theater that aired only MGM classics, where I fell in love with Tracy and Hepburn. But the star attraction, parading out multiple times a day, was the MGM lion—there actually were a few alternate beasts. You would wait in line and be photographed alongside them. Their senses dulled by drugs, declawed, and urged at just the right time to roar.

Snap.

I knew, even as tourists enjoyed the novelty of their interactions with these "show ponies," that my crusade to end this exploitation had begun. When old enough I would ensure the rights of animals. And I haven't eaten a four-legged creature since I was eleven years old.

YEARS LATER, I was invited to a party—rather, an afternoon get-together in Hancock Park, Los Angeles, complete with vegan snacks. It was love at first lecture. I was introduced to Donna Gadomski and Jeffrey Flocken, my touchstones at the International Fund for Animal Welfare. This particular campaign they waged was against the atrocity of the whaling industry. The giant, primordial creatures are at risk every day from countries that still consider whaling an industry, some purely because it is traditional and generational. I would join forces with them, along with Goran Visnjic, Kristin Bauer, Amber Valletta, Heather Morris, Slash, and other animal activists from the entertainment industry. I made a pilgrimage to Washington with Goran (crush) to lobby on the Hill, during the Obama administration.

During this time, a lot of strides were made in terms of

the ivory ban as well. Ivory is historically a symbol of wealth and stature. It was used for piano keys, game boards, the inlay of musical instruments, objets d'art. I remember owning all these things. Connie had jewelry—beautiful ivory necklaces and bracelets—intricately carved. I coveted them. With education, I came to learn that you cannot own these things without the tusk of an elephant. The only way to get an elephant tusk is through the slaughtering of the animal. A gentle, sentient beast that should wander and procreate and survive.

I have, in my passion for the cause, conceived of, produced, and directed a PSA campaign for IFAW that encompasses all the arms of the organization—they generously allowed my creativity to flow, and I gathered together my "animal friends"—the guys from Guns N' Roses, Camryn Manheim, Michelle Monaghan, Kate Mara, Dean Norris, Denise Richards, Cheri Oteri, Goran Visnjic, Amber Valletta, and Mark Feuerstein—to take part in two days of shooting and making our plea. Elephants, whales, companion animals, and big cats. Did you know there are more big cats (lions, and tigers, and leopards, oh my) in captivity in Texas and Dade County, Florida, than in the wild? What?! Those "baby" wild animals in roadside zoos and menageries grow up to be "adult" animals that will one day, no doubt, become dangerous.

We were awarded millions of dollars in airtime and spots in airports all over the world, gratis. Worth the effort and appreciated. I truly believe we contributed to the passage of the ivory ban. I had the distinct honor of attending the very first "Ivory Crush" in Denver, where seven tons of seized ivory was ceremoniously crushed to demonstrate that, unless on the face of an elephant, those useless trinkets that are delivered from ivory are worthless. We "crushed" in November

2013 and China soon followed (they are the number-one country consuming ivory). It was historic and unprecedented. We have a long way to go.

We continue the fight, championing animals like the pangolin, which is the number-one trafficked animal and is endangered. Under the current administration, the threat of the reversal of all the progress we've made in terms of the "animal kingdom" is imminent; thus we continue to fight on their behalf. If the Endangered Species Act falls, we fail.

MY FAMILY'S MANY canines have shaped who I am. I sat with a forlorn Dwight (Debbie's dog) at Debbie and Carrie's memorial. And now, Minnie is gone. I am also hopeful, as I look to my daughters' reactions to the loss of their first animal. The love they show, their sensitivity, feels right in line with how everyone in the family feels about their pets and the animals in the world. Creatures big and small create a balance on the planet and great compassion for all living creatures brings balance in the heart.

Chapter 6

Mother . . . Daughter . . . Sister . . . Fisher

IT'S AN HONOR TO BE nominated.

Oh wait, I haven't been nominated . . .

I haven't been nominated in years.

I was nominated once.

It is an honor to be invited . . . to the parties.

But there is no honor in renting a gown, because you're not a nominee, and the designers haven't sent over their "A" pile. Paying to get your hair and makeup done, and for a car, which this year was an Uber. I mean, everyone's doing it. Especially when there isn't a studio or network paying the ten-hour minimum for a limousine.

I have a love-hate relationship with award shows in general. I am not conflicted about celebrating the year's best performances. But Lord knows, in this family, someone raised up a green (smoky)-eyed monster. In my observation, it's something 97 percent of people feel when watching someone else get the award (or anything) they want. And it doesn't help when you've had your thank-you speech written since childhood. (Let me know if you'd like to hear it . . .) But. There is something grand about getting to forgo the cleanse, stay at home, and eat cheese, watching in mismatched pajamas. I can fast-forward through the thank-you speech of a nemesis, give a standing ovation to my favorites, and ugly-cry through the "in memoriam."

On this night, in 2016, I made the effort. An effort of haute magnitude. These are posturing and posing parties, after all. Even if you're not carrying your statuette, you're supposed to behave like, *Oh, well, we all just happened to be here, looking like this . . . funny running into you . . . I hear you're taking an updated swing at* Murphy Brown *. . . have you found your girl yet? I mean, we do just happen to be here . . . and I have prepared an up-tempo and a ballad.*

I am a former Miss Golden Globe, a second-generation actress chosen because the Hollywood Foreign Press Association felt she would follow along in her mother's double Ds—I mean, they are the Golden *Globes,* after all. I'm often mentioned in the same illustrious company with other former Miss Golden Globes: Marlo Thomas, Laura Dern, and Melanie Griffith. Four actresses who have held the title and gone on to success. And two times I was a presenter. But seriously, it's all been an honor. And Mama can still rock a Halston.

Stroke of Insight

It was January 10, 2016. I was on my way to the Golden Globes. Or at least the after-parties. Glammed up, and ready to slay the red carpet. I got my war paint on at my childhood home, Delfern, as it was only minutes away from the Beverly Hilton hotel's Golden Globe action. My mother was shuffling around . . . even mounting the grand staircase . . . twice . . .

on my behalf, for diamond and emerald earrings she insisted I had to wear. I was doing my spackling and Spanxing there so she could be involved. I knew helping me to get ready for the ball filled her with both a vicarious thrill and a longing for her glory days. And oh, she loved to tell me how to do it better.

"Joely, don't forget to stand up straight in that dress, and suck all this in," Connie said, grandly gesturing, dragging a finger in the air above the large portion of my body she felt I needed to suck.

"No, Mom, tonight I'm going as the letter C in your honor," I said, teasing her as I exaggerated my slouchy shoulders in that way I knew made her crazy.

That's what I get for dressing here. What is it that she sees, when she calls me out for my posture, my tummy, and the myriad of "flaws" she identifies? Is it that she wants me to better represent her, our family? Is it her "seventy-five years of doing this" better? I went there, I sought this torture out, invited it once again . . . Masochistic, right?!

Whatever the motivation, I had to mentally shake off the familiar criticism, put on my game face, and get out the door. Just before I did, I took in my once transcendent and dynamic matriarch in the foyer of the fortress we had all called home, which was on the verge of sale. The same space Meryl Streep and Shirley MacLaine once inhabited in their *Postcards from the Edge* tête-à-têtes, scene after scene representing the relationship of my sister from another mother and . . . her mother. Under financial strain, facing the same Hollywood hurdles I was just beginning to become aware of, which meant that as a seventy-seven-year-old female entertainer (who wasn't Betty White) Connie wasn't going to earn her way out of her problems; we were in bankruptcy proceedings. Still, we were going to simplify, and that would help everything, and 2016 was going to be a good year.

I left, sleek and elegant—my hair chignoned, and my dress a sexy black KaufmanFranco silhouette—and attended the glamorous, coveted HBO party. As soon as I hit the carpet, I heard Connie in my head and stood up straight (and, yes, I sucked). Spirited through the crowd by my plus-one—on this particular night, my current Number-One Gay, Bryant—spirits in hand, I took my rightful place among the other Olympic hopefuls.

At the end of the evening, I got into the car with my driver, who in a loud, thick Israeli accent delivered the news: "David Bowie died."

Saddened by the world's loss, and a little tipsy from the evening's champagne, I passed on stopping back at my mother's house. It was late. I didn't want to wake her. I would pick up my car in the morning, when I'd be able to regale her with tales of the evening's splashiest moments, and the who's who of people sending regards to her.

Little did I know, as my gown fell to the floor and I climbed into bed without removing my lashes, a cluster of strokes had struck my mother's right brain—the pons . . . controlling things like depth perception, the left side of the body, some cognitive stuff, and . . . judgment (and we in this family need all the judgment we can muster). Blood flow and oxygen were cut off from her brain. Not good. Not to mention what it was going to do to me.

I knew, just from talking to her the next morning, that something was wrong. It sounded like she'd had a cocktail. It was ten thirty. I conferred with Tricia, my partner in all things Connie. She'd heard the same altered tone and tempo in Mom's voice.

"Mom, did you take a Percocet by accident?" we asked, on a conference call.

Tricia rushed over to assess the situation, as she lives closer. And of course she got her to the hospital, because things definitely weren't right. I also reached out to the eldest of the Fisher sister trio, because I knew she had gone through a similar situation with Debbie, and she would always have the wisest of words in any situation. Carrie, who was smarter than the average bear and was already well versed in the effects strokes have on mothers, rather than bullshitting me through this, confided:

"I feel as though Debbie is slowly, quietly slipping away from us."

Little did we know that, in the grandest of ironies, they would both be the ones that would slip away from us in less than a year. And they didn't go quietly.

When I arrived at Cedars-Sinai, there were already flowers in Connie's room from Carrie and Debbie. The doctors were assessing her condition. A series of medical professionals came in, one after the other, to give her tests. She couldn't put the numbers on a clock. And she couldn't keep a beat with her left hand. I pictured Connie on hundreds of stages, triumphantly leading her band, signaling the time for her drummer, clapping along. It was devastating to see this being taken from her.

"Are you not able to move your hand, or is your brain telling it to move, and it can't?" I asked her.

"I'm telling it to move, and it won't move," she slurred.

Like a sledgehammer, it hit me in that moment: *This is going to be devastating for Connie. For all of us.*

The diagnosis, according to her doctor, Robert Huizenga, was: stroke.

The prognosis was: who the hell knows?!

This was new territory.

Everything had changed. Nothing had changed.

They came in to ask Connie about her advanced directives (we didn't even know what these were, as Connie always said, "I ain't going anywhere"). So they explained it was a document she needed, containing her wishes about whether or not she wanted to be resuscitated in the chance she became incapacitated. *Holy shit . . . how could they ask that of her . . . like this?*

Connie looked to me, and then to Tricia.

"Make sure you ask the little one," Connie said, slithering through the words and trying to muster a giggle. Was Connie actually, in her current state, implying that I would choose to end her life versus caring for her? Tricia would, naturally, agree to keep her alive, no matter what, like Sunny von Bülow. All of some of this is true. We had a laugh.

Again in this moment, the enormity of what was happening sunk in.

A nurse came in to insert a catheter into Connie's groin.

"You're going to feel a little prick," she said.

"It won't be the first time," I said, delivering the punch line to the roomful of medical professionals. "She was married to Eddie Fisher."

"Joely!" Connie said. She laughed again.

We all laughed. It didn't change anything, really, but it helped. A good Eddie Fisher dig is comedy gold in moments like this.

Over the next sixteen days, I traveled back and forth on the freeways of Los Angeles, preparing for what was coming next.

"Mom, you had a fucking stroke so you wouldn't have to pack, didn't you?" I teased my mother, continuing to be the court jester in the family to keep things light, while feeling crushed by the knowledge that we would have to do the packing, the moving, the living; Tricia and me.

Moving Connie out of Delfern was daunting, impossible, heartbreaking, for so many reasons. But it was the least of what I faced. In the months that followed, while still trying to remain hopeful and optimistic as Connie recovered, I felt myself spiraling into an existential crisis: *What will my world look like without a mother?*

Devastating . . .

And without any Ivy League–type education in any of these fields, I could now practice medicine, law, real estate, estate sales, elder care, and used-car sales, because of this crash course in the cycle of life. Tricia and I assumed our roles. We looked to each other as we signed power of attorney. We took our appropriate parts in the harmony. Once again, I would take the high part (real estate broker, comedienne, disciplinarian). And my more level, cool-headed little sister slid into her role as well (banker, therapist, ambulance driver). With the duties evenly distributed, we pressed on.

Once again, and naturally, I assumed the part of Connie's mother. I'd done it for years already. Provided the voice of reason about inappropriate fans and boyfriends. Played the role of informal road manager. Imaginary grown-up.

Now, I really am the grown-up.

And so, on top of everything else, my mother's health crisis set me off on a whole tangent of superfun speculation: *What if it were me? I have all these children to think about . . . I mean, someday it WILL be me, it is where we're all headed . . . Have I done my job as a mother? Have I accomplished everything I came here to do? Can I depart this life, knowing my offspring will have been well served? Can she? How can she leave me alone to take care of all of this?*

I am not fucking ready for this.

But I had to be. Not only for Connie, but for Tricia, and

of course, for my children. Suddenly, they had to share me with my mother. It was like I'd added another child. And I wanted to be very careful what I showed them about grief. I remembered vividly, viscerally, when Connie's beloved father died when we were living in Malibu. She was inconsolable. She broke down. Her grief took her to such a dark place—a guttural, primordial sound, a loss felt so deeply—it made her sick. She took to her bed. That was the first time I saw it, but not the fucking last. She gets her grief on, that lady. I wanted to be different for my daughters. But what I realized, as I let what had happened wash over me and I took to my own bed: I am no different. I don't actually want to be different. I want them, like Connie, like me, to love deeply, and feel the loss of someone, but to find the strength to move through it and get out of the bed . . . We're all doing the best we can.

ON THE DAILY, I listen for what tone I'm getting when I call my mother, settled into her new, beautiful, modest home. I screen the caller ID for anybody who might be giving me information about her welfare. I haven't heard anything today, so that's good. What I now know is that the lady in the flame sequined dress who captivated everyone she came in contact with, and generously gave to everybody around her to the point where it depleted her of so much—she's never going to return to her former glory. What we have is momentary glimpses of her sparkle and her need to be in control. Her garden, spiritually, and the soil outside her window that reaps giant jewel-toned roses and beautiful plumeria, that's what's important to her now. And we let that be what she focuses on. It's weird to me that she doesn't miss Delfern. If she hadn't had the stroke, I think she would. But it's done a sort of reset for her.

"Well, I'm never going to go onstage again," she says.

OR

"Well, I'm out of the business."

OR

"Did they ask you if I was around?"

It's what she's always called "kidding on the square"—kidding, but not kidding.

Sometimes she just sort of starts to space out, and I can see her go far away.

"Mom, are you okay?"

"I'm just thinking," she says. "I'm so happy everyone's settled."

"That's good. You're happy that they're settled."

"Yeah, because I don't have to take care of everybody anymore."

It's hard to hear. This is a big shift for the lady who, my entire life, wouldn't let me go out the door without staining my lips and cheeks properly.

Women of a Certain Age

They really were of a different breed. Women who came from this era, ladies who married Eddie Fisher. And they duked it out in ways I don't think we dare to (or dare to admit we do) anymore. Like the much talked-about rivalry between iconic actresses Joan Crawford and Bette Davis, rendered in deliciously acute detail in Ryan Murphy's *Feud,* which captures perfectly how we are pitted against each other as women in this business. *As women.* (Everything changes; nothing changes.)

And, of course, as Connie and Debbie. The difference between Connie and Debbie: Debbie was studied and restrained and pure. Connie belted from the gut after straining for the notes with sheer abandon. She wasn't nostalgic. She wanted to press on, to go rogue. To be current, often ahead of her time, musically and in production value. Debbie embraced nostalgia, understood its value for taking people back to better times.

But there were similarities, too. Eddie, for starters. Eddie Fisher had spectacular taste in women, for the most part. Here were these two beautiful, talented actresses that he chose to procreate with (Liz Taylor was sandwiched in between, but unavailable for comment at this moment). And the way they took to mothering, like they were going to do it just like they did everything in their life—the best, better than anyone else. Especially how they reinvented themselves. When my mother wasn't getting the same number of roles or nightclub bookings anymore, she remade herself, launching her own multimillion-dollar skin-care empire, Forever Spring, sold for decades on the Home Shopping Network, earning far more than she ever had as an entertainer. Debbie, until the very end, continued to grace stages all over the country, but also had her Debbie Reynolds Hotel in Las Vegas, and of course, the Debbie Reynolds Dance Studio, which lives on. And she had the good sense to buy up a treasure trove of classic Hollywood costumes, at first displayed in the lobby of her hotel, and then in an entire museum. Later, many of them were sold for a small fortune. She was smart like that. Today Todd continues the mission with his plans to keep the collection alive for future generations, and to add to it many of the mother-daughter duo's belongings.

Bodies by Fisher

In 1999, we took a Fisher girls' trip to Hawaii, the first and only such family outing of its kind. The matriarchs of the clan were there in all their glory—Debbie in diaphanous white, and Connie in head-to-toe tropical regalia. There were the three Fisher sisters: Carrie, smoking and wisecracking by the pool; Tricia, fresh from playing bad girls Hollywood Madam Heidi Fleiss and presidential intern Monica Lewinsky; and me; and then the first third-generation filly of the herd, Carrie's daughter, seven-year-old Billie. All of us satellites of Eddie, but so much more. All entertainers in our own right. Storytellers. Debbie didn't just have the proverbial million stories—she literally had a million of them. My mother was the same. And, of course, Carrie was legendary in this department.

At the hotel, I watched Carrie and Tricia photograph Billie in the dolphin pool, recognizing their posture as the same, and capturing their resemblance in a photo of my own, as they enjoyed Billie's frolicking in the water. On this trip, we sisters realized how much we all physically resembled each other and made a pact that we would forgo the cover-ups—in front of Billie, and for each other—and we'd dance in the sand: *Fuck it, this is what we got*. For a girl who'd never gotten up from a beach chair without sneakily pulling my towel around me to cover up, I delighted in throwing away my sarong. Years later, on a Miami beach, after giving birth to my second child, I again retrained myself to be bold for my own daughters.

I got something special from all these women. Not always easy. That's not how gifts work, especially of the family legacy variety. It's complicated. Sometimes painful and fraught because of what they make us see in ourselves. But their value is what I've been holding on to in light of everything that's happened. Because it stays, even when the person who gave it has gone on. In digging through the dowry I've been given, this is what I've observed.

I WAS HYPNOTIZED by Connie, and everything I did was tempered by her version of femininity. My mother was the chronicler of our family narrative—oh, the fables, the exaggerations, the folklore, it was fantastic. She was also the primary female image I internalized, and that I would refer to for comparison throughout my life. She was my watermark. At some point, I began to assess my mother's weaknesses and strengths, and decided what I wanted to emulate, and determined how far to stray from my home movies. I knew all of this before age twelve.

I watched this magical radiant creature spread her wings, from the wings. I watched her get as much from what she was doing to an audience as what she got at home (sometimes more), and if she didn't have that outlet—there was an emptiness, jealousy, competitiveness. Something I was already beginning to emulate. Next came my struggle with who I was physically. And with the following-in-the-footsteps part. 'Cause I wasn't blond, and blue eyed, and thin, I felt like a redheaded stepchild a lot (I actually dyed my hair in response, and became known as a redhead) . . . Now I like to think I have more substance, but at that time, there were too many pressures for me to ignore them completely. Or I'd make myself feel guilty. A lot of body image stuff. Connie held "image" up to us girls as a value . . . and what defined our value . . . It takes a really long time to redefine those kinds of ideals for yourself.

She was a crazy role model. I bore witness to a seesaw, from egotism to self-deprecation. At a time that was most crucial, I could've benefited from someone who accepted herself, it didn't go unnoticed by a teenage me . . . she needed a little self-love. One message that I got was that if you're successful in the entertainment business . . . you are loved (but I saw it wasn't enough). Another was that thinner equaled better. And that you are only as good as your next (to last) job. Connie used to introduce Tricia and me like so:

"These are my daughters, who are more beautiful on the inside than they are out. Joely got a part in a movie with the great James L. Brooks as director. She's playing with the big kids now. Tricia signed a record deal with ATCO records."

I loved the celebration of my accomplishments, but then, what am I when I don't have a gig? Not to mention that she was taking credit for our external and internal beauty (which, by the way, she does get credit for). And that's why it's so difficult for me to see the state she's in now. Especially because it hasn't softened her inner critic. She came to see me in Laguna, poststroke, performing in the play *Sleeping Beauty and Her Winter Knight*. And she gave me notes. I was playing Carabosse, a Maleficent-inspired evil queen—horns and all. There was a part where I kicked my leg up at the end of a number . . . and what did she say?

"When you go downstage left, when you do the thing with the kick . . . make sure your toes are pointed."

My inner monologue: *I'm wearing boots up to there. No one can see my toes.*

"Okay, Mom," I said. I pointed my toes.

I caught a glimpse of my naked form, getting out of the shower the other day, and even though I stand six full inches taller than my mother, and she's got thirty years on me, I flinched as I saw the beginnings of my own transformation.

What happens when beauty fades? When you gaze into the looking glass and what you see displeases you, or you are inundated with images, memorabilia, and social media chronicling your progress, your dismantling . . . we've all seen it, participated in it.

This is an area where I couldn't commiserate with Connie (who's still telling me to "send my photos to *Vogue*," as if that's still a thing *one does*—okay, Connie, right to Anna Wintour). Or delivering bons mots like this (from a hospital bed, no less, after she had a cardiac event in 2008), when I told her about a part I'd just tested for.

"Ooh, is it a good part?"

"Perfect. Single mom, smart, sexy . . ."

She stopped me.

"Well, you haven't been sexy in years," she said. "You've been married so long, you're stale. Just because you have your boobs hanging out doesn't make you sexy."

I looked at her in her current state and remained silent.

On a scale of one to Mommie Dearest, in that moment, she was off the charts.

Mirror, Mirror on the Wall

When I needed a sympathetic sounding board, thank God I was lucky enough to be related to a woman who thumbed her nose at the slings and arrows: my sister Carrie. She was the one who said: "Don't tell me that I haven't aged well. I've had enough trouble my whole life, being the age that I am." John Steinbeck wrote in *The Grapes of Wrath:* "It was her habit to build laughter out of inadequate materials." Her material was more than adequate and she made laughter habit-forming for certain. It's really fascinating and sad to me that she only made it to sixty. What gems would we have had upon her arrival at seventy . . . or eighty? We've been robbed! She made it okay to talk about flaws. She made it okay to wear them on the outside—and add glitter—and that's heroic to me, even though I think she only saw herself as part-time heroic. She was just fine to . . . survive? And then, in the end she . . . didn't.

Our last text exchange was full of talk about aging . . .

"I'm losing my jawline, how about alive, and suddenly 60?" she texted.

My response: "Crazy but you've never looked better. I'm coming up on 50, but I'm dancing around in a cat suit like I'm not."

"I WISH I WAS 50."

Ironic. It really was true; she had never looked better.

And of course, Carrie came from multiple generations of this stuff, just like I did. I don't know how Carrie saw Debbie when she was a child. I can only imagine that my older sister watched her own mother be Unsinkable (Molly Brown) through similar lenses as those through which I viewed Connie. And what she took from a woman who, all of her life, looked impeccable, had a similar impact on her as the ways in which I absorbed and rebelled against Connie's radiance. There's no way any of this would go unnoticed by any of us.

I first watched *Postcards from the Edge* in a theater full of people. They laughed and were charmed and moved by the great performances of Meryl, Shirley MacLaine, and everyone. But I was processing the experience of watching a slice of my sister's life that I was not yet privy to—it was in the years after this that she let everyone in, including me—with my childhood home as the backdrop. But what I saw bore a resemblance to what I knew. I felt a sadness in that movie, as if I were watching the future of my own mother-daughter relationship, even though I wasn't. There was just something that was profoundly uncomfortable, on a cellular level, in that scene where Meryl Streep climbs on top of Shirley MacLaine in a hospital bed and draws on eyebrows to prepare her for the awaiting paparazzi. That was like, in part, watching my own story, a future that had yet to unfold. It was like a gift; I didn't know what a strange gift I was being given . . . foresight.

As a ten-year-old girl in the darkness of a theater in Westwood, this familial love affair had first begun. In a forty-foot close-up of the gun-toting Princess in white diaphanous robes—a partial English accent, a smart deepness in those chocolate-brown eyes. A cinematic communion that caused me to swell with pride; this must mean that this chubby almost ten-year-old (me) must be part princess—half princess, all Fisher.

My recollection is that Connie reached out and a "play date" was made. Carrie would arrive some time shortly after to *Star Wars* playing in the background—normal? It was the beginning of that love affair—I had a big sister—a famous one.

Of course, over the years, famous would be a trait relegated to the bottom of the pile. What really enamored me was Carrie's ability to give chapter and verse to the nebulousness of flaws and faults. Creating chasms out of cracks. And sealing them with clever creative caulking. Like that art form I love, kintsugi: the Japanese art of fixing broken things with gold. Kind of like taking a broken heart and turning it into art.

ele

Tricia Leigh Fisher

My sister, Tricia, the one that's still here, the one that Connie gave me to save me.

Tricia and I both came out of Connie's vagina and were unfathered by Eddie. Sure, we are alike, in that we are musical, we are writers, we are creative, we are seekers, and we think our children are our everything.

But our lives have been very different from the start.

We are only fourteen months apart, but in some ways, I was always raising her. Mom never missed a school play, but she never helped with any of our school projects—she wouldn't have been able to assist with trigonometry anyway. So I was responsible for Tricia in many ways. Just picture me at thirteen, Tricia twelve. I took Connie's Mercedes 450 SLC, with the license plate that read WILDFL, with Tricia in the passenger seat beside me, winding through the broad boulevards of Beverly Hills. Not for some teenage joyride, but because Tricia had a dentist appointment and there was no one else to take us on that particular day. I cared about trying to maintain that kind of normalcy for my little sis, to keep life running with some degree of regularity. (*Home Alone: The Prequel.*)

I was a pretty good parent for many years. And then, I had kids.

Tricia and I have a special bond because of that—a bond that is unbreakable. Our styles—in fashion and communication—

may have varied and evolved. But we both instinctively knew how to divide and conquer in our shared familial duties:

"Joely, you wanna take this?"

"Why, of course . . . Tricia, this one feels more like you."

A no-brainer of epically reassuring proportions. We speak too many times a day, on occasion, just to hear the tone of each other's voice on the other end.

From the very start, I imagine dealing with my boisterousness, my raucousness, my presence, may have been tough. TLF had first to deal with our mother, no father, a far-off sister, and the ever-present, and in her face—Joely.

On a spiritual, existential level—and literally—I wasn't going anywhere. Nor did I want to. I wanted to be everything to this person, half my person, double my person, double the fun.

I demanded the proverbial (and the actual) spotlight, far more than she. It would be completely unconscious—and yet untruthful for me to say I wasn't aware of this.

Tricia Leigh. Wanted so desperately as a do-over, and definitely a playmate for me. I have a memory—far off—of my older sister speaking French and cradling me in her arms. Now I would get to return the favor, pass on my linguistic skills to this darling little premature, hairy creature. Connie and Eddie had once again tried to repair things with a sperm and egg scramble (the term coined by Carrie). They would never get it quite right, but what a fantastic gift for Joely—a five-pound, five-ounce plaything to provide endless hours of entertainment. Over the years she would do infinitely more than that. This little girl—yes, she is still my junior, in age, height, and weight—would be my friend, my confidante, my partner in crime, my accomplice, my duet partner, my witness, my bridesmaid of honor, my doula, my mirror. We've been dreamers and schemers our whole lives—first playing elaborate games, building forts, playing family (I was always the mom; it's fascinating when a child plays family and it looks nothing like their own).

She would see me through the absolutely most heinous of times (Connie's boyfriends, breakups, and one bad perm), talk me off actual, literal ledges, and be my creative counterpart for so much. We've been each other's witness for this lifetime, and it's her I want to tell my side of the story if I'm not around. What would Lucy do without Ethel? Laverne without Shirley? Mary without Rhoda? Ellen without Paige? We would never catfight, and always yin and yang, about who got to be who.

When she was first to land a leading role in a film (*Pretty Smart*—a girls-gone-wild-style coming-of-age film set in Greece—don't you dare go to YouTube), I was cast alongside her, and we had an incredible summer of firsts. Ever since, I've wanted her to be a part of almost everything I've done in my career. Whenever an appropriate guest spot came up—on *Ellen* and *Wild Card* and *'Til Death*—I instantly knew Tricia would be perfect, and she always delivered. Having been asked to direct my first movie, when the script needed a rewrite, I immediately thought to enlist Tricia. She's an incredible writer, and I knew she would elevate the material and make the project shine. The script is fantastic. I always want her around.

It Takes a Brothel . . . I Mean a Village

There is also a stunning brigade of "the other women"—no, not Eddie's mistresses—the other women in my life, who by default, or perhaps by design, have mothered me. These incredible women—friends, friends of Mom, friends of Bill—these ladies are my teachers, and I still, at near half a century, call them "aunties." I have chosen to turn to them in free fall—for their kindness, their experience, their wisdom, their shared love of our art, my mother . . . or just me.

"It takes a village" may sound a bit cliché, but on some occasions it just fucking applies. I watched the effect my mother had on men my entire life, but it didn't go unnoticed that women adored her as well. For all of her beauty, her sensuality, her feminine wiles, women never felt threatened. She was inclusive and generous—there have been those who stuck around for the meals, travels, and perks, sure. But these are her angels: the separate-check girls—these old broads—you haven't lived until you've seen Lainie Kazan, Diane Ladd, Renée Taylor, and Connie with the late Shelley Winters, in makeshift bathing costumes (bras and panties), kicking around on a hot day in the Delfern pool, or at our Mexican house, Casa Siempre Joven (Forever Young) in Puerto Vallarta. I like to think, although her dearest of friends, they were hand-selected to the collective for the benefit of the girls (Tricia and me)—to offer a change in perspective, inspiration, and a demonstration of healthy competition. Tricia and I have lived and worked with these ladies on many occasions—Valerie Harper has played both of our TV mothers—Lainie Kazan has also been my surrogate and TV mother. Frances Fisher is my sister from another mister (and mother). And Diane Ladd officiated when Chris and I had our tenth wedding anniversary renewal of our vows. Renée Taylor, married for fifty-two years to the late, great Joe Bologna, not only makes me laugh but is a stunning example of how to commit to a marriage and work alongside the one you love. My mother chose wisely these women who surrounded us.

One of my touchstones, my go-to, my "sage," came at me in an altogether different way. One fateful day . . . we were living in Malibu and having one of those signature parties Connie liked to throw. It was always a mash-up of people she had worked with over the years, and lovers, and random sorts—they all knew she gave good party. In walked O. J. and Nicole Brown Simpson. She was stunning. Frankly, they both were. She had on a clingy white dress, and it left nothing to the imagination—especially if you imagined underwear. Tricia and I ran around and kept trying to get another glimpse of this "specimen." I was thrilled and shocked and couldn't stop looking. Then I lost interest.

I sat out on the sand, and my mother's friend, *Hollywood Reporter* columnist Sue Cameron, came and sat beside me. To hear her tell it, I was the most interesting, mature, articulate guest at the party. I *loved* that. She went on to be my agent, my manager, and one of my best friends . . . and is twenty years my senior (she's gonna kill me for saying that).

I have made it my mission to in turn surround my daughters with women from every walk of life—my posse are of every color, shape, creed, and mind-set, except if you voted for Trump . . . that's a no-no!

My girlfriends, the women in my life, are fierce. They know what they want, they support each other and me. I look to them for how to be. I rely on them to keep me in check. They are activists, artists, and passionate players in the game of life. We find the ways in which we are alike and (mostly) embrace our differences. Like friends of Connie's, I've watched the girls transition to women, to wives and partners, and revel in their rearing of children.

You have all come into my life in such unique ways. The ways I suppose you were meant to . . . so, perfect. I have always tried to be a good friend to you, times change, we change, but there are those of you who have stayed constant. From the school yard to the road, miles across this country, even across the sea. In casting offices, and on sets, prenatal yoga, mommy and me, you are colleagues, even passersby. We have sat up nights, saving each other, stood up for each other, laughed ourselves into tears, and covered up the occasional misstep. As life goes by, our careers and partnerships devour the time we used to have together, but know that it's what continues to drive me forward, and sometimes I long for it; you are all pieces of me. I pray that you all know I would do anything for you (as long as it's legal). If I've ever done anything to make you mistrust me . . . forgive my trespasses, I know not what I do. Let's find our way back through the craziness, the darkness, and the divisiveness of this time in the world, for we are strong women and we learned it from the best. It is out of the ashes that the phoenix . . . okay, you get it. I'm here for you.

Daughters

Now I have three female children. They're so different from one another. I watch them closely and am careful to overcompensate (you heard that right) when it comes to building up their confidence and self-esteem. Early on, I made sure to find each one of my girls' gifts, and I've made sure to celebrate them often for these qualities. Every time I see Skylar Grace dance, as I look at her onstage and through the camera lens (much as Connie did at Our Lady of Malibu all those years ago), I sob with pride. She is thoughtful and loyal. True Harlowe came into the world at home on my bed and never stops surprising me with her out-of-the-box thinking. She's smart, Presidential Award–winning smart. Olivia Luna, whom we chose to complete our family, has the sass and quick wit to follow along in the family's comedic tradition. And takes pride in her role in our tribe.

Every day presents me with new challenges and celebrations of them, and I make it my mission to instill some real wisdom in them about this business of being female. And to teach them what assets they have in each other. I may no longer have Carrie, but I have the memory of her, and her humor, and her wisdom. And I have Tricia. In the same way I have given my three daughters the gift of each other, so they can be mirrors for each other, as my sisters have been for me.

Unfortunately, I didn't have a spectacular, cherished relationship with my grandmother. Although she was funny and brash, I always felt uncomfortable around her. This is not what I wished for my children. My mom is still very much active in my mind and in my life, and she's active in theirs, too. I once heard Carrie's daughter, Billie, joke in an interview that Debbie insisted Billie be known as Debbie Reynolds's granddaughter, not Carrie Fisher's daughter. I think my mom's aligned with Debbie in this. She wants the girls to see a little vintage Connie Stevens in their "nana."

Unsurprisingly, the way they grandparent is similar to the way they parented. They are sure they're going to do it the best. Or maybe it's that they want some of the firsts with their grandkids (Connie wanted to take Skylar to her first ballet and teach her how to drive) in order to make up for the firsts they missed with their own kids. It's a complicated realization for me to have, filled as it is with all that I lost in that equation. Up until the end, they've shown themselves to be the same women they always were, full of moxie and genuinely affectionate, maybe even more than they were with their own children.

My mother recently saw a photo of my daughter Skylar in a formal, flesh-colored dress. She was gorgeous. Could not have looked better. Mind you, my daughter is over five foot eight, a dancer, and sometimes stands a little hunched (the familiar "C" that can feel like it stands for "comparison" when your mother is larger than life). My mom looked up from the photo and had that expression on her face I knew so well.

"Are you going to tell her about her tummy?" Connie said.

Inner monologue: *Tell her what about her tummy?! Tell her that she's a fucking beautiful creature from God?!*

"No, I am absolutely not going to tell her anything about her tummy."

But I know better than to argue. I also didn't pass this warped perspective on to my daughter. I simply basked in her beauty and modeled that for her, so she can do the same.

And my mom, bless her, does acknowledge this mothering talent within me.

"You're so good, you're that girl that will braid three heads of hair and make three separate lunches," Connie said to me.

Yes, yes I will. Gladly. Gratefully. (Okay, most of the time.)

Tricia has become the crafty mommy, the room mom, the mom who can always be counted on (by her kids and by my kids, too). And Carrie definitely picked the right person with whom to co-parent, almost as if she knew what was coming for her, and that she wasn't going to be able to get up and make the sandwiches.

Well, we must have turned out okay, because our children are turning out spectacularly. Maybe none of them will write a memoir. Maybe all of them will. Certainly, my girls will talk about me in their lives. And they'll stand up straight.

Chapter 7

243 Delfern

ALL OVER THE GREATER LOS Angeles area, people have treasures from my childhood home, Delfern, in their houses.

Not that the agents who helped us to organize our estate sale in the spring of 2016 saw our belongings as "treasures." Now, try and imagine a complete stranger coming into your childhood home—while your mother is recovering from a stroke across town, and it's unclear if she'll ever be able to live on her own again—and peering over your mom's prominently displayed china. Connie had bought it at auction from the legendary Beverly Hills restaurant Chasen's, when it closed, and used it for many parties.

"You can get rid of all of these," she says. "I mean, how many more dinner parties is your mom really going to have?"

You didn't really just say that, did you?

All I can see when I look at the plates is Christmas Eve dinner at Delfern, as we file through the narrow hallway adjacent to the kitchen, where we've all placed our signature dishes. Connie loves it when Aunt Ava makes the sweet potatoes with the caramelized marshmallows. And Sue Cameron always brings the green bean casserole with the crispy fried onions. And I, of course, always make the brussels sprouts and a novelty stuffing, and fresh-bake a homemade apple pie just at dinner's end. And Tricia will do the salad and her famous pumpkin bread. We will each cook a turkey. Connie carefully places a Post-it note—written in her handwriting—in front of each chafing dish, to identify what it is and who prepared it. And each one of us grabs one of these buffet plates and fills it, as we watch our children run in and out of the room—all they really want is pasta—piling on our family holiday meal. So, okay, yes, I will get rid of the fucking plates, but there will be dinner parties, goddamn it. Our real priority is to have Connie back at the table again . . . we'll use my plates.

Cut to the quick: Tricia and I did move forward with the estate sale (in my opinion, an experience only enjoyed by the dead). Now, this wasn't the first time we'd had an "eight-car" garage sale at Delfern. But this time we were about to sell the property, which had been in our family since 1975. *Everything must go!*

Mom had been in the hospital for nearly a month, and Tricia and I weren't sure of her long-term prognosis. Or where she would live while convalescing. We just knew she couldn't return to Delfern. None of us could. Soon it wouldn't be ours anymore. So we rallied—with a small group of amazing, loyal friends—to tackle Delfern's massive accumulation of junk, memorabilia, and very valuable *things*.

You know, the Native American memorabilia, the Red Skelton clown painting, the white convertible Corvette, and that pink Lucite bear my mom keeps asking me about, as if I should have known how attached to it she was. There are pieces that Connie randomly has flashes of need for, and they're gone now.

Why not unload some of it, and make a little money?

Here's why not.

Times being what they are, I used social media to advertise—that's one way to drum up business. The day of the sale, I saw a Facebook comment, something along the lines of: *We went to the Connie Stevens estate sale. I got two vases that will sit prominently on display in my home. The Mackies were divine. And the crowds, up and down the staircases like cattle. But it felt like a funeral. And what a shame Connie Stevens has lost everything, and they have to move out of that home that was so important to the girls.*

Well, he didn't really write *all* of that. But he did use the word "funeral." And I read between the lines. What had been fodder for his Facebook post, the staircases everyone had walked up and down at the sale, which he'd described online in this cavalier way, were the same staircases where I'd watched my children take their first steps; the wood floors that had changed from whitewash in the eighties, and caramel color in the nineties, to deep mahogany in the present day, were still the same floorboards . . . our floorboards.

I asked for the comment to be deleted. But that was just one comment. I felt the same energy from the hundreds of people who walked through our home, passing judgment, muttering under their breath: "Isn't this excessive?"

Yes, it was excessive. But they were *our* things. It comes with the territory, I guess. We were selling stuff at bargain basement prices that we paid good, well-earned American dollars for. They couldn't see all of that *stuff* through my eyes, when I'd passed through the house in the days leading up to the sale; everything had stories (and now price tags). The bronze sculpture on the bar that was a miniature replica of the sculpture *Nostalgia,* by Jose Ramiz Barquet, located on El Malecón in Puerto Vallarta, where we always walked when we visited our home there. I know it sold for much less than its value, and Connie still talks about it, determined to buy it back. No one who came to the sale could see how everything was a part of Connie's legacy, our inheritance, the places and the people that had made up our life, a chapter of which was now ending.

So naturally I contacted a friend at the TV show *The Insider.* To add insult to injury, I would take to the airwaves and draw more traffic the day of the sale by inviting the world to commiserate. (And, yes, we do take credit cards!) We agreed I'd walk around the property and tell family anecdotes, but I drew the line at sporting my mom's Bob Mackie gown, as had been suggested.

"Oh, I don't think I can do that," I said, recoiling at the thought of squeezing into my mother's size 2 and spinning for the cameras.

So I had Connie sign the original sketch of the gown, for the two to be sold together. My hope was that it would fetch a pretty penny. I'm not sure that it did, frankly. I had reached a point of "Just get rid of all of it. I can't look at it anymore."

When the cameras were rolling, Debbie Matenopoulos kept pressing me:

"But, really, how do you feel? Losing everything?"

That's not *exactly* how she phrased her question, but that's how I heard it. And the one thing I didn't want to do was stand there and weep about loss when I was feeling so much of it. We were standing on the third floor on the balcony. When perched there, the whole of the property is visible: the tennis court, where I could still see all of the soirees held there in full swing; the swimming pool, where Esther Williams swam; the complete two and a half acres we called the forest, where, as children, we'd reenacted our version of *Lord of the Flies,* although we had been told it was off-limits.

So in order to get through it, I put on a brave face, for the interview, for the sale, for my mother. I was asked to give the viewers at home a tour of the property.

"Well, what are great stories about the house?" Debbie asked me.

The stories are too numerous to jam into a three-minute magazine segment, and not all necessarily fit for prime time. So let's start at the beginning . . .

It was 1974 when Connie bought our family homestead on Delfern Drive in the small pocket between Bel Air and Beverly Hills, the very exclusive Holmby Hills neighborhood, also home to the Playboy Mansion, Aaron Spelling, and Betsy Bloomingdale. The house had been designed by the first prominent black architect, Paul Williams, (sung to the tune of "We've Only Just Begun") and was a stunner. The poor Italian Catholic kid from Brooklyn had purchased her Tara, and it remained a destination spot on the tours and maps of stars' homes until just last year (we used to wave to the tour buses as kids, and we would extort money from tourists for our high-priced lemonade—made with lemons from the property).

The house had previously been owned by legendary ice skater and movie star Sonja Henie, who had died five years earlier. Her widower, Niels Onstad, whom my mom called "the Viking," took us around the property.

Sonja had always wanted to have children, and the Viking was enamored with the idea that a loving family would reside there. He sold the house to Connie for $350,000. In 1975, we moved in, when I was eight. Connie marked the occasion by having the date intricately carved into the grand rosewood mantel of the fireplace, a focal point of the formal living room.

Frosted Malt

During the era when we first moved into Delfern, in the mid-seventies, my father only came to the house once or twice. Unlike Carrie, I don't have family photos of the American Gothic persuasion. No, I take that back. There is one, taken on one of these rare occasions when Eddie visited in that first Delfern year. It is worn, and the hues are as faded as my memory of posing for it. Both Tricia and I have hair that is long and styled. We are both smiling, but my smile is that of an already aware girl who knew this uncomfortable faux family shot wasn't the norm.

Connie is rocking the polyester high-waisted, wide-legged pant—come to think of it, so is Eddie. It's like a beautiful, magazine-worthy editorial for Courrèges or Paco Rabanne. Connie has great hair, always. She's Italian and Irish, and a little bit Native American. (And she's a little bit country, and a little bit rock 'n' roll.) She only counts the Italian. It's blond and curly and huge—platinum. Her lashes are dark and full—bottom and top. Her milk-chocolate liner and shimmery, malted lipstick—actually called frosted malt (which she bought in bulk when Revlon discontinued it and then brought back as "Sexy" with her own makeup line, Forever Spring). I can smell the Fidji perfume emanating from her image.

I think my mom wanted to show Eddie she was surviving and thriving without him. On that day he visited, she showed off, and the photo captures this feeling in the look on her face—she had triumphed.

Connie's Special Place

A classic Hollywood estate, on two and a half acres, with an Olympic-size swimming pool and a tennis court, it was a traditional house with a circular brick driveway. My mom especially loved the striped awning above the front door (where, years later, I took my wedding photos). Over the threshold was a majestic foyer crowned by a striking chandelier, and that iconic grand staircase. To the left was a classic, old-fashioned library with beautiful, lit wooden shelves that, for years, housed books, movies, and memorabilia. There were two bathrooms, one on either side of the front entryway, one pegged for men and the other—the ladies'—featuring a gorgeous metallic chevron wallpaper and mirrored built-in vanity that was most likely, on more than one occasion, used for cocaine. The dining room, which was of the time, had padded, fabric-covered walls and another gorgeous chandelier. The back staircase had a chair lift—the "elevator"—installed for someone with an injury, which was how we carted luggage up and down the stairs. The kitchen was where the women of the family gathered to make ravioli for holiday meals. From the very first moment we saw the property, Tricia and I ran upstairs to the master suite, with its fireplace and two giant sliding doors opening onto a patio that Connie called her "special place."

"This is Mommy's room!" Tricia and I exclaimed, excitedly.

The third floor featured panoramic trompe l'oeil paintings of Sonja Henie's Norwegian childhood, complete with fairy tales and nursery rhymes. It had once housed pipes for an ice rink, where she must have anticipated one day having children skate. Mom removed the apparatus for the ice rink and put down flooring for us to roller-skate, and that became our playroom. It was located above the bedrooms occupied by Tricia and me.

We became accustomed to hearing our house ghost, whom we assumed was Sonja. Although Sonja had died on a flight to her homeland of Norway, not at the house, we felt like she was there with us. Maybe it was just Connie's way of making her children feel comfortable with the supernatural, but I can't remember a time when we didn't consider Sonja part of the family. Connie even sold a pair of my old ice skates once at a yard sale, claiming they had belonged to legendary skater Sonja Henie.

When we pulled in or out of the driveway, we would see the lights on the top floor turn on. In my bathroom, when I opened a drawer on the right side, the corresponding drawer on the left would open by itself. We could often smell food cooking downstairs. Toys we'd left in disarray in our playroom were moved to one side and lined up neatly.

"There's Sonja, at it again," we said, comfortable with the idea that she'd cleaned up because she liked to keep the space tidy and needed to skate.

ele

The Menagerie

Tricia and I weren't really sleepover-at-other-houses girls. Was this the result of living in this fabulous place? Maybe. Was it the result of not wanting to be apart from our mother when she was home from the road? Definitely. And so, Delfern became a safe haven and a hotbed for giant sleepovers with our friends. Any given weekend, the hang was always on. In lieu of us going to camp in the summer, Connie got us big tents, and we camped out on the Delfern lawn—many times.

We weren't the only ones who had sleepovers. My single, sassy mother entertained from time to time as well. From my window, one morning, I saw the collateral damage of a wild seventies party, and all that entailed, including a souvenir of the night's revelry, Chuck Mangione, playing his flugelhorn by the pool, wearing only his trademark hat . . . and a pair of socks.

The pool house, which my mom called the Moroccan den, was done up with fabric on the ceiling, beautiful rugs, beanbags, and the smell of ganja in the air. It was where Connie went to party. On one occasion, the Moroccan den was home to one of those "friends helping friends" pyramid parties. Every decade or so these schemes seem to come around. A dozen people were invited over with their initiation monies—ten thousand dollars in this case—and were served chardonnay and finger sandwiches while hearing the pitch. For weeks after that, people came in and out with their shoeboxes full of cash. At some point, as happens, the "investors" dry up, and it stops—not everybody gets to the top of the pyramid.

Connie was hot stuff. At one point, she caught the eye—and the attention—of a Saudi prince. He was completely head over heels in love with her, and he came to her with a six-carat diamond.

"I can't possibly accept that," she said.

And then he came to her with a Lamborghini.

"I can't possibly accept that," she said.

And then he came to her with a llama.

"That I'll accept," she said.

After that, Fernando Llama lived in the backyard of Delfern. The problem was that he was irritated that he lived in Holmby Hills, and not wherever llamas live. At first he started spitting at us, then he started biting us. My sister and I turned a cardboard wardrobe box into a vehicle we'd climb into, in order to travel through the backyard, with its metal arm sticking out the front of it, in case the llama came near us. It fell apart in the middle of the grass, and we all took a screaming run toward the bar area. The llama bit me. So, naturally, it was donated to our pediatrician's office on Sunset Boulevard for a time, before it went to a petting zoo in Valencia.

But we still always had a wild pack of Siberian huskies on the estate. Because, you know, when you have two and a half acres in Holmby Hills, you need a pack of wolves.

ele

Foreclosure Is a Four-Letter Word

As a single working mom, who'd never gotten any support from Eddie, Connie strove to support her family but couldn't always keep us in the style to which we were accustomed. A year after we bought Delfern, I came home in my Catholic schoolgirl uniform to find my mom lying on her bed with her then-manager. That was the first time I heard the word "foreclosure" being tossed around. I didn't know what it meant. But then she leaned over and whispered in her manager's ear, and I could see her mouth form the word "trampoline." Unable to afford the mortgage, we leased Delfern to Herb and Lani Alpert, who remained there for seven or eight years. This sent us to a modest tropical-looking beach house, which we leased, on the shores of Malibu, and yes, it had a trampoline.

DELFERN PROVED TO be a reliable investment over the course of the next forty years. It went from being our on-and-off primary residence to being leased several times, which allowed us to buy other properties, accumulating real estate over the years. Although Delfern was, for decades, the primary place we called home, Connie instilled in us the idea that as long as we were all together, we were home. So as much as I loved the house, and wish that we still owned the property for the next generation, moving in and out of it as a family wasn't associated with the same loss it would be years later, when we prepared to leave the property for the last time in 2016.

WHEN WE NEXT moved back into Delfern Tricia and I were in high school. Connie was still often on the road, and we were old enough that, if we wanted to go away and join her, we would. But more and more, we wanted to stay home and be with our friends or act in school plays. Connie felt we were beyond the need for the constant supervision of a nanny or governess. And we had Dora. She came from El Salvador when we were very young, with fifty dollars tucked into her bra, crossed the border into the United States, and found her way to us, becoming a part of the family. When one thinks of the Delfern house, Dora is there, a constant presence. Thirty-six years! Her amazing smile, and her wisdom, superseded the fact that she never spoke English very well. She would have done anything for my mother. And did everything for my mother. Everybody loved her. When we lost Dora in 2011, we had a big memorial for her. The house would never be the same.

ele

Camp Windfeather

My mom had established a charity called Windfeather. She recognized a need for underserved Native Americans in our country, being a quarter Iroquois herself. She raised money to build wells on reservations and to send Native American kids to college (nearly a hundred children benefited over the years). And during two summers, in the mid-seventies and the mid-eighties, Connie decided she would bring a few dozen Native American children to stay at our house. Delfern became Camp Windfeather. So these scores of children from different Indian nations around the country had their "horizons" broadened—they went to Disneyland and the circus, and some saw the ocean for the first time. My mom gave them clothing and sleeping bags and got haircuts for those who wanted them.

During the first go-round, Tricia and I were just kids ourselves. But during the second Camp Windfeather, we were old enough to be enlisted as counselors. For better or worse, we were put in charge of groups of children at Disneyland (if I'm recalling correctly, I did lose my children for a spell).

Imagine feeding that many kids. We set up a big outdoor kitchen in the driveway and shuttled three square meals a day toward hungry kids beside the pool. Our friend Carol Tamburino served as short-order cook. We'd repeatedly run back to her, shouting our orders ahead of us.

"Fifteen more . . . of everything!"

Wearing her fluffy yellow robe, Carol flipped eggs and cooked bacon.

"Fifteen more," she shouted back in her thick South Philly accent.

Looking back, it's hard to imagine what it must have been like for these children to be dropped into Hollywood luxury for the briefest of moments and then returned to their normal lives. But I know Connie did so with the best intentions, and as a teaching moment for her own children, to bring us in touch with the disadvantaged, and remind us of how fortunate we were. "There but for the grace of God go we," Connie often said. There isn't any way the lives of these children went unchanged. This may have been one of the inspirations for my need to help others as an adult. I would return to this idea of giving back throughout my life.

ele

Postcards from the Edge

With her birdies imminently flying the coop, Connie decided that Delfern was too vast a home for her to rattle around in alone. Forever Spring was in its infancy, and Connie wasn't yet flush, and the house would again fetch a large amount of money as a rental. She leased the property, this time to a couple who said they were doctors. They paid first, last, and whatever, and their paperwork seemed up to snuff. They had planned a lavish wedding to be held on the grounds. Whether or not that event took place we'll never know. Not long into their year lease, they stopped paying rent. And we couldn't get them out. They put all the furniture and everything—including the toilet seats—out on the lawn. We finally got them out, but we learned that they had done this before in four other states. We realized a lawsuit would be unfruitful, as we would be the last in line to recoup any damages from people who really had nothing.

My mother had purchased another home, on Cherokee Lane in Beverly Hills. While living there, she continued to rent out Delfern. Around this time, they were location-scouting for the film version of Carrie's book *Postcards from the Edge,* and Delfern was in the running. When Carrie and director Mike Nichols saw the pictures, they knew immediately this was their "hero" (a film term for the perfect selection). It was only then that Carrie learned the house belonged to her ex-stepmother Connie.

During filming, my childhood bedroom became Mike

Nichols's private office. For me, it's impossible to separate the movie's iconic scenes from those of my own life—there was the one filmed against the bank of curved windows in the formal living room area that always housed our piano (and our Christmas tree). In the movie, Shirley MacLaine's Doris Mann (in head-to-toe red bugle beads) welcomes her daughter Suzanne—home from rehab—with a party where she proceeds to steal the show. As if acting on a totally spontaneous instinct, she belts out a well-rehearsed rendition of "I'm Still Here," hopping up on the piano—my mom's piano, on which, legend has it, Henry Mancini, our neighbor directly across the street, first plunked out the strains of "Moon River." Another iconic scene was filmed on the grand staircase, the one where Suzanne accuses her mom of having flashed the crowd at a childhood party. "It twirled up," Doris retorts in her own defense. Years later, I posed for wedding photos on said staircase, jokingly spinning around in my virginal white, so that it "twirled up." Then there was the scene filmed on the floral-print banquette couch, where Doris awaits the return of her wayward daughter—the same couch on which my mother had, on occasion, waited up for me. In keeping with what's known as a "locations agreement" in film, the production paid to give the property a little face-lift before returning it to us. We moved back in promptly after her nip and tuck.

WHEN I RETURNED to L.A. after college, I lived in a rental property with my boyfriend, Dean, and a few friends. While I was embarking on my acting career, Connie put me in charge of the Cherokee Lane house, letting me be the landlord and keep the money. So I found some women to be my tenants. On their application, one was in PR, one was a flight attendant, and one was a "model"—of course. I had my landlord help me run TRW credit checks, and he said they'd all come back fine. They paid first and last month's rent—in cash.

And then they stopped paying rent.

In order to evict them from the property, we ended up sending in the marshal, and one of the girls resisted, so she was hog-tied. The girls had to be physically removed from the property. When I went in to see what they'd been doing in the house, I'd never seen so many pairs of underwear in my entire life. It was panties, panties, and more panties. And there was a little black book—with men's names in it. Yes, they were hookers, and not just any hookers but girls who worked for the infamous "Hollywood Madam," Heidi Fleiss. And, yes, they'd turned our home into a whorehouse. After that I turned the house of ill repute into a girls' dorm and moved in with several female friends. One roommate, my friend Spike, was a massage therapist with a chocolate chip cookie business on the side. The house smelled like cookies, and there were massages, so yeah, not much had changed.

When I returned to live at Delfern for the last time, I was now an adult. The doors always remained unlocked. Everybody entered through the side door, which was flanked by overgrown ferns and gardenia bushes. When I entered the door, I'd let the screen door slam behind me, making sure whatever dog was there at the time didn't escape.

"Mom! I'm here!" I'd yell.

I could tell where in the house she was by the decibel level of her reply: "JF."

It was like the Beverly Hills boardinghouse. It really was. Essentially, it became the house for wayward divorcées and single friends. With the return of the prodigal daughters, Connie decided to add on, so it would feel like we had our own places, building matching two-story condo-style apartments for Tricia and me, which shared a kitchen in between. These became home to us as single gals, and with our various paramours from those years. At the same time Connie also added a structure that housed a recording studio, editing bay, and rehearsal space, complete with dance barre and mirror. That would later become the space used for telemarketing by Forever Spring.

It was while living at Delfern that I landed my role on *Ellen*. Within the first year, I bought my first house, in the Hollywood Hills. Although I lived on my own after that, Delfern remained the hub for milestones and celebrations in our family and among our friends. Among the greatest hits from these twenty years are:

For those big decade-marking birthdays, I created a nightclub atmosphere out of my mom's tennis court and invited all my talented friends to perform for me. And of course, the birthday girl always closed the show. They were great parties. We give good party. Or we used to. Not so much lately.

Connie and her besties, Renée Taylor and Lainie Kazan, would serve as beautiful bridesmaids for Diane Ladd's wedding, held on the lawn. I spent the night before my own wedding in my childhood bedroom. My mother had her famous August birthday soiree there every year, with all the comedians competing for attention, outjoking each other, and arguing over which story was whose. (My own favorite story is the time I enjoyed a rare cigar with Uncle Milty—Milton Berle—when I was in my early twenties. He jokingly pulled me down onto his lap and said: "Aw, I remember the last time you sat on my lap—you were just a wee thing." I giggled. "You wet me," he said. And then, with great shared comedic timing, we both delivered the punch line: "Would you do it again?" he asked, just as I said, "Want me to do it again?") Esther Williams's birthday was the same day as my mom's (August 8), and one year, to celebrate, we had the women's Olympic synchronized swimming team perform in our Olympic-size pool. Many benefits for HIV/AIDS research and awareness, spearheaded by me, were held there.

Delfern served as the location for several music videos, including one for a single from Tricia's album, which my husband, Chris, shot, setting the pool on fire. The Delfern pool was also used as a location for a pilot Tricia recently wrote and filmed.

Medium Kim Russo came a-calling with cameras, to visit with Connie and me and investigate Delfern for her show *The Haunting of* . . . and naturally, we were visited by both Sonja and Dora on this hallowed ground where we'd all cohabitated for so many years.

"Did you always lose your keys?" Kim said. "Dory?"

"Dora," I immediately corrected her.

"She's saying, with a giggle, 'Miss Connie, it was Sonja who always hid the keys,'" Kim elaborated.

Kim stood in several different places in the house and felt the presence and vibrations of a male relative.

"Connie, who was the . . . it's a male . . . was it an older brother or a father?" Kim asked.

Connie looked at me and replied, "Could be either."

"He's telling you," Kim said. "He's thanking you for . . . did he live on the first floor . . . or he's showing me . . . he's thanking you for caring for him. And he's showing me the room over here. He's telling me to tell you . . . you did enough."

She pointed to the library.

My mom collapsed. I filled the group in:

"Grandpa Teddy convalesced in a makeshift hospital room in that library."

What had started off to be a lighthearted trip down memory lane moved my mom to her core. Seeing the direction of the reading, and wanting to protect my mom, I shifted the focus onto myself. I took Kim to the third floor, Sonja's room, and naturally she felt her presence in the space as we stood together. This brought up a tremendous amount of emotion for me, in turn, as I stood in my former playroom, flooded with memories.

Kim, Connie, and I sat down in a room we called the solarium and talked about the presence of all these people who watched over us. And we were comforted by it.

Then, at the end of the day of filming, as I walked Kim out, she turned to me.

"I know it's very fresh," she said. "And I didn't know if you wanted me to say anything on camera, but your dad did come through."

Eddie had just passed away, within the previous year.

"Well, I'm glad to see he's hovering around," I said.

Having nothing left unsaid with Eddie, I inquired, "What did he say?"

"He's showing me . . . did you recently get a tattoo?"

"Yes," I replied.

"Your father said, 'Thank you for including me in your tattoo.'"

So I showed her my arm for the first time and described the design. My tattoo is the word "family" in seven languages—those of my descent, the languages I speak—and I described how I'd sat with the tattoo artist and told her we had to include the Hebrew—*משפחה לילדים* (*mishpachah*)—for my father.

Like my mother, the experience shook me to my core—not with sadness, exactly, but with wonder at the cycle of life . . . and I do believe in ghosts.

IN THE WEEKS leading up to the estate sale in the spring of 2016, Tricia and I sifted through the selection of items we thought would bring happiness to our mother, wherever she would land. I think we chose wisely. We know her very well. We know the beautiful things she always loved, and her go-tos, and we got rid of everything else. This was no small feat.

One room was filled with items that my mom hoarded away for gift giving. Every closet, in every room in the house, was full to the brim with Connie's coats, gowns, and assorted other clothing. We pulled it all together into Tricia's childhood bedroom, where it was all stacked up on the bed and hung on sixteen racks of clothing. We called a variety of people—friends, the costume designers from assorted shows, including *The Goldbergs*—to come over and select from among the choice eighties items, in all their shoulder-padded, sequined, jeweled glory. We tried to shine some shit in those difficult days by inviting people over, and being silly, and trying on the most ostentatious of all the clothes. Giving away what we could to the right homes made it feel like we were doing some good. But every day went from manic hilarity to sheer and utter despair and back again. It was three weeks of feeling buried and traumatized, every single day—tearing off scabs, putting a Band-Aid on an artery, swimming upstream, trudging through the impossible. Tricia and I did all of that without Mom, for Mom, to spare her the pain of that experience.

You can understand why twenty-five dollars for the Limoges china seemed like a fair market value, when I was worried about my mom's very survival. And you can even understand why I didn't get the significance of the pink Lucite bear.

SO OUR HOUSE at 243 Delfern Drive has just popped back on the MLS. Despite the fact that those who purchased it from us for a hefty sum (most of which we owed back to the bank)—a family prominent in the restaurant and finance worlds in Beverly Hills who were fans of Connie's—purposefully circled the property while promising to maintain the integrity of this iconic Hollywood home and to restore it to its vintage glory. They broke their promise. Where seventies chic had reigned, it's now modern and cold, full of black marble, metal, chrome, and stainless steel. Maybe it needed another face-lift, but it's unrecognizable. They uprooted the fruit trees Connie had named for her grandchildren, took down her favorite striped awning. I swipe right through the photos, conceal the images of what our home looks like today from my mother—it's like another death in the family.

Chapter 8

Always a Soubrette, Never an Ingénue

SOUBRETTE (n): the flirtatious, mischievous, comedic confidante of the ingénue; second banana

SO IMAGINE IF YOU WILL, and I'm sure that by now you will, being the daughter of a successful, beautiful, talented icon—a sixties sex kitten, a huge international star. And also, from a young age, it appeared that all the female offspring in the family wanted stardom, too, and wanted it badly, so there was a second level of competition as well.

When I was in fifth grade, Connie directed the Our Lady of Malibu school musical: *The King and I*. She cast me in the plum role of Tuptim, the lovelorn slave girl. I had seen Yul Brynner perform as the iconic King of Siam, taking a triumphant yet excessive nine curtain calls. This was my first foray into my dream of gracing the Broadway stage . . . in the multipurpose room of a Malibu Catholic school. Connie said she looked through the lens of her bulky seventies camcorder as she filmed, and not only could I hit the notes, but I had something special. This was going to be my career.

The bug had bitten. In those days, *The Hollywood Reporter* and *Variety* used to be delivered to our house every day, jampacked with reviews and all the latest industry news, and in the back, a list of upcoming auditions. When I was fourteen, I pilfered one of the *Hollywood Reporters* and perused the ads in back. My eye was immediately drawn to an open call for the L.A. cast of *Annie*. Without telling my mother, I got myself to the audition, at the United Methodist Church on Franklin and Highland in Hollywood, dressed in my Marymount Junior School kilt and saddle shoes, and I tried out for *Annie*.

I got called back. Prepubescents lined the basement of the Shubert Theater in Century City and, one by one, belted out "*The sun will come out tomorrow . . .*" My mom-ager, actually just my mom, drove me to said callback. The producers suggested they would love for me to jump into the role of the swing orphan. As a mother who knew better, she didn't allow me to take the position, which would have meant being the understudy for *all* the orphans in the cast and on standby every single night. There was no way Connie would allow this.

From then on, my career in high school and college musicals was much like you'd imagine. I did them all. When you study musical theater in college, everyone there was Maria in their high school production of *The Sound of Music*. I arrived in Boston to a mélange of Marias. So you're suddenly competing for roles against other people who are just as talented—and just as used to getting the part. How do you solve a problem like . . . I just met a girl named Maria? Sing out, Louise.

Girls Gone Greek

When we were in high school, Tricia got discovered at a hockey game at the Forum. She went in the next day for an audition and ended up being cast as Burt Reynolds's daughter in a movie called *Stick,* released in 1985. Connie had gone on a few dates with Burt back in the day, so everyone involved loved the synchronicity at play. Except for me. I was really pissed that Tricia had a movie and I didn't. But even I had to admit I didn't look like Burt Reynolds. I looked more like Troy Donahue. At that time, Connie came up with an idea to split any money Tricia and I earned equally between our trusts. It was part of her whole Three Musketeers philosophy: all for one and one for all. Connie told a *People* magazine reporter who came to the house to do a story on the three of us: "We're in this together. If one wins, the other wins, too." Once the earning scale shifted dramatically, the arrangement changed.

Tricia and I didn't go on a lot of auditions yet. My mom wasn't going to be a stage mom, and she wanted us to have some semblance of a childhood, so she didn't want us to be working constantly. If something came up that seemed like it would be a great, fun thing to do, then we would. And the fact that we were going to get paid for it, too, was a bonus. It wasn't about the money at that point in our lives.

I toyed with the idea of forgoing college to stay in L.A. and act. But then, at the last minute, I decided I wanted to go away to school after all. Emerson College in Boston was the only school that had saved my place, so that's where I went. I liked having something the rest of my immediate family didn't—I was getting a college education. I wasn't going on auditions because I knew what I wanted, and boy, would a musical theater degree help me. I put on the freshman fifteen at the same time—my introduction to the Hollywood standard of beauty, which began my lifetime struggle with weight and body image. When I came home on school breaks, my jealousy ignited because I found that, during my absence, Tricia had gained momentum in her fledgling career. It was always a big decision whether to return for another year of school or to make a go of it myself.

The summer after my freshman year, in 1986, Tricia was cast in the starring role alongside a young Patricia Arquette in *Pretty Smart,* set at a private girls' school in Greece. When they made the deal for Tricia's part, there were all sorts of female parts available. Her agent suggested that I take one of them, and the director and producers happily agreed I would play a part alongside my sister. I was going to Greece, too. Jackpot!

Connie had decided that, since we were going to a foreign country, she should send someone along with us who could serve as a bodyguard. So Jeff Speakman, a friend of my mother's boyfriend at the time and a martial arts expert, was corralled. He ended up getting a small part in the movie, which led to a short-lived career in action films.

There were about a dozen of us young actresses—mostly from L.A., but a few from around the world—who descended on Athens. We were put up in a gorgeous hotel. We had a per diem. We got to act. That right there would have been enough to convince us we were living La Dolce Vita Loca. It was learning by doing. It was a ridiculously cool first experience on a set like that—cliché . . . and fantastic. We spent the summer running around the Greek isles, shooting a movie.

The whole experience was magic. Sisters working side by side, drinking, dancing, and carrying on—what everyone thinks it's like to be on a movie set as a young woman—and more. Or what people might even fantasize about. So let's not pole dance around the fact that this movie was soft-core porn. I mean, nearly everybody was naked for much of the movie. Boobs were everywhere. No, not mine and not the two Tricias' boobs. We shot two different versions of some of the scenes—one with clothes on, for TV; and one with bare breasts, for film. They had stickers to cover everybody's nipples and bits. And when cameras stopped rolling for the day, I even kissed a girl and I liked it. I mean, I *really* liked it.

The evil headmaster—that's right, the evil headmaster—was played by Dennis Cole, who was Troy Donahue's stand-in during the years when he was my mom's frequent costar. Often in our careers Tricia and I would find ourselves working alongside people that had worked with one of our parents, and it made for some camaraderie and fun.

My love interest in the film, "the tennis pro," was played by actor Nick Celozzi, who *also* happened to be a family friend. We had a bathtub scene. Bubbles and boobs. I still felt like I hadn't come into my adult body yet, so this was a very big deal for me. Here I was, even if only giving the illusion of nudity on the big screen, sitting in the bathtub, up to my neck in bubbles. Nick always laughs when he recounts this part of the story. He came in, as directed, stood over the bathtub, then dropped his towel.

"You never took your eyes off my eyes," he says, laughing. "You never looked down."

I thought I looked seductive and casual and cool, but apparently I wasn't able to hide my sheer terror at seeing my friend's junk.

He got into the tub with me, and we kissed. As soon as the director yelled, "Cut!" I fashioned a bubble cover-up and popped out of that tub as quickly as I could. And yeah, as I recall, there's absolutely nothing sexy about the scene (don't you dare look it up).

I watched Tricia play the lead. She was great and sparkly in the part. But I felt a pang of jealousy. Being number eight or nine on the call sheet only served as a motivation to eventually make it to number one myself. I only realized then that this feeling had been ingrained in me by Connie. I'd heard her kvetch my whole life about actresses of her generation who'd achieved greater critical acclaim—"Jane Fonda got another fucking part . . . Why does Blythe Danner get all those roles?" It's embedded in my cellular makeup (and it's been modeled for me) to be jealous. And I always have been when it comes to my career. But I took it in a different direction (not that I don't whine and kvetch in private sometimes, of course). But instead of becoming bitter and resentful of others' success, it drove me to decide: *Well, fuck, I'm going to get my own shit.*

I'll Do Anything

My mom believes there are stepping-stones to wherever you get to in life, and this is definitely a role she'd point to as a major stepping-stone in my early career. As she described it (gleefully, to anyone who would listen): "Joely got to play with the big kids."

But first I had to get the part. I'd left Emerson, a few credits shy of graduation, in 1988, and moved back to L.A. I had the feeling that everyone knew who my parents were. I tried to combat any urge toward nepotism, because I wanted to be seen for me. And walking in singing "Oh My Papa" or "Kookie, Kookie, Lend Me Your Comb" didn't feel like it would grant me much mileage.

Going into the 1989 Academy Awards ceremony, both Tricia and I were tapped by producer Allan Carr and director Kenny Ortega to represent a future generation of statuette winners. The material: "Gee but It's Great to Be an Oscar Winner," written by Marvin Hamlisch, who conducted that night. The cast: Ricki Lake, Christian Slater, Chad Lowe, Patrick Dempsey, Savion Glover, Tyrone Power Jr., and the late Carrie Hamilton, Carol Burnett's daughter, and a few other up-and-comers and children of stars. We rehearsed for two weeks to do a montage of dirty dancing, tap dancing, and swashbuckling—the number ended with all of us giving our acceptance speeches en masse (no, really, if you want to hear it . . . go to YouTube). On Oscar night, we were introduced by the legends Lucille Ball and Bob Hope but were outshined by the opening number, in which the more famous Lowe brother, Rob, incongruously paired with Snow White in a musical opener that was a laughingstock.

Oscars are always during pilot season, so it was a good high-visibility opportunity. The following day I was called in to read for a part—they'd had trouble casting the role of Rosalie, the soubrette, a whiny Italian from Queens, in *Mulberry Street,* which was the television version of *Moonstruck,* with Cher's role played by Connie Sellecca (the 1980s TV star equivalent of the Oscar winner, and with equally great hair). I was eventually cast in my first regular role in a series.

I had momentum, which meant I'd had a taste of victory and had gotten to that stage every actor must go through—the millions of auditions. This was the beginning of my hooker-with-a-spleen-of-gold stage. I did some guest roles—everything from a cop undercover as a hooker on *Blossom* to a waitress with a shotgun on *Something Is Out There* and a recurring role as a preschool teacher on *Growing Pains*—oh, and come to think of it . . . another hooker on *Golden Palace.*

James L. Brooks was writing and directing a movie, *I'll Do Anything.* I went to the Sony lot to audition for casting director Paula Herold. It was just what you'd think it would be like, now that everybody has seen *La La Land*. The Sony lot looked exactly like that, with these cute little bungalows.

The film was a musical, so for my audition I had to sing sixteen bars of something, then do a scene. This was a big studio movie with the acclaimed James L. Brooks. And they'd already cast Nick Nolte and Tracey Ullman. So naturally, I sang "Someone to Watch Over Me," which I never felt unsure about, and did the scene. And then, I didn't hear anything. Some time passed, and they were getting to the point where they'd begun shooting, and they were filling in these smaller roles. So they brought me in again, this time to read for Jim. Then I got another callback, where I had to dance for choreographer extraordinaire Twyla Tharp (no pressure) at a studio in Culver City. There was a bizarre, wonderful combination of talents contributing to this cinematic soup.

I felt like I was getting closer, and yet the anticipation was unbearable. They had cast the first part I'd been auditioning for, but there was a splashier role that had not yet been filled. So I went back, yet again, to meet Paula Herold and Jim, this time in Jim's private office. The room was lined with little red velvet seats—almost like a movie theater. So as I delivered the final notes of my song, I instinctually, but impulsively, did a full layout on one of the chairs for a final tableau. It made Jim laugh, and he has a very distinctive laugh.

I'm going to get this role, I thought, triumphantly.

Apparently they weren't as sure as I was. A little bit more time passed with no word, and then I was told to come to the set. (Insert traditional fanfare here.) When I arrived at the studio, we were taken to an adjacent set, where they had already started shooting. Yes, I said "we." I was thrown in with my competition—Mariska Hargitay, Liz Vassey, and Michelle Nicastro. While we all nervously awaited our turn up at bat,

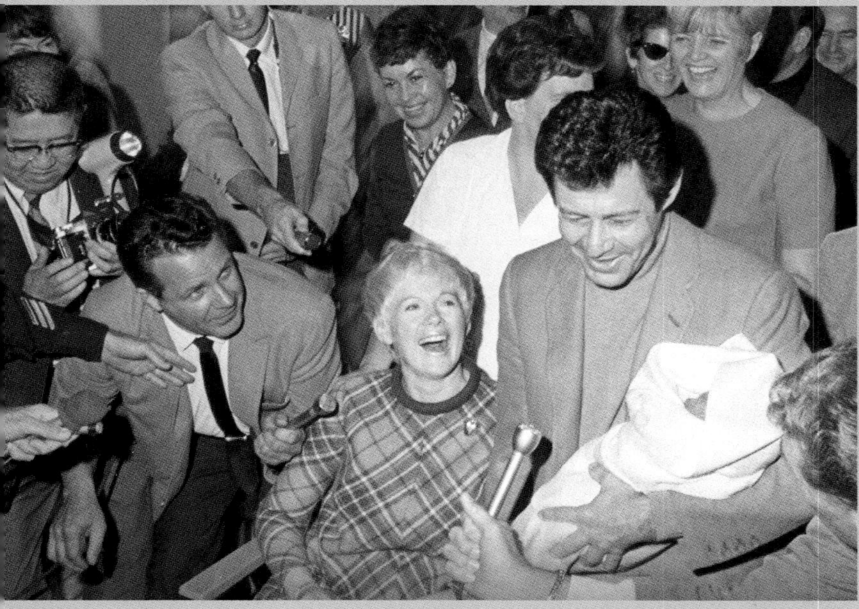

TOP LEFT: Connie—always ahead of her time . . . TOP RIGHT: Eddie, whom Connie still describes as "delicious" BOTTOM: All eyes on Connie and Eddie as they exit the hospital with baby Joely, October 1967 (*© Bettmann / Getty Images*)

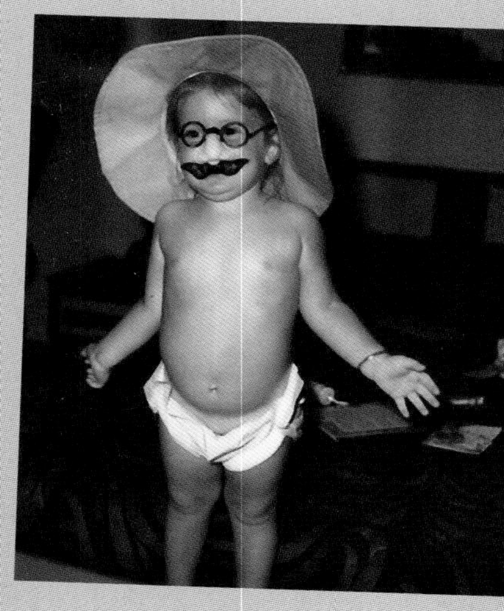

TOP LEFT: Connie's mother, Eleanor—Grandma enjoying a smoke with baby Joely. Times have changed . . . TOP RIGHT: My first gig as a stand-up . . . finding the funny MIDDLE LEFT: Baby Joely with her new playmate, Tricia Leigh BOTTOM LEFT: American Gothic: a rare family portrait BOTTOM RIGHT: Connie and the girls . . . and their hair, always in good company

TOP LEFT: As Tuptim in *The King and I*, live and direct from the multipurpose room at Our Lady of Malibu TOP RIGHT: It's all Greek to me . . . as Lysistrata at Beverly Hills High, 1985 BOTTOM LEFT: In a production of *Anything Goes* at Beverly Hills High School, cast alongside David Schwimmer BOTTOM RIGHT: Young Joely joins the act—not always the fashionista she is now

TOP: Emerson College parents' weekend—after a decade apart, Eddie and Connie show up in the same sassy sweater BOTTOM: After a triumphant performance in San Francisco with proud Mom and Dad in the audience

Facing Page TOP LEFT: Clearly Eddie's excited about showing off his daughter to royalty, pictured here with Queen Farah of Iran TOP RIGHT: With Eddie on a summer adventure in the South of France MIDDLE LEFT: Posing with Dad in front of Tony Bennett's portrait of Eddie, at Tony's art opening in L.A. MIDDLE RIGHT: Noodling around with oh my papa—no extra charge for the mullet and tie BOTTOM LEFT: Shoe shopping at Fred Segal, one of our favorite pastimes BOTTOM RIGHT: Eddie's first meeting with granddaughter Skylar

TOP: Connie guest stars on my Lifetime show, *Wild Card* MIDDLE LEFT: Connie costars as my mother in *Search Engines* MIDDLE RIGHT: Two divas painting up for a night out BOTTOM: The separate-check girls—Lainie Kazan, Connie, Diane Ladd, and Renée Taylor

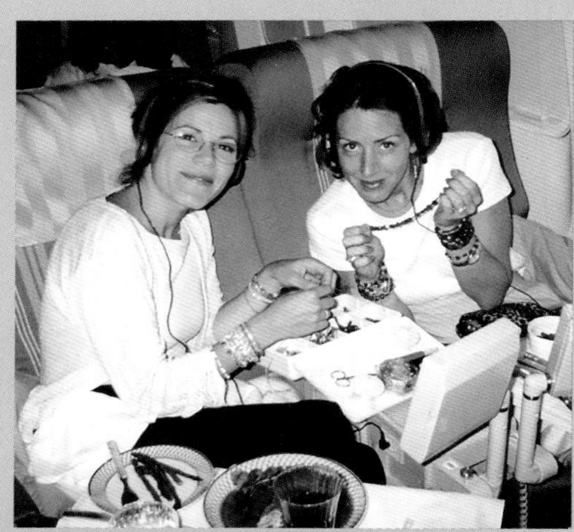

Facing Page TOP LEFT: Sisters and their hair TOP MIDDLE: The sisters emulate Heart, one of our favorite '80s bands TOP RIGHT: Happy times with our governess Helena MIDDLE LEFT: With Tricia, making jewelry on a transcontinental flight, naturally MIDDLE RIGHT: On a spectacular emotional pilgrimage to Mozambique with Save the Children BOTTOM LEFT: Supporting big sis Carrie at the *Star Wars: The Force Awakens* premiere BOTTOM RIGHT: Doing what we do best . . . together

TOP LEFT: I attended the father-daughter dance with Connie's boyfriend Ralph Forbes. Weird TOP RIGHT: Ready to hit the stage with some of our favorite members of Connie's band BOTTOM LEFT: My view of Sandra Seacat and the group post the emotional, life-changing heart mandala acting exercise in Montecatini, Italy BOTTOM RIGHT: With Tricia Leigh and Patricia Arquette during the filming of *Pretty Smart*

TOP LEFT: Clearly he had my heart; David Styne proposes TOP RIGHT: My date for the senior prom, Wade Weller, whom I imported straight from Oklahoma for the occasion MIDDLE LEFT: Me and Dean during our Emerson days, Boston MIDDLE RIGHT: "This one I like"—Daddy approved of Humberto. Oh the irony . . . BOTTOM: Joining my main squeeze Humberto at the studio

TOP LEFT: Carrie gets little Billie ready to be a flower girl at Auntie Joely's wedding TOP RIGHT: At a Delfern celebration, waiting to welcome baby Holden BOTTOM LEFT: Proud auntie at Billie's high school graduation BOTTOM RIGHT: My and Carrie's firstborn daughters, Skylar and Billie

TOP: Debbie and Connie, Eddie's exes/supermoms/sisterwives/divas/friends *(© Dan Callister / Getty Images)* MIDDLE LEFT: With Mama Debs sharing a moment at Carrie's "Fifties Farewell" party BOTTOM RIGHT: Sisters at a luncheon honoring Debbie for her work with the Thalians BOTTOM LEFT: Tricia and I celebrate Todd's birthday

TOP LEFT: A moment of shared admiration at the Fox upfronts, New York City *(© Evan Agostini / Getty Images)* TOP RIGHT: All the Fisher sibs at the *Star Wars* premiere MIDDLE: The last time the Fisher sisters were all together BOTTOM: The family supports Carrie at the *Wishful Drinking* premier, Los Angeles *(© Tinseltown / Shutterstock.com)*

Still crazy after all these years. The gang celebrates after the twenty-year anniversary of "The Puppy Episode," and runs into James Corden . . . A true Hollywood story

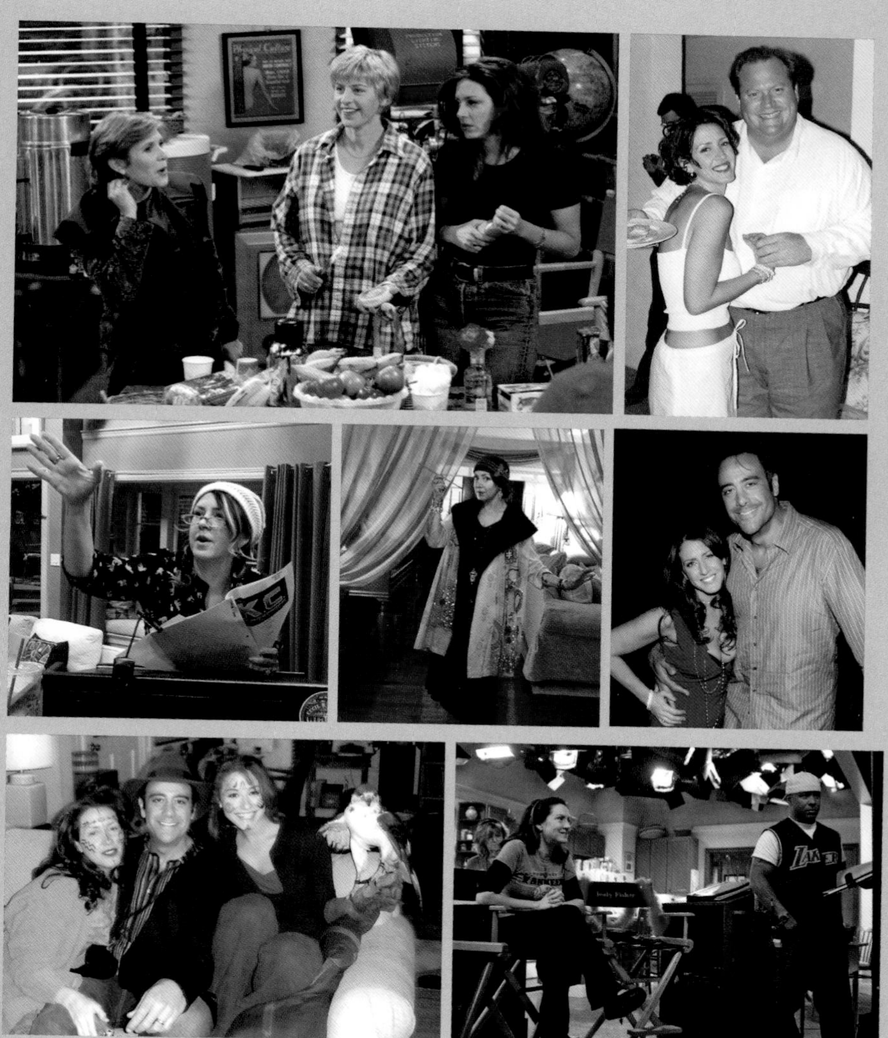

TOP LEFT: "The Movie Show"; Carrie Fisher stars as herself alongside me and Ellen *(© Bob Riha Jr / ABC Photo Archives/ Getty Images)* TOP RIGHT: With John Carrabino MIDDLE LEFT: Taking my rightful position behind the podium directing Disney Channel's *K.C. Undercover* MIDDLE: Woody Allen said no to this. Auditioning for *Bullets Over Broadway* MIDDLE RIGHT: With Brad Garrett, my TV husband and gentle giant BOTTOM LEFT: On the set of *'Til Death* with Brad, Kat Foster, and a falcon. This also is not normal BOTTOM RIGHT: Television directorial debut on the set of *'Til Death*, Sony Pictures, California

TOP LEFT: I got to play with Robert Patrick on the set of *Scorpion* TOP RIGHT: With the ladies of What a Pair!, True plays the part of baby Simba in *The Lion King*'s "Circle of Life"—*Us Magazine* called this "not normal" MIDDLE LEFT: Behind the scenes in *Inspector Gadget* with Matthew Broderick MIDDLE RIGHT: Learning choreography from Adam Shankman, *Inspector Gadget* BOTTOM LEFT: Go Go Gadget Blue Goo (the original slime)—crazy day on location in Pittsburgh BOTTOM RIGHT: The cast of *Inspector Gadget* with producer Jordan Kerner and the legendary late Stan Winston we could hear music from next door, where they were shooting a musical number. Prince was on the set, as he had written the ballad. Julie Kavner (who happens to be the voice of Marge Simpson) was singing to Albert Brooks. Twyla's troupe was performing on tables in the bar set. It was Felliniesque.

We were in the surrealest of circumstances—none of us had ever met before, but one of us was going to get cast and have a job the next day. Instead of being catty about this, we bonded and laughed and told stories, until one by one, each of us was called in to audition.

"You're going to get it."

"No, you're going to get it."

"*Maybe* I'll get it. No, you're going to get it."

"Let's call each other," we said as we finally left the set hours later.

The next morning, I called Mariska.

"You got it," she said.

"I did."

"All right. You get this one."

It was the beginning of a lifelong friendship, and clearly, she would get hers in the grandest of ways.

Connie was right—I was playing with the big kids, indeed.

It was my first experience of working on a big movie where the craft service budget was unlimited, and everything felt very cushy. I did have to share a double banger—a trailer built for two—with Vicki Lewis, who has also turned out to be one of my dear, dear friends and makes me laugh harder than anyone I know. Nick Nolte often came to our trailer to eat lunch with us, and they ended up being a couple for years after.

It was a big-budget movie in an ambitious genre—*La La Land* long before its time. We did the big musical numbers at this movie theater in Agoura, with Joely Richardson, Vicki

Lewis, Jeb Brown, and I tap-dancing down the road behind a profusely sweating Albert Brooks, who played our boss, and Twyla's troupe bringing up the rear. I was the D girl (my character was written without a name, but I decided to call her Rachel). "D" stands for development, not what you might think it does—those overachieving, entitled young men and women in the movie industry who are given an enormous amount of responsibility, even though they don't really have the experience. They read a script and become a producer on it because . . . who knows? But I did get what I thought was the best line in the movie, when Albert Brooks asks the group of us, after viewing Nick Nolte's character's screen test, "But would you fuck him?" And I responded: "Well, six years ago, maybe."

The anticipation of its release was amazing . . . until its release. So the nearly fifty-million-dollar budget was an expensive experiment . . . it flopped. Ironically, the movie about how movies get made, which included a musical number about audience testing, tested badly. No matter; I'd had the incredible experience of working with one of the greats, James L. Brooks.

And at least there was some buzz about all of us young actors, which definitely helped us in our careers. Vicki went on to win a Tony Award, and you might recognize her from the TV show *NewsRadio*. Anne Heche's career took off not long after that. And *moi*? In a very short amount of time, I worked with Jim Carrey on *The Mask*. I worked with Nora Ephron on her film *Mixed Nuts,* which starred Steve Martin and featured every funny person in Hollywood, from Madeline Kahn and Adam Sandler to Rita Wilson and Parker Posey. So I found myself in the land of big directors, big cinematographers, big costars, and even if I wasn't the star, it felt like I was getting notches on a belt. But I would have to remind myself: *it's a marathon, not a sprint*. I was definitely encouraged—I had the feeling that opportunities were bubbling up, and all of this was on its way to being a career . . . and then, later that year, I got a little television show. (Insert double fanfare.)

SO YEAH, FOR the last few decades, I've enjoyed a healthy, packed resumé, chock-full of soubrette roles. But I still hear this jealous, competitive voice in my head—the voice of Connie. For all the wins, and the enviable position I could be in, and the roles other actresses would give a limb for, it has been a lifetime of feeling less-than, of getting the consolation prize. Because Connie didn't get it from her parents, she lived in a vacuum that was: *you're not validated unless you're working*. She felt that way about herself—so why shouldn't we, her daughters?

Also highly motivational, of course. If a little crazy making? For sure. I became very self-directed when it came to show business, from a young age. Was that because I thought Connie would like me better if I made it? Or because I wanted to get her attention? Or the attention of the world—or I'd like myself better? And there it is . . . that self-love thing.

It's definitely gotten me out to auditions and kept me stretching myself. But it's also meant that I've had to do some fancy mental footwork when I haven't gotten the part, or when I haven't made it to the top of the marquee—challenging during the many years when I've been the soubrette, and not the ingénue or the leading lady. Historically, because I want it so badly, I go to great lengths to be prepared for my auditions—I've made a definite decision about who the character is. I've done my dream work. Where does she come from? What moves her? Who moves her? I've decided what she'd be wearing—is this woman heavily made up, is she natural? All that preparation pays off, I am her.

When in Rome (or Tuscany)

I realized early on that preparation was the key to everything. Once again my partner in crime, Tricia, and I had the good fortune to venture to Italy to study with renowned acting coach Sandra Seacat (for many years Jessica Lange always drew on her expertise to prepare for roles—that was enough for me). This may sound cliché, because it was cliché—we literally ate, drank, slept, learned, and sweated together in this beautiful villa. Italy changed my whole trajectory. My tools and how I use them. I was there with thirty other actors, and we all engaged in self-discovery at its utmost. We went to the studio at nine in the morning and came home at nine at night, and we hung out after hours, drinking wine, smoking cigarettes, letting our hair grow (including the hair on our legs and in our pits). It was everything. But on our occasional days off, Tricia and I would grab our Eurail passes and take off from our home base of Montecatini, famous for its healing mud. We explored the country—Capri, the Amalfi coast, and Firenze—that's Florence to you and me. On one of these crazy jaunts with my friend—now interior designer extraordinaire—Mary Rae McDonald, she finagled a stay for the weekend at one of Florence's famous luxury hotels, as mutual friends from L.A. were vacationing there. It was a welcome, sexy distraction from the intense work we were doing. I had a playful, fun tryst of a weekend with an eventual A-lister.

The class included two other teachers from the Actors Studio, but Sandra's work was the deep excavation of the heart mandala—the year of the heart mandala happens between the age of ten and a half and eleven and a half. It's when you begin to develop autonomy, when you learn how to say no, when you look at relationships, and you see where you come from, and it all starts to inform who you're going to be.

The exercise starts with writing yourself a letter at bedtime:

> Dear inner self,
>
> If it is thy will, please reveal to me, in a dream, my heart mandala.
>
> Love and Respect,
> *Joely*

Universal subconscious picked these images in order to reveal to me my true inner self: and of course, in my dream . . . I was sitting in the center square of the *Hollywood Squares* game show set, together with my mother. *Hello, subconscious!* Here I was, *sharing* a square with Connie. *Don't I get my own square? Why am I in a square? A HOLLYWOOD SQUARE?!*

So next up, we were assigned to do a ritual in order to shed the burden of our dream, so we could fully know ourselves and move on, and therefore be able to do the same excavation for roles in our acting. We should include things that came from the earth in our ritual—flowers, corn silk, water. I found a piece of marble on the ground for my ritual. I still have it. I tied myself up with silk stockings, and I was trying to get free, get free, get free, and I snottily ugly-cried through my ritual, and I finally did . . . get free. There's something about creating a public ceremony that puts some physicality to this process of release that definitely rids you of that which has been holding you back. My life changed. And although Tricia had a different dream, and a different ritual, she feels the same way. I can't stress enough how incredible that was. And it completely changed my approach to my craft—it *gave* me my approach to my craft, really. It remains the foundation for everything I've done since—and everything I know I have in me yet to express.

Another part of the curriculum that summer was called a Private Moment, which was ironic because it was in front of forty-five people. We each got paired off to explore what our private moment might be. I sat with one of the other actors in our little, hot, sweaty room, with the mosquito coil smell and the sound bleeding in of other people doing their thing in their rooms. The whole challenge was to be as private as you can be onstage, in front of others, without being an exhibitionist—no masturbating, no showboating. It has to be something that's really scary, really private, like for someone else, it might be picking a zit in the mirror, having an intimate talk with yourself, or singing.

We met up at our courtyard studio where class took place, summer heat gusting in through open windows. I knew what my scariest choice could be, even though I really didn't want to do it. I took my time, as I was supposed to, really getting private in front of people. I kind of meandered around in my space and tried to block out, as best I could, the fact that anybody was watching. And then, I slowly undressed. I did it as if I was alone, and I really was able to undress myself—literally and figuratively. I imagined a mirror where the audience was, so it was as if I was looking at my reflection, as opposed to being watched by all these people. As I stripped myself, it brought up tremendous emotion. I was very uncomfortable being exposed like that. All my insecurity from a lifetime of comparing myself to my beautiful mother came up. As I write this, I feel compassion toward a woman who I never saw—literally or figuratively—stripped down, a woman who covered her body in front of her own children. And I couldn't imagine her going to a place of such vulnerability.

But this was exactly what I wanted to do. I wanted to go deeper. And I wanted to be freer and more at peace with what my body looked like, and felt like, and to take this through into being able to bare myself later in my work.

ele

Maybe This Time

When I returned from Italy, I felt different about the tools I had at my disposal to prepare for a role. I felt like I knew what I was doing. Over the course of a career, there have been two handfuls of female characters with which I have put this work to good use. In 1999, I was given the distinct pleasure of playing one of the most coveted and iconic roles in musical theater—Sally Bowles in *Cabaret*. Choreographer-director Rob Marshall and director Sam Mendes were at the helm of a Broadway revival. I auditioned for them. After a small slew of Sallys, I was asked to go into the role. In eleven days, I got a crash course in all things *Cabaret*, from Rob's right hand (and foot), Cynthia Onrubia, and the assistant director, J. V. Mercanti. Rob Marshall and Sam Mendes came in to fine-tune and nuance my performance before sending me out in the part. They would watch, from time to time, and give me notes: "You're self-indulgent in this scene, give a little less."

But the real preparation I did was my dream work. I did the same heart mandala exercise I'd learned in Italy in order to tap into the essence of Sally. In my dream of her, I was out-of-control roller-skating through a crowd in New York City, and when I woke up, I thought: *That's Sally . . . she's out of control on roller skates in a crowd.* So that's how I started to build the character, from that emotional place.

Once I had learned the part and begun to really embody the character, Rob gave me a big-picture note: "You need to do on-screen what you're doing onstage every night, because it's fucking real."

It's hard to describe how satisfying it is to find yourself in the perfect role that comes along at just the right time, and then really nail it. Fucking incredible, for starters. But then, the difficulty was in finding a way to do it every night for a year. About three months into the run, I began having trouble. It was such a dark part, and I was so deep inside it. Rob Marshall saw the show and then came back to my dressing room.

I was in pretty rough shape, and I couldn't hide it anymore. Every night, onstage, I was having the experience of the junkie girl who was lost and roller-skating amid the crowd, who just wanted to be loved, and I felt what she felt, and it was so hard.

"I don't know what to do, because I don't know if I can do it again," I said.

"You've done it already, so when you go onstage, you embody that character, so you don't have to physically have the experience every night like you do," he said. "You *are* her. You don't have to excavate that stuff every time. Relax. It's going to be fine. It's funny. I've had this conversation with several other Sallys. It happens, always, at the same point—you are her now, so you don't have to work so hard."

I did three hundred performances as Sally Bowles. Having to do the show that many times, I welcomed occasional input, especially when it came from a member of my talented family. I particularly loved hearing when Carrie said I had the characterization down and sang better than any of us. Sistah, not sister, Sharon Stone, who came to my opening night in San Francisco, offered a couple of unsolicited "notes," one of which was to change my body language in an opening tableau. I tried it. She was right. And it was always a balm to see a familiar face in the audience, as when my manager of many years, John Carrabino, flew out to surprise me at several tour stops. Ellen came to see me on Broadway, and I upped my game that night even just a little more.

Some shows were better than others, but even the shows that didn't go so well had their moments. I remember Ellen used to say to me, "When I was doing comedy, and everybody was laughing, but there's the one person who was sitting there with his arms crossed, I told my jokes right to him." I had that same experience when I was in *Cabaret*. If anybody in the audience was not feeling me, I would work harder, and I could usually reach them, and that felt amazing. And also, it was the feeling of becoming Sally. Because that's what she did, too. Sally Bowles wanted the love. I knew how that felt, and for the year I was in the show, I finally felt like I was receiving the love. I'd done the work, and I was enough, and I was okay. That's a very difficult place to get to as an actress, as a woman, as a human.

ele

Woody, or Won't He?

This approach has worked for me for many, many years. Unfortunately, for every experience I've had where it all came together, I've also had the opposite happen. I've had those moments where life, or your own internal workings, get the best of you, and the results are far messier. Even when you have the tools, life takes you in different directions, and you can't always deliver. You get sloppy.

Partly, it's the industry. For all the good work you do, sometimes it's just never going to happen. Those auditions where I was the best square, but they wanted round, so I just didn't fit, no matter what.

Then there were the times when I did it to myself. Like that time in my twenties when I was flown across the country to audition for a musical. It was a really important audition for a really big show, and I stayed up all night partying and sabotaged myself. And I still don't know why. When I wanted it more desperately than anyone else I knew, why not just have an up-tempo and a ballad prepared? (Like I do right now.)

In recent years, I've had a few resurgences of the old internal melodrama. Maybe it was the financial setbacks I experienced. Maybe it was getting older and finding I had to audition for parts that would have been offered only earlier on—when there were parts at all (the drought when it comes to parts for older actresses is no joke). Even just a few years ago, I flew to New York for an audition for Woody Allen's Broadway adaptation of his film, *Bullets over Broadway.* It wasn't a big, open casting call—they were only seeing a few people. So it was a big deal. It was for a part that I could play in my sleep. It was a high-profile job I could have really used right then.

But.

My internal voice started self-sabotaging right away.

When I heard the music I thought, *Oh. I kind of don't love this song. It's not really my thing.*

But then, the other side of the argument came in: *But. Dianne Wiest played it in the movie, and she was so, "Don't speak. Don't speak." I want to do that so badly. The part is so great. Maybe the song will change, or maybe I'll be able to put my stamp on it.*

I'm not really a trained singer; I've got chops and I'm a great song stylist. Until recently, I was lazy when it came to keeping up that part of my instrument. Even though I started landing the leads in school musicals in fifth grade. And I studied musical theater in college. And I'm Joely with a Z, who really thought the cornerstone of my career was going to be singing and doing musicals. But I haven't always done the work to support that dream. Because it is my responsibility to have a dozen songs ready to go, and to go study with different teachers, and to take care of myself—no cigarettes, no alcohol—to be vigilant over my vocal cords. I wasn't back then, and I'm still not always, which is weird. Why have I found myself at so many auditions, wondering: *Why didn't I take six months to prepare and go to the gym? Why do I only go to my very expensive vocal coach the day before I have to sing? Why don't I warm up? Why did I ever smoke?* Well, I'll tell you why: because after an audition I can blame something . . . other than that I wasn't the best one for the role.

So when I flew to New York for this Woody Allen audition, I actually got sick on the plane. Or depending on how you look at it, I made myself sick on the plane. So that, when I went to sing, I had a little bit less to draw on than what I normally would have. And there it was: I had an excuse if I didn't get the part. I did that many times in my life, where, postaudition, when everybody assumed I would get the role, except me, and would automatically be asking: "When do rehearsals start?" I had the perfect way to extricate myself from the disappointment.

"Oh, you're not going to believe it . . . I got sick on the plane."

Well, if I'm not feeling well, then I have an excuse to not be perfect.

When I arrived in New York, they had me work with the musical director.

"You have those chops?" he said, impressed.

"Yeah, you can hear it's a little scratchy," I said.

"You'll be fine tomorrow."

That's what I thought. So I went to dinner with friends, had a little wine, went home kind of late. Looked at the scenes and thought, *Oh God, this is a lot more than I thought it was. Why didn't I do my dream work? Vocalize? Memorize? I must not really want this one.*

The place where I auditioned was consummate New York—this skinny little elevator that opened right onto a Broadway rehearsal space, with the sound of people singing scales up and down the halls. It's so cliché, but for me, still thrilling. I *want* to be in this world. I absolutely looked the part—full period costume, the little cap with the big jewel. Maybe that was just enough to get by. I was on deck, and I heard a Broadway diva singing the song—just absolutely to the rafters. *I should run . . . back to a cushy television job.*

I walked into a room with the director, Susan Stroman, Woody Allen's sister and longtime producer, Letty Aronson, and Woody, whom you can't talk to directly. Even though I had met him on the street. He knew I was Carrie's sister, and he had once gone in for an open-mouth kiss in front of the Ivy on Robertson. (Natch.)

Susan gave me a hug and said, "We're so happy to have you here." The musical director winked—*you're going to be great.* Woody Allen leaned on the table, framing his face with his hands—he was looking at me as if through a camera lens, instead of the broadness of the Broadway stage. Maybe it threw me.

There's no way to candy-coat it, I sucked.

I had gone to New York for that audition. But I'd given myself the perfect excuse to not land the part. This is the essence of my struggle. We can do the work, and learn our craft, and gain valuable insights from the best directors in the business, and stockpile experience, and we're still battling whatever our original fear is—maybe, in my case, the little girl who will never be the beautiful star her mother was. Or maybe, possibly, not to eclipse her star. Mostly, in recent years, I win the day, and the little girl doesn't. But it can still be hard and uncomfortable. When I sing at a benefit event, with a lineup of other entertainers, there's still a part of me that wonders: *Do I belong here?* And then, I hear the opening notes of my song, the curtains part, and my confidence returns as I walk toward the microphone and into the spotlight. I realize I am a star. I realize what I have—an ability to move people; it's poetic, it's transcendent—I've always had it. It's a gift and a responsibility. So the question still remains: *What is it that's keeping me from my rightful place?* I'm not a lazy person. I've always been driven. It still thrills me . . . every . . . time. So what the fuck?

Perhaps I shouldn't overthink it, and just take my mother's well-meaning and fantastic advice: "When all else fails, Joely, just sing the song."

Chapter 9

I'm Not a Lesbian . . . But I Play with One on TV

AS I MAKE THE "DRIVE of shame" back to Ellen's house, her locked cell phone in my left hand and my balled-up Spanx in my right, I realize how truly I have missed this woman's presence in my life. This is how I remember us, crawling in traffic, chauffeured by assistants . . . ol' cell phone 'n' Spanx herself . . . returning to the scene of the crime.

The previous day, we had reconnoitered for a brief moment, for the momentous and emotional twentieth-anniversary celebration of "The Puppy Episode" of our show. The Reunion! I had been invited back into the folds—no, not the lady folds—get your mind out of the gutter, Ellen and I have always just been friends, despite what Howard Stern may have once implied, when I appeared on his show, about Ellen scheduling our wardrobe fittings at the same time. Back into the inner sanctum, up close to the intimate triumphs and travails of a true entertainment magnate.

We'd been on-screen besties for four years, real-life friends for longer than that—she'd introduced me to my husband and had been at our wedding—but in the ensuing years, our time together had been relegated to her big white talk-show chairs. My friend, who was never one for jewelry, was awarded the

Medal of Freedom by President Barack Obama in 2016, a giant medal placed around her neck by an elegant, effective president—my president. And how I'd openly wept. I was alone with my husband. We sobbed as we recalled our first meeting, orchestrated by her.

Moments before we would all reconvene as a cast on Ellen's talk show, I was standing in the greenroom at Warner Bros. I wore a hot-pink cocktail dress with a tight silhouette, pretty sure Ellen wouldn't be wearing the same thing. I'd even done a cleanse leading up to the show, to appear at my sveltest, as this was another historic TV moment—honoring the iconic first coming-out of a gay character on a network TV show. I looked at my onetime castmates, Clea Lewis and David Anthony Higgins, and I realized my hands were shaking. I don't get nervous about anything, except for going to the dentist and flying on airplanes. There was a vibration, not unlike the one we felt that night that Ellen DeGeneres, and her sitcom alter ego Ellen Morgan, both came out on *Ellen*.

The show started with Oprah's interview (in the original series, she played Ellen's therapist, whom Ellen actually came out to first, during one of their sessions) . . . because Oprah. And then, Laura Dern, who played the object of Ellen's affection, was interviewed. And then coming back from commercial break, there were clips of memorable moments of the cast teasing the idea that Ellen would finally come out. The thought crossed my mind to do a pratfall, always the physical comedienne, but I opted to saucily sashay my way to the front of the couch.

As we sat together, well coiffed and painted—concealing the ravages of age with . . . well, concealer—hair did and makeup on, with millions of people watching yet again—the air, the atmosphere was charged. The producers, writers, and some former Disney executives were in the audience, along with people whose life had been changed forever by the coming-out narrative. We gathered together, joined by the memory and sheer honor of taking part in this historic moment in television, and in the life of Ellen D. I knew, I'd heard on many occasions, from the horse's mouth, how she didn't wish to be the poster child for the gay movement . . . but how could she not be?

Ellen, as the host of her successful, long-running talk show, would get to recount the triumph and the aftermath of "The Puppy Episode." And for four seasons, I'd gotten to be the bestie, Paige Clarke . . . and a gay icon in my own right. An honor that meant as much to me as any of the other accolades that came along at any time in my career.

One of the men who produced the anniversary segment was clearly a fan of our on-screen relationship. It was easy to tell. He knew the specific episodes, and he reminisced about them as if the characters had really been us, and had really been his friends: ". . . remember when she rode your train down the aisle . . . then, oh, when she kissed you . . . ? You were like Laverne and Shirley," he said. "Lucy and Ethel." I was tickled at the comparison to my favorite female comic duos.

It's true that we had that *thing*. That physical comedy rapport, that timing. I believe it's because we genuinely liked each other, and respected each other, and got a kick out of each other. For me, I would say that's the case. One of the most telling memories of the show happened when Ellen and I switched clothes in an episode. Not only did we don each other's wardrobe, but we each entered the way we thought the other one would have. We put on a physicality, and a facial expression, to how we saw each other—it wasn't at all negative or mean, just playfully overt—and telling. We loved each other, we just didn't want to *be* each other.

But, I'll be honest, when I first landed the part of Paige, I was simply glad for the work. I'd been building my Hollywood resumé for the past eight years, but the most recent round of auditions had been *rough*—enough near misses nearly breaks your heart, but my spirit wasn't broken, and I forged on.

ele

She's Not Sexy

That particular year, 1994, I auditioned for twenty-nine pilots. I had even shot a pilot or two, but none of them had gotten picked up. I had not yet made a name for myself. But I think, maybe, there was beginning to be a bit of a buzz around town. I was definitely among a handful of women who were on a short list for all the hot shows. It was the year of *Friends*. I was brought in to read several times for all three female roles. But the universe had something else in mind for me.

Now, when I say I auditioned for pilots, sometimes I went in one time, met all the producers, and that was it. Sometimes I went in three times, tested at the network, and that was it. So I experienced all varying levels of rejection. The show I auditioned for right before I got cast on *Ellen* starred a comedian named Carlos Mencia, and it was going to be the new Ricky and Lucy. Right in my wheelhouse, a fun, young married couple—lots of physical comedy—I felt it was a great part for me.

I wasn't the only one.

"You're our first choice, we want you for this," the casting director and producers said to me.

All I had to do was the final step in pilot casting—get network approval. At that time, I was running from being the hooker with a heart of gold at one audition to being a young mom with three toddlers at another. It was so crazy. Actors could be seen changing clothes, reading lines, nervously lipsticking, in their cars, going from one end of L.A. to the other, from studio to studio. But now it was time for me to test at Fox for this part. I went and got my hair done, something I normally wouldn't have done, but I really wanted to be perfect.

Now, there's a whole methodology to how casting directors and producers present their top choices to the network, so they choreographed the whole thing, and they assured me I was a shoo-in.

Here's what the president of Fox, Sandy Grushow, had to say: "She's just not sexy."

Ouch, says the woman who James L. Brooks called "Jugs."

"Joely, I don't know what to tell you," the producer said. "We did not cast the role, so when they do the next round of testing, we want you to come back in again. And we're going to tell you exactly what to wear this time."

Apparently, I hadn't learned how to sexy-dress myself.

In preparation for my audition the following day, I went to the lot where they were. I literally jumped out of my car, pressed myself against a chain link fence, holding potential outfits up for the producer and casting director to approve.

"What do you guys think?" I asked.

"Wear the skirt," Gilda Stratton, the casting director, said.

"Wear your hair down," Marco Pennette, the producer, said.

The scenes were there. I know they were. But this guy just didn't have it for me. He was the president of the network. So he nixed me.

So that's Hollywood, baby. What is beauty? How is beauty defined? What is sexuality? How is sensuality defined? Usually, the man in charge gets to say. And for this particular guy at the top, I wasn't it. So I didn't get to be Lucy . . . that time around. Apparently the universe really did have other plans for me . . .

ele

These Friends of Mine

Back to the back-lot shuffle, my spirit still unbroken (barely), I went on an audition for the first season of Ellen's sitcom, only at that point, the show was called *These Friends of Mine*. For whatever reason, at that time, I didn't get the job. They shot thirteen episodes. And with a midseason pickup, and a retooling of the show, the character of Paige Clark was added in the place of the ladies who were previously cast. They were looking for someone sexy, and naturally, they thought of me. Ha! Did they think I was sexy? We were about to find out. I went to test at the network—ABC—which was in Century City at the time.

I'll never forget the room. Almost always, at the networks, these rooms are dark theaters, with rows and rows of seats . . . or even a brightly lit conference room . . . but always, they are filled with executives and people who have all different roles at the network—everyone turns up to watch these auditions.

I showed up, and Ellen and I did several scenes together (the same scenes I'd auditioned with the previous year—I really had them down by now).

I made Ellen laugh in the middle of a scene.

I got the job, that same day, at five o'clock.

I was at a friend's house, going over music for my live performance at an upcoming fund-raiser, when I got the call. This composer and I were standing there when the phone rang.

"I got it," I said.

I just knew. And I also knew that my life had changed forever.

Although the show had only done half a season at that point, I'd heard a buzz about it. And it was getting picked up (!) so getting this job meant I had a real, actual job—not just a pilot where we shot the one episode and then waited to see if it stuck. I had been cast in my first on-air sitcom, one that would clearly alter the trajectory of my career.

ele

The Caustic Best Friend

From the start of the second season, in September 1994, when the show was relaunched as *Ellen,* with the addition of *moi,* the new configuration seemed to be working. We had heat. I played Ellen's childhood best friend, Paige Clark, a brassy, self-centered-but-ultimately-devoted personality with a capital "P," who couldn't seem to help but stir up trouble. The ensemble cast would also grow to include masterful comic talent—Clea Lewis came in to do one episode and ended up being a regular; David Anthony Higgins was a fixture at the bookstore-coffeehouse; Arye Gross was Ellen's roommate; later Jeremy Piven was added as Ellen's cousin, Spence, Paige's eventual main squeeze. Soon enough, everyone wanted to be a guest star on the show, and A-listers gravitated toward it.

We were the cool kids, and it was the club everyone wanted to be a part of—every show opened with a different surprise guest, from the Captain and Tennille and the Bee Gees (that was fucking rad) to Oscar De La Hoya and Devo. Memorable guest stars who played a part in the storylines included Martha Stewart, Trisha Yearwood, Bonnie Raitt, and a full cast of Fishers. Tricia guest-starred on the "Lobster Diary" episode, alongside Mary Tyler Moore. Eddie guest-starred, playing himself, in the "Parent Trap" episode, in which Ellen tried to re-create her parents' honeymoon in Cuba, complete with a performance by Eddie Fisher—naturally, when you don't want your parents to get divorced, bring in Eddie Fisher.

The producers approached me going into an episode called "The Movie Show." Names had been bandied about for who would be a fantastic guest star. One producer suggested Carrie Fisher. She asked me, "Do you think Carrie would do it?"

"I can ask her," I said.

Carrie obliged and played herself. In the episode, my character, Paige, had landed a job as a development executive at a studio, and I wrangled my best friend Ellen into letting me use her business as the set for my film.

Only, in reality, Paige hadn't been able to get the bookstore she'd wanted as her location, and so she'd manipulated Ellen into helping her out. The whole joke was about what it felt like for Carrie to *not* be Meg Ryan. Carrie, ironically, repaired Ellen and Paige's relationship in a scene she'd rewritten herself, elevating the material. She was so rooted in herself, and in this episode she got to poke fun at all that, talking about how she was the sardonic best friend, and Meg Ryan always got the guy and she didn't—which was all true, of course. Fucking hilarious. And genuinely authentic. Especially at the end of the episode, where Carrie rewrote some lines featuring ideas borrowed from the eighties Ron Perlman movie *Quest for Fire* into material that is quintessentially her.

"Years ago, there were tribes that roamed the earth, and every tribe had a magic person. Well, now the tribes have been dispersed, but every so often, you meet someone from your tribe, and the trick is, when you do, is to know that person all your life."

Of course, there are few titles that describe Carrie better than "magic person," and so getting to act in those scenes with her is one of the career moments I most cherish. This would continue to be the way Carrie and I described our family, and we both referred to each other, within the family and to others, as magic people of our tribe.

The show was working so well. It vibrated. The scripts were great. There was just something that wasn't quite clicking. For all the chemistry, and the great writing, we had reached a point that Ellen needed to live in her truth as a human being, and her character would obviously need to follow suit.

The Puppy Episode

I was watching *Transparent* recently, and I got to thinking about how progressive it is—only "progressive" isn't even the right word. It's real, and authentic, and blatant, and daring. It is *really* daring. Times have changed. Of course, not everybody loves it . . . not everybody's even seen it. But it did get the attention of the industry, and it's rightfully collected a lot of statuettes. It has this feeling of being at the forefront of something important, something that can't be denied any longer. It made me think back to twenty years ago, when Ellen came out, and what a big deal that was on television. Before then, we had seen gay characters on TV, sure, but never the female lead. We paved the way for *Will & Grace, The Fosters,* and *Modern Family.* And we had never seen the process, and the evolution, of actually coming out in front of your friends and family, and all the emotional ups and downs of that sometimes-frightening process.

It was a process, and an evolution, just to get the green light for Ellen to come out on the show. ABC was now owned by Disney, which was then led by Michael Eisner and Mike Ovitz, whom I affectionately called Me and Mo. Season after season, Ellen, and whoever the writers and producers were that season, would agonize over how to make the show sing. Everyone knew that Ellen was gay, and the dating episodes featuring guys clearly didn't work—well, they worked in that Ellen is fantastically funny, and she could pull it off. But everyone could tell there was something missing—the dialogue was great, she was funny, the guys were cute, but there wasn't any chemistry. I think it was just that thing of her, like anybody, wanting to live in her truth, and to be who she really was, and to love who she really loved. Those of us who worked on the show always knew Ellen's girlfriends, but the world at large didn't. It's not like we were told not to say anything, but there was an unwritten blanket respect that everybody had for her and her privacy.

Finally in 1996 there was a meeting . . . Ellen wants to come out.

"Why doesn't she just get a puppy?"

After the meeting, Ellen was very emotional, distraught.

Yeah, sure, a puppy would fix everything.

So then it became a joke. Every week, when we worked on

the script, we'd point out: "Here's where we'll get the puppy." We did our best to scratch the surface of social issues, but this was a different time. It was still the multi-camera sitcom era, and we could only take it so far. People loved the show. Clearly, there may have been people in the audience who felt that *thing* that was missing. Maybe without even fully knowing it. We could feel it on the set. Ellen could feel it. Disney, and ABC, and Ellen, continued to replace writers, trying to make the show work better. Whole entire teams were replaced every year. Not because she couldn't get along with people, but because she wanted more. She wanted her show to be provocative. She wanted it to be real. Without coming out, I believe, she felt unable to do that.

And then, in the middle of filming that season, Ellen came back from yet another Me and Mo meeting, this time completely transformed—there was this light in her face, and this change in her body language and her gait, representing this gift she'd been given.

Finally, she was going to be able to come out on the show.

Of course, the coming-out episode *had* to be called "The Puppy Episode." It was a special hour-long episode that aired on April 30, 1997, and was watched by forty-one million people. The night ABC aired the coming-out show, I was in New York City, sitting in a giant gay bar with my husband and my castmate Clea. They were playing the episode on a big screen, and everyone in the room was obviously nerved up and excited . . . it was loud. We couldn't always hear all the jokes over lesbians screaming in anticipation. Clea and I knew what the jokes were, of course, and that for this one night, perhaps it wasn't about punch lines anyhow.

Once it happened, it felt amazing. There was this mood of *Let's see how far we can go with this. Let's see how challenging of stereotypes we can be.* Now we were really the cool kids, and everybody wanted to be a part of it—the Indigo Girls, Emma Thompson, Sean Penn. Most of all, it was clear how exceptional the experience was for Ellen. It was stunning to watch the bird let out of the cage—I think she even used that analogy herself; she said it was like being caged up, and then having the doors open wide, and being able to fly and go as you please after that.

I still don't know what changed for the powers that be. But the result was white-hot. And it was incredible to be a part of the magic. Not only because LGBT equality was something I believed in deeply, and because now it would be properly represented on TV, but because I was given what I thought was the most interesting role in the whole drama. My character, Paige, had trouble adjusting to the truth of Ellen's sexuality, and it was complicated and rich and real to play that. When we read the script for the first time at the table read, the character of Ellen's gay friend (played by Patrick Bristow) said: "I'm so proud of you!" And Clea's character's response was: "Well, I for one think it's super." While Jeremy Piven's character, obviously, said: "Ellen, I love and respect whatever you do . . . and if you want to bring a woman home, I'm cool with that. Very cool."

The reactions were mostly accepting . . . and very PC. Paige's reaction was different, more complicated, more real, and I actually felt like it represented a lot of people in the world—you're my friend, and I love you, but if this is something you didn't feel like you could tell me, I don't know if we're really friends. Of course, Paige would make it about herself. Not to give it too much weight, but I think a lot of friends in the same situation actually do feel that way. Even if they're not totally truthful about it. I represented a large part of the audience. I earned my Golden Globe nomination for the episode where Paige did finally come around . . . and got a hell of a kiss.

When I do talk-show interviews about *Ellen,* I always joke on the air that it was really great of Ellen to be the star of *my* show. Or I say, with feeling, that Ellen had this tumultuous journey, and I got to be her sidekick, her foil. Between the two of those, something in there is true.

As I've heard again and again over the years, a lot of women love them some Paige. They've since found the show in syndication. Or by being a fan of Ellen's talk show—perhaps they didn't even know she did a sitcom, because they're too young. When I was in New York earlier this year, I got to meet up with a fan I'd met through Instagram—a young man who was a superfan of Paige, because the show kept him going during his darkest period. Growing up in Kosovo, as a young gay boy who was severely beaten and attacked, and kicked out of his house, for being gay, he would watch VHS tapes of *Ellen* to laugh and feel sane. It meant the world to both of us to acknowledge that our little-show-that-could had an effect like that.

Of course, not everyone was ready. We did have death threats, and that meant a regular bomb sweep before every show. It was a frightening time for all of us, and sobering that some people could be so filled with hate that we had to live like that, even just as a precaution.

But those of us who were so proud to be working on the show were still riding the high. Not long after Ellen came out, I was invited back to my alma mater, Emerson College, to receive an honorary degree. When I got off the plane, I realized I hadn't been in Boston since I went to school there. It felt crazy. So much had changed—in the city's landscape, and in the landscape of my own life and career.

I was staying at a hotel in Copley Square, right in the heart

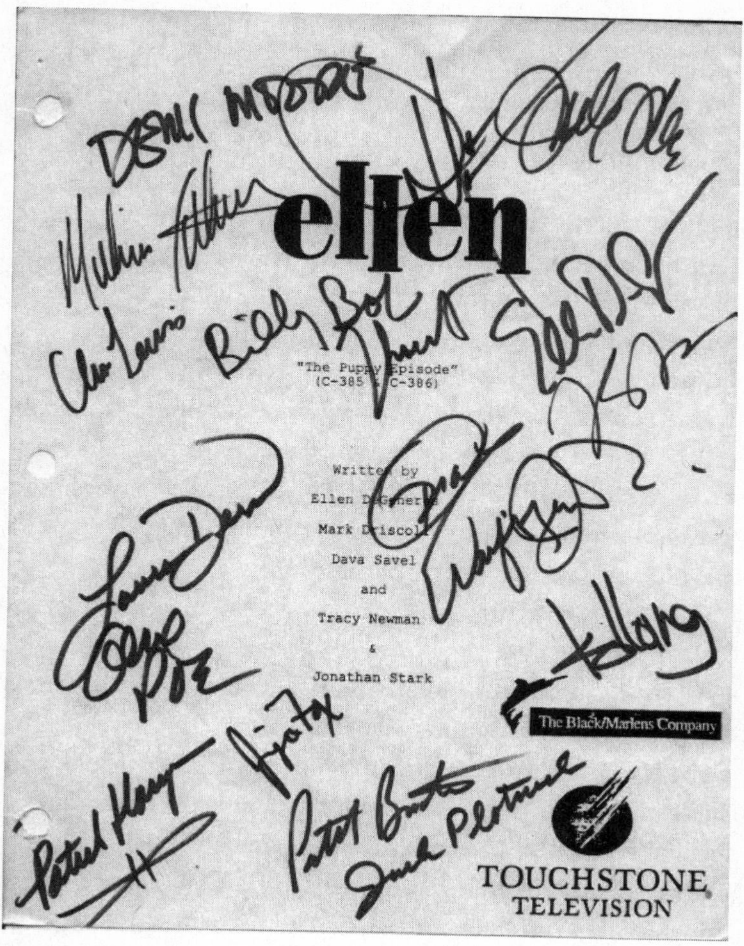
ellen

"The Puppy Episode"
(C-385 & C-386)

Written by
Ellen DeGeneres
Mark Driscoll
Dava Savel
and
Tracy Newman
&
Jonathan Stark

The Black/Marlens Company

TOUCHSTONE
TELEVISION

of the city. I landed at night and went right to bed, and when I got up in the morning, I went out to explore my old stomping grounds. I stepped right into the heart of a gay pride march—drag queens, and rainbows, and lesbians . . . oh my. As soon as I walked out, remarkably, people in the crowd recognized me, and they were so excited that I was there with them. So I walked along as part of the parade for a time, and I just sobbed, because I was so moved by this recognition from people who were on the front lines of the fight for LGBT equality in their daily lives. It wasn't my first march, and it sure wouldn't be my last.

The experience was very full circle, and very cathartic, and the perfect segue for me to go receive the Alumni of Distinction Award that night. Leo Nickole, who was the head of the musical theater department during my time at the school, was still there. It was wonderful to feel like I'd done him proud. Hometown girl makes good. When I walked out and was handed my award, I held it as I started to talk. And just like that, bam, the microphone fell. But since I have ninja-level skills in the art of the quick recovery, and my Fisher feline reflexes, I did what came naturally to me. I started tap-dancing. (And got the laugh.)

EVERYTHING WAS RISING, and then the wave wasn't cresting anymore; we were on the downside of it. Ellen's character got a girlfriend. It became more difficult to integrate a happy and successful Ellen—in a relationship—and the cast of characters around her, and it became less funny. It also suffered from a scathing backlash. We were protested by conservative right-wing people. You know the ones. The network felt obligated to slap an unwarranted warning on the front of the show, deeming it sexually explicit, which it wasn't. The ratings began to decline.

For me personally, for my character, there was just not enough for Paige to do . . . no Paige on the page. It was frustrating, as an actor and somebody who had been there since the beginning, and been an integral part of the show's landscape, to go from being in every episode to opening up a script at a table read and seeing that I only had two lines in that entire episode. Or none at all. I felt underutilized, during what was a tumultuous time overall. And then, in the middle of season 5, in the summer of 1998, we were canceled.

When the show ended, I was cautiously optimistic. I'd had a high-profile part on one of the hottest shows, and I'd been nominated for a Golden Globe, so you would assume there'd be something waiting for me. Spinoff? There was a sort of "development deal." I would do a pilot called *In the Loop* and if it didn't get picked up, they'd either find another part for me or I'd get bought out of my deal. So either way, I would get paid. I couldn't wait to get back to work. I really wanted to be back on a good show.

In the Loop was *Friends*-ish, but a little bit older and set in Chicago. It was a very cute part and totally different for me. I played a ditzy blonde, the type of role my mom built a career on. Fun. I was acting alongside Lisa Edelstein (currently the star of *Girlfriends' Guide to Divorce*) as well as Tom Verica, who most recently has been on *How to Get Away with Murder* and is currently an executive producer and head director on *Scandal*, and Jeff Garlin of *Curb Your Enthusiasm* and *The Goldbergs*. Basically, everybody went on to have careers, even though the show was never seen.

I got the best "consolation prize" ever when I was cast in *Inspector Gadget* later that year. As with any big-budget Disney movie, they auditioned every actress in town. It was my first big screen test. I found myself back on the stage where I'd shot *Ellen*. Kismet. I was being tested along with a couple other actresses that day. The cinematographer who would shoot the film, Adam Greenberg, lit the set. I did several scenes with Matthew Broderick and left feeling good about what I had done. It was one of those moments I talk about, where I felt like my life would change and it did. Mere hours later, I got a call from Jordan Kerner, the producer, saying: "You're our girl." *I was their girl.* For more than a year of my life, I would work with an actor I had been a longtime fan of, and I really upped my game in terms of learning another dialect of the language of acting.

I DON'T THINK it's any coincidence that I found myself surrounded by people who were open in their sexuality, not just on *Ellen,* but in all areas of my life. I'd like to think that, for as long as I can remember, I've been sexually fluid. That's not just a fancy way to say I like girls, too. It's the person, or the soul, that I'm attracted to—not necessarily the gender.

There were childhood friends, even the children of close family friends, who helped lead the investigation, and this created an atmosphere of comfort and confidence in the constant exploration of my sexuality. All the C words! Where there were make-outs with Dannys, there were also make-outs with Danielles. And as early as age nineteen, in addition to my boyfriends, I've had what in classic Hollywood parlance are called gal pals. (Hey you, with the confused look on your face—that means I've had female lovers.) And this goes beyond getting caught "shopping" or "dirty dancing" in a club on Santa Monica Boulevard. In fact, timing is everything in life. There was, and still is, a woman with whom—had I not found my husband, married him, and started a family—I might have pursued a permanent relationship. Our connection was deep, and smart, and sexy, and went beyond friendship. In the same way that the men in my life have done, she shaped who I am as a lover, as a woman, as a mother. This is something that Chris knows has always been a part of me, and he doesn't feel threatened by it. In fact, he jokes, if I ever left him, it would be for a woman. Perhaps this woman. Truth be told, my respect and love for her meant that I had to set her free, as much as it hurt my own heart, so she could have her own happily every after. Everyone involved knows I'm not going anywhere. And so she and I always know that we can take it just so far—which makes it exciting, taboo, forbidden, but safe, because we all know how deep my commitment to my family is.

And so, there is an organic, authentic reason I actively crusade for the LGBTQ community (we've recently added a "Q," maybe for me). It sounds almost silly or condescending when I hear myself saying it, because I desperately yearn for a time when we are collectively inclusive and straight up just human beings—oops, I said "straight up." My daughters are on the precipice of exploring their sexuality, as I did, and should they find themselves defined by any one of these letters, I am a mother who will without hesitation support their happiness. My gravitational pull toward everything interplanetary and intersexual began early in life. Perhaps it was that curiosity . . . which would suggest the "cat" was sacrificed. I'm not altogether sure "pussy" was harmed in the process. It was true attraction, the "B" part of LGBT is an authentic part of who I am. (And I am a bitch.)

In April 2000, we went to Washington, D.C., for the Millennium March for Equality to promote LGBT rights, human rights. Just post my Broadway run in *Cabaret* I met up with Ellen and her then-girlfriend, Anne Heche, in New York City. They invited me to climb onto Ellen's tour bus, as she was doing stand-up across the country. And it seemed apropos to join them for the march. I knew I wanted to be part of it—I felt like it was going to change the world. There we were, marching at the head of a million people, carrying this enormous banner, alongside Matthew Shepard's family, Melissa Etheridge, and Ellen and Anne. It was just wild—an overwhelmingly powerful feeling. We were all so proud, holding the banner. Even though I'd never gone public with any of my female lovers, there were all those box lunches I've enjoyed at the Hollywood Bowl. And there was no question of what I had gained from these women over the years, and what identifying as part of this community and movement meant to me.

My mother always had a dance company backing her, and all those boys were gay. She often laments, "Thirty-seven of my dancers died of AIDS. My whole dance company is gone. They all died."

Of course, she's the great exaggerator. And that's not literally true. But clearly we did lose a generation of men who had shared the stage with Connie, with Debbie, with that whole class of performers. The boys were vibrant and beautiful, and then gone.

My uncle, my mom's youngest brother, the character actor John Megna, died of AIDS in 1995. He was a really fascinating guy—smart and quirky—and she was very close to him. He debuted on Broadway at age six in Frank Loesser's musical *Greenwillow.* Most notably he played Dill, the character loosely based on Truman Capote, in *To Kill a Mockingbird,* opposite Gregory Peck. We were all very close to him. No matter how close we all were in this family, he never felt comfortable enough to come out as homosexual. If only he had been alive to see the impact of that moment on *Ellen,* perhaps it would have been different. The loss ripped through my mother, and also through me. I wanted his approval. I had acted in a few scenes with him in small plays, and I wanted him to know I was going to be this great actress and a big star. When he passed, my role on *Ellen* was in full swing. I feel confident that he left having seen me.

His death is a family story, but also, on a broader scale, propelled me into being very active in the fight against HIV/AIDS. I've raised money and awareness as a spokesperson and a producer and host of events, and I've made an appearance at every benefit I could, singing my lungs out, because I had a personal connection and commitment to the cause. There are so many causes we are asked to lend our name to. Today with HIV/AIDS, there seems to be a complacency—because it is possible to survive and live with the disease—but the fight isn't over.

Reunion

I had been on Ellen's talk show several times over the years, but we really hadn't seen each other in a while, going into the twentieth-anniversary special. The morning we taped the show, I dressed carefully in my fuchsia dress. I had my friend Laurent D. there to style my hair. He's been cutting my hair since I was fifteen. I used to go to the Jose Eber salon in my Catholic school uniform and sit up on phone books. He was with me the night I got married and we celebrate every milestone together. He's a very dear friend. So of course he was there, as my stylist and my confidant.

I was a little nervous when I got to the set. But nervous for me is different than nervous for other people. It can energize me—make me cocky, even. Of course, it couldn't live up to my expectations. I was so proud to be there, to have been there twenty years earlier. It was natural for me to slip back into the role of sidekick. I've come so far in my life, but in her presence, I naturally assume the position.

So on April 30, the morning "The Puppy Episode" anniversary aired, I was driving my daughters to school when my youngest, Luna, spoke up.

"Are you on that *Ellen* show today?" she asked.

"Luna, it's the anniversary of the show that Mommy and Ellen did together," my middle daughter, True, said.

"Oh," said Luna.

Oh, I thought. *Yeah, that's right.*

"Do you know why it was such a big deal?" I asked them. "There was a time when people on television didn't talk about being gay. It was just not accepted."

They gave me blank looks.

"What's the big deal?" they asked.

With a proud grin, I replied, "Exactly."

It's a very difficult thing for me to explain to my kids, because they are so unconditionally loving of everyone. They really are.

And for me, this speaks to so much—the human beings that they are, what I've done as a mother, and the real legacy of what we did on *Ellen*.

Chapter 10

The Courtship of Eddie's Daughter

THE PORTRAIT OF FAMILY LOOKS different for everyone, means something different, and it has evolved over time. Maybe creating a family is a way to try to have what you think "family" should be. Connie did that. And I believe Debbie did as well. Eddie loved the chase and the getting married part, but never understood or embraced what came next, family, in the standard sense of the word. Later in life, he loved the idea that all these people were his children, as if he had something more than biology to do with it, but he regrettably missed out on their development and the real cohesiveness of family life, putting career and addiction first. Definitely not anyone's idea of a traditional father. Insert *Eddie Knows Best* joke.

Universally, there are people who think settling down, or perhaps "settling," is going to make things different. If I have a family with this person, I will become a parent. For a moment, Connie really thought about Eddie that way. I'm going to be the one that's going to make him different. She had a fantasy about him, given all the loss and volatility in her own childhood. Debbie admitted to doing this several times, in her relationship with Eddie and with others. Carrie as well.

So for me, family means stability—or my portrait of a family. I still love what the road and working does for me—it makes me alive—but now, it's a balance, and I wouldn't have that without what I have at home. And it also makes me better equipped as an actress and director and makes it more profound. There's definitely something that has made me stay in it longer than anyone else in my family—twenty years and counting. As Connie says, "I'll never see twenty years with anyone." Maybe it's because, as I often say, I chose someone who could not be further from Eddie. My husband Chris can't sing and he's a true partner in the parenting process. But before Mr. Right, there were a few Mr. Right Nows.

Seven Minutes in Heaven

Fifth grade was a big year. There were many firsts. It was our first year in Malibu. We lived at 22002 Pacific Coast Highway. Right next door to the comedian Flip Wilson. We became instant besties with his daughters, Tamara and Stacey Wilson. Tricia and I started the Dynamite Club with them, later initiating Nikka Costa, daughter of composer and arranger Don Costa. I was the president *and* the social director (prepubescent control freak). Nikka was the mascot. It was very exclusive.

Tricia and I were enrolled at Our Lady of Malibu. As usual, our house was the hang. A big group of kids came over after school. You could always see surfboards and skateboards, leaning up against the exterior of our tropical, tiki-like abode. We were intent on organizing games of Spin the Bottle and Truth or Dare. My only mission was to wind up in a closet (Seven Minutes in Heaven) with Danny Webb. Luck was on my side, and the bottle landed on me and my crush, Danny.

We nervously rendezvoused in the closet while trying to appear totally nonchalant (for fifth graders). Here's the thing—seven minutes is a *long* time when you're that age. Well, any age. Actually, seven minutes sounds about right these days. We mostly just giggled, but we did share a first kiss.

ele

Sibling Rivalry on the Shores of Kaanapali

Given that Tricia and I were only fourteen months apart in age, it's kind of miraculous that we never really fought over boys. Maybe we had different taste. Maybe it was wired deeply into our DNA that we were going to be there for each other throughout our lives, and were therefore much more important than any stupid guy. The only time we ever came close to going head-to-head over someone was a boy named David. Back then, the holidays would often take us to the shores of Kaanapali, Maui, Hawaii. Our accommodations varied over the years, but the hub was always the Hyatt Regency.

We were too young to invite boys we liked back to our rooms (until we weren't), so after dinner, while the adults hung out in the hotel bar and finally went to bed, we'd flirt and circle around each other in the tropic fervor of the hotel lobby, with its lush jungle of plants and subdued piped-in island Muzak. Romances were constantly blooming and breaking off, sometimes within a single night, and often without anyone—even the couple directly involved—really understanding what had kept the relationship from spanning further than the six hours between dining and bed.

So, one particular evening, David took a shine to Tricia. He romanced her by walking her along the beach by moonlight while holding her hand, and even kissing her as the waves lapped the shores beside them. Very teen beach movie. When she got back to our hotel room later that night, she was dreamy and stirred up the way teenage girls get when they're on the cusp of a new romance. There was a sense of anticipation going into the next night's gathering of teens—would the previous evening's beach stroll be repeated? Would yet another base be reached? Would a relationship blossom? Not exactly. When we met up with David that night, he hardly seemed to register Tricia's presence and suddenly had eyes only for me. Being the seventeen-year-old girl that I was, rather than defending my sister's delicate heart, I took the bait and allowed myself to be wooed with a similar oceanside walk and kiss. By the time of breakfast the next morning, when Connie registered the nuclear-level strife brewing between her daughters, our rivalry for David's affection had become as intense as "Summer Lovin'," or in this case holiday lovin', can get. Connie immediately set us straight, never having had the same rivalry with her own sister, but wanting to prepare us for the future of our relationship and knowing that the testosterone-laden vacation version of this kid would never amount to anything back on the mainland. "Boys and men will come and go, but your sister is your sister for life, and if I teach you anything it would be to never let anyone jeopardize that. They're not worth it. No one's worth what you girls have."

Having kicked him to the shore, our sisterly bond reaffirmed, and possessing the newly honed insight that maybe a guy who romanced two sisters on back-to-back nights wasn't exactly the prince charming we'd fashioned him to be, as hard as it was, we moved on. In retrospect, the whole affair seems more school yard than steamy, but both Tricia and I took the lesson to heart and we never again let a man come between us, and would be each other's maid of honor.

ele

The Serial Monogamist

Maybe I was born craving the promise that someone was going to stick around, or at least, the fear that they wouldn't was embedded in my psyche at a young age. I mean, I got married for the first time when I was six years old, to David Styne, during one of those family trips to Hawaii. And for all of my sexual fluidity and acting out, I always seemed to be in a relationship from the time I was in high school, until, well . . . today.

I was a serial monogamist. I think that urge for romantic stability was an obvious, direct result of not having ever seen a relationship that worked . . . ever. I loved so deeply, and so hard, and the moment I fell in love, I was hooked. I was determined to prove that this love I'd found was going to be something bigger—and longer lasting—than what my mother and father had experienced. Ah, the follies of youth!

ele

I'll Buy a Bird for You, if You'll Just Care for Me

When I landed in my triple dorm room at Emerson, I started meeting the good people of the seventh floor of the Charlesgate dormitory, a former brothel, now an upscale condo building. Directly across the hall was a fella named Dean. A transfer student who was four years older than me, cute, and Jewish. The first week of school, we experienced Hurricane Gloria. We were alerted to stay indoors and tape our windows with *X*'s, and of course this provided the atmosphere for shenanigans to ensue. We played Seven Minutes in a Dorm Room, and from that moment on, we were inseparable. We really fell for each other, but I always felt like I was chasing him, and as I would discover, there was a reason why.

When it came time for breaks, he went back to his home state of Florida. Here's the advantage to having a showbiz mom who spent much of her career on the road, performing. It made it pretty easy to finagle reasons to just "happen" to be in Florida when I was missing Dean and wanted to see him.

There were a remarkable number of legitimate reasons for Connie to go to Florida, and then I just had to join the traveling show, which was how we'd always rolled. In 1987, she starred with all of her old cohorts in *Back to the Beach*—a spoof of sixties beach party films—with Frankie Avalon and Annette Funicello. Around the release of the film, they did a tour of Florida (I guess its fan base was localized in its many retirement villas) that included Connie, Frankie, Herman's Hermits, Jan and Dean, and one Beach Boy. We must have played every dog track and racetrack from Fort Lauderdale to Tampa, and we did a big show on the beach in Miami.

While we were in Miami, we were staying at the Fontainebleau. Dean's family lived in Palm Beach, which was an hour away. The whole family came out to see our show. I was close to his family, including his two brothers and his sister Tara, whom I'm still friends with today. Think about that, it's thirty years ago. That's another thing about being on a set and changing schools fourteen times, and being in people's lives . . . I have that need and that ability to have those relationships. His mother, Jackie, who still leaves me voice mails as "Mom from Florida," was so great and a total character. Her line was, "We've got to go get your nails done. How are you ever going to get a nice ring if you don't have nice nails?"

While I was in Florida, I had an open invitation to stay with them on their yacht, which was an amazing four-bedroom boat on which they cruised up and down the Intracoastal Waterway around Fort Lauderdale and Miami and to the Bahamas.

When I arrived at the boat, they weren't there, but it was normal for me to come and go as I pleased. I took a shower and got settled. And then the phone rang. I thought it might be Dean, or Mom, so I answered it. Well, it was my nemesis, Stephanie, his "ex-girlfriend"—I had always felt like I was competing with her memory. I'd occasionally spoken to her very briefly because she'd called the dorms during the school year. *Why was she calling the dorms?* you might ask.

She was just checking in on him because they were still friends, right? I thought.

Anyhow, when we found ourselves on the phone this time, I didn't need to introduce myself.

"Hey, Stephanie, it's Joely," I said.

"What are you doing there?" she asked.

"I'm here because I'm working with my mom. I'm singing backgrounds."

"Yeah, maybe I did hear that you were there."

"It's actually great to finally really talk to you," I said, feeling like I could be more candid because there was no one around to hear me. There was a little small talk, and then I said, "I don't mind that you two are still friends. The only thing that would really bother me is if you guys were still sleeping together."

There was a long silence on the other end of the phone. I heard everything I needed to know in that silence.

"Can you come over here right now?" I asked.

She picked me up and drove me back to the Fontainebleau Hotel. We ordered room service, hung out, and dished the dirt with nervous giddiness. Obviously, Dean had thought we'd never meet, and so we'd never find out the true depths of his duplicity. But now his cover was blown, and we were not going to let this go quietly. We decided to call Dean—together. I got to bust him in such a big way, but it really wasn't much of a consolation. As I soon learned, his family had known about Stephanie and me. And they had kept telling him, "You can't do this to these two girls." But he did.

I got my heart really broken for the first time. I was betrayed. I don't think my mom offered much in the way of advice. I feel bad even saying this about her, but her response was to want to fill that pain and emptiness by buying me something. Not that I didn't already know about that side of her personality. I had already seen her do that for herself, but I was struck by her offer to do it for me.

Then Dean picked me, saying I was the only one he loved. When he graduated, I left Emerson at the end of my junior year, and he ended up moving to L.A. with me. After he chose me, I felt secure in the relationship. For a minute. We really tried to make a go of it. I *especially* tried to make a go of it. That was my first real, deep love for somebody—somebody who wasn't capable of making a choice about who he loved. That really hurt my self-esteem. Not only that I had to fight for him, but also that he'd lied to me. It made me spin out. Hasn't everybody done some version of this to get the one you want? *I'm not enough. I'll try to have nice nails, I'll try to have a different color hair. Or maybe I need to be thinner. Or I'll be into the music that he's into.*

I bought a bird. I had a pet bird because of him—an African gray parrot named Dylan, which is not a goldfish in a bowl. It's like having a child. *Dean loves birds,* I thought. Okay, sure!

But a degree in broadcast journalism and hopes of a career in TV news took him to Missoula, Montana, and Chico, California, and finally, back home to Palm Beach as the weatherman, and it became clear that the long distance wasn't going to work. He married a nice Jewish girl. We were young . . .

Learning to Hit the High Notes

There was the A-list director whom I never got to work with but who chased me for years; the record-holding football player who gave me his gate code, which I used a few times; a casting director; the Olympic swimmer; a stunning Italian composer. And the saxophone player—you know what they say about men who play sax. These delicious diversions between serious relationships aside, I was generally a one-man woman. I wouldn't say I *leapt* right into my next relationship, but it didn't take me long to be fully head over heels and committed once again.

His name was Humberto. He was as dashing as his moniker might suggest, a real Latin lover, and he was thirty-eight years old to my twenty-two. Although he was considerably older, I wouldn't say he was a father figure to me. To really break it down, he was almost more of a mother figure. (But much, much sexier than that might suggest.) He booked fabulous trips for us, bought me expensive gifts, and just *knew* that I was really blond (well, gentlemen *do* prefer blondes, so I added highlights). I basked in his attention and the thrill of being pulled into his dynamic orbit. He was a successful music producer and engineer, and we definitely came together, in part, around our shared passion for music. I spent hours—and days—at various recording studios around the world with him.

"Come over, my mish," he summoned me, using the nickname he'd given me because I was his "Main Mission." "I'm at Record Plant."

"I'm at Ground Control."

"I'm at Ocean Way."

If I didn't have an audition or job that day, I'd hop in my car and head over, and often I'd be there until three in the morning. The whole experience was magic. Music had literally been a part of my life since birth, and I loved it—from the inside—with a fierce ardor that allowed me to be mesmerized by every minute detail of its production. (Plus, I adored the feeling of being tucked away in the studio with Humberto while he was working, so there was that, too.) And he worked with some incredibly talented musicians, so that made it fun and inspiring for me as a young singer and artist.

I got to witness recording sessions by a supergroup formed by members of the Go-Go's and the Bangles. I played pool all night with Scott Weiland (RIP). I had the supreme thrill of sitting in the sound booth and witnessing the divine Streisand lay down tracks for her first Broadway album. She even came over and sat on my lap, which was as cool as it sounds. Oh my God, I had a meltdown (the good kind). Humberto made a special cassette copy of the "TV mixes" for me (the music with all her vocals stripped out), so I could sing along. I cherish it and still have it to this day. I got to sing live in the room at the iconic studio at Capitol Records . . . with a hundred musicians playing behind me. Humberto was the copilot to Dr. Eugene Landy, who produced his patient Brian Wilson's album. As Humberto laid down the vocals, doubling them in order to create the harmony part, we heard a mystery vocal line join the eight tracks that were already recorded.

"Where is that part coming from?" Humberto asked me.

I shook my head in wonder. We both turned around, just in time to see Brian nonchalantly spinning in his chair, adding yet another layer of perfect vocal harmony. Musical genius.

The atmosphere of rarefied talents and creative expression was similar to the atmosphere in which I'd grown up, and I felt right at home. It was what people would imagine, the Hollywood aspect of it—how I'd sat in on sets with my mom, as Carrie had sat in on sets with Debbie. This was my rock-and-roll version of that. And it was even better, now that I'd found a way to create my own version of the world I adored—with the man I loved. He was always flying me off to exotic locales with him—the Montreux Jazz Festival in Switzerland, where I got to enjoy all the fabulous perks of being involved with a man like this. He often worked with Celine Dion. I was his date for her lavish Montreal wedding to the late René Angélil. She was like Canadian royalty—their Princess Diana—and that wedding was over the top, with all these parties, each more lavish and beautiful than the last. That was a beautiful experience. Even better was being in the studio with her on many occasions. And when Humberto called me at eleven o'clock at night, at my little house I'd bought for myself in the Hollywood Hills when I landed my part on *Ellen*.

"I'm down here at Ocean Way," he said. "Celine left, and I need a couple of lines sung. Just double her, quickly. Can you come . . . right now?"

Of course I went, for all the reasons you would imagine. And it was a thrill.

During one recording session, she was singing a remake of Eric Carmen's "All By Myself." I was glued to my seat, just in absolute awe of the talent of this woman (and we Fishers can sing!). I soaked up every crumb of wisdom she so generously tossed my way.

"I'll tell you how you get to the high notes," she said in her thick French Canadian accent. "You imagine a string. And it goes from all the way in the sky, and all the way down into the ground. So you plant your feet, firmly, on the ground. And you imagine the line . . . from here to here . . . through here . . . all the way up."

As she gave me this advice, she presented the string from bottom to top, from her bits, along the axis of her body and up above her head, raising her arm in the air with a dramatic flourish, and absolutely nailing the high note. I got chills. On occasion, when reaching for a high note, I think: *What would Celine do?*

It was not unusual to find us in the private jets and lavish homes of music icons Neil Diamond and Julio Iglesias. The Iglesias family Thanksgiving dinner was a real showstopper—Enrique, Julio Jr., and the entire family gathered around a beautiful table, with treasures from the most incredible wine cellar I've ever seen. There were eight glasses in front us, and if we didn't like anything we were poured, Julio would instruct us to spill it onto the grass. I jokingly asked for a straw. None of them tasted bad to me.

Of course, both Eddie and Connie loved that I was dating a successful music industry pro. No doubt Eddie wanted Humberto to produce an album for him. While many of the people in my life were concerned about the age difference between Humberto and me, it didn't even pop into my dad's head, ever. (Obviously a sixteen-year age difference was nothing for Eddie.)

I loved that Eddie loved Humberto. I think because Eddie hadn't been around much until just a few years before I'd started dating him, part of me liked that having Hum as a partner might impress Eddie. Or at least make an impression on him. I cared about having closeness—and commonality—with my dad, and so I liked aspects of myself that got his attention—my voice, my talent, my success. I knew I didn't need my father's approval—and a part of me even rebelled against wanting it—but I definitely felt pleased when I earned it. With many areas of my life—relationships, roles—there was a part of me that wondered: *Let's see what Eddie's going to think about this.* The fact that he thought so highly of Humberto made me happy.

Humberto never worked with Eddie, but when Connie set out to release a family Christmas album in the early nineties, he did step up to coproduce and engineer. (Although who could really produce anything with Connie at the helm?) Tricia and I soon realized that Connie had given us such autonomy growing up—our opinions really had mattered to her, in terms of *Where should we go for trips? Should we buy this house? Let's talk about it.* But when it came to this artistic collaboration, she was the mother, and she'd worked hard her whole life. She didn't want to hear anyone else's thoughts. She respected us just enough to allow us to be a part of her Christmas album. Called *Tradition: A Family at Christmas,* it was fraught with anxiety and competition, like so many holiday family traditions. Despite the tensions, from "Rockin' Around the Christmas Tree" to the a cappella harmonies of "Auld Lang Syne," we put artistic differences aside to create a holiday classic.

When Humberto and I were together and living the high life, it made me feel like I was engaged in my best life. But it wasn't always like this.

The truth was: Humberto was married. I was his mistress.

I didn't believe that reality to be true about myself. Because he always insisted that his marriage was over. Because he always insisted his divorce just needed to be finalized. Because he always insisted he loved me. Because I knew I loved him. Because I was young and hungry, and on my way to a successful career, and yet I lacked the ability at that age to see myself as deserving of more than just being the other woman.

But the truth of my status in his life obviously had a major impact on our relationship, even if I didn't want to admit it at the time. This was why he always wanted me in the studio with him. And on the road with him. Because these were moments when he wasn't at home with his wife and kids. It's hard for me to own all of this now, but I believe we all must forgive our younger selves, and forgive the people who teach us our lessons, and make our reparations by doing better next time.

I could trick myself that I was okay with how things were, until I couldn't. We were in Amsterdam, where he was working with major producers, in Mutt Lange's studio, on the new Air Supply album. Humberto had a break from the studio, and we were tucked up together in our gorgeous, luxurious hotel room.

When he stepped out onto the balcony.

To call his wife.

It hurt like a punch to the gut.

What am I doing? What am I doing? What am I doing? I asked myself the whole time he was gone.

For the first few years we were together, I thought I'd marry Humberto. By this point in our relationship, I knew he wasn't divorced yet and wasn't in any hurry to be. But the promise of a future with him was still too alluring to let go of, at first, even with my dawning knowledge of the full reality of our situation.

And then, as my career progressed, I began to feel more confident and more comfortable in my skin. After my first year of playing Paige on *Ellen,* I made my Broadway debut as Rizzo in *Grease.* No biggie—just the realization of a lifelong dream. The culmination of a desire I'd had since my fifth-grade stage debut back in Malibu. And a career highlight both Eddie and Connie had racked up. They both came to see me on opening night, as did Tricia, which felt like a huge triumph for me. (Technically, I made my Broadway debut when I was in utero, as Connie appeared in Neil Simon's *The Star-Spangled Girl* until she was seven months pregnant with me.) I was realistic about the fact that producers were putting TV stars in Broadway shows to sell tickets, and that's why they'd offered it to me. But I also knew I was deserving of the role.

During the months I was in New York, I was away from Humberto. He could be very critical, sometimes even almost malicious. So this time apart—of my doing, not his—had an important impact on me. It was the beginning of my autonomy. I didn't need a Svengali. I was beginning to have my own career and my own success, and suddenly I found I didn't care so much about what he thought of me. He came to visit me, saw the play. He didn't critique it, but he was snobby about it. I could see him from the stage, sitting in the second row. His unspoken response: *Meh, it's* Grease. *You're jumping around, playing a teenage girl.* He stayed for the weekend, but this time the dynamic was different, because he was staying in *my* apartment. And when he left, I felt the profound sadness of still loving someone I'd outgrown, and now realizing how much more I deserved.

There had been a time, in the beginning, when I'll admit that my role as the younger, sassier woman—not the wife, but the hot young girlfriend—made me feel powerful. But then I grew, and that wasn't enough for me anymore. And what he was giving me wasn't nearly enough. That hurt. When I think back to that time, I can feel myself back in my body at that age, and feel just how terribly lonely and sad it was to love someone who was unwilling—or unable—to really, truly be mine. And how it made me doubt myself . . . and my self-worth. For the first time, I could see my pattern, with Humberto, with Dean, with my first love in high school—I'd loved them, and they'd all had other women in their lives. I wasn't number one. Suddenly, that wasn't good enough for me anymore. And I couldn't stand the thought that I was coming between him and his wife and the family he had committed to.

I returned home to L.A. in September, in order to start shooting the second season of *Ellen,* which was a hit. I finally felt strong enough to begin to separate myself from Humberto. I had my sweet house in the Hollywood Hills, which was my sanctuary, and I had a full, busy life that was giving me plenty of thrills, without him.

A week or so before my birthday on October 29, I was talking to Humberto on the phone while I was taking a bath.

"Why am I not coming to your birthday dinner?" he asked.

"Because . . . it's on my birthday, and I don't want to spend my birthday making sure you're okay. Or making sure you're entertained. Or making sure you're anything. It's my day."

For the first time, I was the one who said the first good-bye when we were signing off at the end of our call. "I don't want you to call me," I said.

I ended my relationship with him.

Hung up the phone.

And sobbed.

In the bubbles.

And met Chris, my husband of twenty years, the next day.

ele

The One

There's this feeling you get when you meet someone. Some people call it chemistry, which seems accurate—your pheromones, theirs—eye contact, body language. You move differently, lean into them, thrust your overactive center forward—your best bits. Then you deprive them of it all by glancing, or even turning away completely—sneaking a glance back. *Did it work? Did I successfully lure him in?* If so, you gravitate toward each other, playfully, nonchalantly, until you are in each other's orbit.

Yes, my dear ones, that is the feeling of attraction . . . real attraction . . . the kind that can last for two decades . . . and more . . . and I was about to experience it. Big time.

Sitcoms work three weeks on, then take one week off for writing. It was a hiatus week. Ellen was working on a film, *Ellen's Energy Crisis,* for a ride at Epcot Center. It was an educational ride about energy—but not in a dry, boring way like in school. It was a big deal for her, because it was Disney, and *Ellen* was on ABC, which was owned by Disney, and so there was this expectation for her to hit it out of the amusement park.

At the same time, filming green-screen material is very time-consuming and tedious. She got bored between takes on the set and called me.

"Why don't you come visit?!" she asked.

Go sit on a set during my hiatus week? I thought. *Really?*

But she was my friend, and I knew I should just go over for a few hours and keep her company between takes. So I agreed and drove down to where she was filming— stage 1 at Raleigh Studios in Hollywood. When I walked onto the set, opposite the biggest green screen I'd ever seen, there was a crane. The arm was extended into the air, and a man was balanced atop the crane, looking into the camera, in profile . . . I could only see his profile . . . and his silver hair.

Silver fox.

Ellen was hanging to my left, in a helicopter, on the soundstage, in front of said green screen. It was a big huge wall of green. The scene featured her and Tim Conway. She was blow-drying her hair as the action of the scene.

"Cut!" the director yelled.

She looked at me, and we exchanged one of those loaded glances like two girlfriends will do. Me: *Who's the silver fox on the crane?*

She indicated with a wink, a grin, and raised eyebrows—all the silly matchmaker specials—that she got where I was going with this, and she was going to hook me up later.

They broke for a minute. She came down. We got right to what was important.

"Find out about him," I said.

Then, of course, the hair and makeup team got involved, as they always do.

There was a chorus of: "You should talk to him! You should talk to him!"

It was literally like high school.

I went over to talk to him.

True story: He had never seen the *Ellen* show. So he had no idea who I was. As I learned later, he just thought that I was Ellen's sexy redhead friend. (Clearly, he was perceptive.)

He was very shy. He kept his head down while we talked, and he kind of kicked the floor, as if he was a kid, kicking the dirt on the playground.

"What's up? What's your name?"

You know, all that awkward small talk. Meanwhile, everyone else was giggling off to the side, just radiating the excitement of: *Oh my God, it's such a cute match.*

"All right, well, I'll see you around," he said.

Then he walked away.

See you around? See you around?! That's not a good way to end this moment.

Ellen and I went to her trailer. And I proceeded to write him a note:

In case I don't see you around, here's my number.

With a flourish, I applied the smack of a lipstick imprint. I know, very brazen of me. Very hussy. But what if I didn't see him around? I had to make a move.

So, Ellen had that note burning a hole in her pocket all day. Before she could give it to him, I left and went home to change for an event I was going to that night. Then I just *happened* to return to the set, wearing thigh-high boots and a miniskirt. And a supertight sweater. And, you know, maybe I used the girls to get his attention. (He noticed and later used to tease me: "You could knock an eye out with those things.")

As he tells it, he almost fell off the crane.

He *still* didn't ask me out, so I was really counting on Ellen giving him my note. This is how he tells the story of when she finally worked her magic. They walked onto the set at the same time. She strolled over and put the note in his pocket. Everybody on the set saw it happen (especially hair and makeup) and knew intrigue was afoot.

"What was that?" people were asking. "What'd she give you?"

"I don't know," he said. "Leave me alone."

He ended up calling me, and I asked him out. Wait, wait, before you tell me to follow "the Rules," or whatever, I had a really good excuse. My agent at the time had invited me to go see R.E.M. two days before my birthday. Although I liked R.E.M., I'll admit that I wasn't exactly *desperate* to see R.E.M. But it was the perfect low-pressure excuse to get us together for a night to see if we clicked.

"Do you want to be my plus-one?" I asked him.

The only hitch was that the show was in Anaheim—a forty-five-minute drive, each way. The thing about a situation like that is it gives you lots of time to get to know each other, which is what you should be doing on a first date anyhow. He told me that he had been married, and he had two sons. My heart sank. This reminded me of the relationship I'd just left, and that sounded major warning bells for me. It was a very different situation, in that he'd been divorced for eight years. But I had this feeling at the time that, when I had a baby, I wanted my husband to say: "That's the most amazing thing I've ever seen." Not ". . . other than the first two times I saw it." I really stopped and wondered: *Do I want to be with someone who's already experienced so many of the big, exciting firsts I've got coming up?*

Panicky inner dialogue aside, it ended up being a great first date.

I'd already planned a big birthday party, and I didn't invite him because I felt like we were too new to introduce him to everyone yet. But we saw each other the day after that. I soon realized that his boys were an amazing gift in my life and that we were embarking on a very different relationship than his first marriage. There would be plenty of firsts for us, too, and we'd both share the same excitement and passion for the life we were building together.

I ended up meeting his children the weekend of December 6, which was his son Cameron's birthday. I made myself climb over a big, tall fence at a baseball field (in high-heeled boots, of course), to go hang out with the family (and to try to impress everyone—I never would have been such a daredevil on my own steam). I soon realized I didn't need to impress anyone—I was already part of the family.

My relationship with Chris was a revelation for me. I had been in these relationships where I had been not less adored, but less at the center of something that really matters—a partnership, a family. In Chris, I could sense a stability, a quiet strength. He didn't challenge me to prove I was worth loving, a pressure you feel when someone always keeps you at somewhat of a distance. He challenged me, by inspiring me, to be my best self, and he made me feel safe. After years of absent men in my life, he could not have been more present. I knew this was where the good stuff started for me—marriage, family, partnership. We've basically never been apart after that, for twenty years and counting.

ele

Here Comes the . . .

The word on lovers' lane was that Chris and I couldn't keep our hands off each other. We were crazy about each other. A few months in, we were already looking ahead to our future—together. My mother's dear friends Renée Taylor and Joe Bologna had a wedding every decade to renew their vows and celebrate their love (an inspiring fifty-two years). Chris went as my date to their thirtieth wedding party with my mom. The ceremony was held at the Nikko Hotel on La Cienega, and it was officiated by a Tibetan monk. The bridesmaids—Barbara Hershey, Diane Ladd, Michelle Lee, Lainie Kazan, and my mom—donned jewel-toned dresses, and it was a beautiful evening. During the reception, Chris and I were sitting at a table with Connie and Tricia.

Over the din of the celebration, Chris turned to my mom.

"I want to marry your daughter," he said.

My mom and Tricia both cried. We all cried.

We also drove to San Francisco so Chris could ask Eddie for his blessing, but we all knew Connie was the real head of the family. Everyone was absolutely thrilled for us. My mother threw me a beautiful, amazing, everything-I-ever-wanted wedding. We planned the big day for New Year's Eve 1996. We knew it was a big ask to have people give over their New Year's Eves to us, but spiritually, it felt like it was the beginning of something wonderful for everyone.

On the night of our rehearsal dinner, we all went to this tiny little restaurant in West L.A., Carmine's, which is owned by one of Chris's childhood friends. It has since become one of our favorite spots. The rehearsal dinner was like its own small wedding. Literally every cousin and family member was there. We all sang. My mother and father even sang together. My mom was feeding him the words. It was so funny and sweet. In that moment I truly did not feel any sourness about having grown up without Eddie. It didn't matter, because I knew he hadn't been capable of it, and now I had him in my life.

For our wedding the next night, the number of people Chris and I (and, honestly, Connie) wanted to include in the evening's delights wouldn't have fit into even the largest ballroom. So we found ourselves back at the scene of the crime. We decided to tie the proverbial knot on the same soundstage where we'd first met. I married a cinematographer, so of course we'd be beautifully lit.

It was like a movie. I had a bevy of stunning bridesmaids (twelve!), including my dearest childhood friends, Stacey and Tamara Wilson, Flip's daughters, Mariska Hargitay, and of course, Tricia Leigh as my maid of honor, as well as my best friends and cousins, and a tiny Billie Lourd as one of my flower girls. We planned everything with extreme care—the food, the flowers, the décor, and, of course, the musical choices.

Isn't it every little girl's dream to have her father walk her down the aisle? Even with his absence during my childhood, I envisioned and created a way to have Eddie be a part of this ritual, while never diminishing the fact that my mother truly had been my only parent for all of my life. I knew just what to do.

A curtain parted, the room was hushed and brimming with anticipation. The air felt different, still, and full of promise. We walked out to "Nessun Dorma." My father was on my left, my mother on my right. We walked halfway down the aisle together, and then, dramatically, my mother leaned across me to kiss my father. I turned and, picking up my veil slightly, kissed my dad. He sat down, and my mother walked me the rest of the way down the aisle, then gave me away. It was symbolic of how my life was and had always been. The moment was spectacular—perfectly choreographed, like a true Stevens-Fisher production. When the music ended, I was standing across from Chris, with Father Terrance Sweeney between us, ready to officiate.

"Now, that's what I call an entrance," Father Sweeney said.

It was a wedding to rival the royals—pure magic. It was New Year's Eve, and we had 650 guests, wining and dining and ready to usher in 1997. When we'd been planning everything, my mom had told me: "We're Italian. Everybody's going to have their shoes off, and we're going to throw sandwiches."

"What?! That's like something that happens at Italian weddings?"

I think what she meant was how at the end of a big Italian party, when people are still reveling into the wee hours, you order in the meatball subs, and the chicken parms, and you yell out into the crowd, "Who wants chicken parm?" And people raise their hands, and you toss them a sandwich. We didn't quite do that, but we sort of did. I did change into something sexier by Donna Karan. And at the end of the night, we sent all the leftover food in a refrigerated truck to feed the homeless.

Because I'd grown up so much in my mother's world, it was very old Hollywood. It's bittersweet to think back on the guest list, because so many of those who attended are no longer with us: Milton Berle, Flip Wilson, Jack Carter, and many other old-time comedians. Entertainment journalists, including Army Archerd and George Christy, who had written about my mom for years and years, covering her weddings, and her career, and the birth of her children—covering my birth and now my career. Her dear old friends and castmates from *Hawaiian Eye* attended, including her costar, Robert Conrad, and a Hawaiian actor from the show, Poncie Ponce, with whom she sang "The Hawaiian Wedding Song." For the reception, we had the Les Brown Orchestra, and then a funky band that played until well into the next morning. It was spectacular. Connie was proud that she was able to give her firstborn daughter the wedding of her dreams. It was inclusive, and gorgeous, and a little bit over the top, and people who were there still describe it as one of the most beautiful weddings they've ever attended.

Leading Man

I had found a true life partner and we both knew we wanted to have children together. And I had a little practice. We had partial custody of Chris's sons, Cameron and Collin. I loved the boys and I feel like they came into my life at a time when I could influence them still, even though I didn't give birth to them, as an integral part of their parenting, as their mother often says. I had just turned twenty-eight, the year of the Saturn return, an important milestone in life. *Ellen* was at the height of its popularity, and when it ended, I had the chance to step into my dream role in *Cabaret* and did the big Disney film *Inspector Gadget*. We were in no rush to settle down *too much*. My eldest daughter, Skylar, was poking around in the family archives recently.

"We were wild," her dad and I joked to her.

She did the math in her mind and stopped short.

"So, wait, Mom," she said. "You got married when you

were twenty-eight, and you didn't have me until you were thirty-three?"

"Yep," I said. "We had four really good, fun running-around years together first."

I had met my match (in the positive way), and we were enjoying every aspect of our shared life. He let me shine. He was the first person who adored watching me own my place in the spotlight—never threatened by it. He loved seeing what it did to me.

Connie had very old-fashioned ideas about gender roles. Which was weird, since she definitely wore the pants in all her relationships. Men were supposed to pay. They were supposed to take care of things. I have no idea where she got this idea, since I don't think she ever had a man in her life who did these things for her.

"Let Chris drive," she would say to me when we would all pile into the car together.

Um, okay. She certainly hadn't raised me that way. And, ironically, all she wants to do now is to "drive" herself—to be in control.

Yes, Tricia and I both married and started families. Yes, we did break up the band to a certain extent. But really, we were still the Three Musketeers. And Tricia and I never looked at it as breaking up the band. We looked at it as creating a symphony.

I always valued and was interested in what Connie had to say on all subjects. She was still the queen.

So it was interesting for the woman who was the best at everything to suddenly stumble upon the one area in her life where there was no questioning the fact that both of her daughters had eclipsed her. As the years go by, one by one, and Tricia and I both remain married to our husbands, we have long surpassed my mom's longest legal marriage, of three years. And, for once, she wasn't defensive about this. I think she's proud that we've been able to sustain relationships. And it makes her philosophical.

"I think you 'marry' . . . " she once said to me, making air quotes around the word, ". . . several people in your life. Even though I never married Ralph, he was one of those relationships in my life. Even though I never married Bill. Even though I never married Charlie. Officially . . . in a ceremony."

I knew exactly what she meant. They were marriages, in a way. She spent years with each of those men, which is a long time to spend with somebody. And she remained friends with Charlie and Bill for years after they were no longer involved. I was at her house recently when Bill called her to say hello. They talked, and then there's this thing they still do at the end of their calls, when neither one of them wants to say goodbye. They go . . . "Three, two, one," and then they both hang up at exactly the same time, because neither one of them can bear to hang up first. Even though they haven't been together in decades. Even though he's married, has children and grandchildren. They still have that connection.

I agree with my mom that a special connection is a special connection, and it doesn't require a wedding ring to make it so. The years that I spent with each of my longest relationships would shape who I would be as a wife eventually. But there's also something next level about actually committing to someone—in front of your family, friends, God, and everyone—and actually sticking it out, together, day after day after day after day. Because the truth is, as anyone who's been married knows, it's fucking hard. Even when you have the good fortune and blind luck to meet and marry a truly great guy, like

I did. Not a day goes by that I don't yell out to Chris: "I don't deserve you." And mean it.

But.

Still . . . it's hard.

I've often joked (but I wasn't *really* joking) that the institution of marriage was invented when we lived until we were twenty-six. So, back then, if you got married at fifteen or sixteen, and you died a decade later, you upheld your promise of till death do us part. Ten great years together, and then you're in the box. A lifetime together these days is a whole different story, because over decades together, we do change. The plan is to grow together, and not grow apart. When George Harrison was asked, "What's the secret to a twenty-three-year marriage?" he answered, "Don't get divorced." (And do sleep with groupies.) Well, as long as your spouse sanctions them, ménage à trois trysts can be super hot and sexy, and can bring you closer together. Surrogates can keep it spicy. And being able to fully express your sexuality—and your personality—within your marriage can keep it healthy and strong. Just a little friendly advice from the Fisher-Duddy boudoir.

Some people remodel a kitchen and get divorced. The things that have been thrown at us the past seven years—Connie's bankruptcy, my financial woes, the ebb and flow of our careers, the loss of Eddie, Connie's stroke, the loss of Carrie, the loss of Debbie, all the tremendous heartbreak, and every little difficult bullshit thing these events set in motion—have put a strain on my marriage. Not because we're so special. But because that's life. Tragedy, moving house—several times, back to back, under great financial duress—and having intense family obligations, can be a real strain that could cause a couple who had less at stake to break up. We've survived. And we still laugh every day. And he still thinks I have a great rack.

Chapter 11

The Apple Doesn't Fall Apart Very Far from the Tree

I KNOW WHAT IT'S LIKE to stay awake and alert and alive until the sun comes up. Or rather, to crawl out of dark, smoke-filled, coke-filled rooms. Back rooms of bars and clubs, clandestine, *clan*-destined (if the genes fit . . . a velvet voice . . . a penchant for altered states and emotions masked), clenched jaw, pupils like saucers, best-friend-making, life-altering—wait, mind-altering—*wait, where was I?*

Oh, the paraphernalia—the mirrors, the straws, the rolled-up bills, any page of a magazine, preferably a gorgeous sea—or a black anything—so the coke would show up against the background like sparkling champagne. Like a quarry, a discovery of gems, deposited into my bra, the grail, the hiding spot, the irony—no one will think to look there. I am holding, like in the eighties, tucked away into my décolletage, nearest to my heart, which beats fast. No matter the plunge of the neckline, there, concealed, I am committed to the increase of its beats and here for the party.

Hi, my name is Joely. And I'm an alcoholic.

"Hi, Joely . . ."

Gosh, that felt good. But it's a lot more complicated than that. Isn't it always? Let's take you back. There was no escaping the need for speed. Everyone in my family liked to get sideways once in a while. Some of us more often than that.

Now, let's *really* take you back.

My first experience with drug use was as a toddler. I had a baby's-eye view of my own father tying off, prepping a needle, and injecting drugs into his veins. I was propped up in an inappropriate proximity to Oh My Papa. I have a letter to back it up, one Eddie wrote to me on yellow legal paper when I was a child, out of severe guilt and remorse, and of course, higher than a kite. As he said in the missive, I was supposed to be the one to "clean things up." What a fucking huge responsibility. It was such an addict move. He was trying to make his behavior okay, justify it, explain it away, but he couldn't. Not for a long time. Many years later, when I came across the letter, it was as a young woman who could find compassion—by then, I knew my father and I shared some of the same demons. Before this letter, I had only seen Eddie Fisher's autograph, so this was the most of his handwriting I'd ever held. And it was an attempt at an apology, one I would eventually accept.

Along with the letter I found what would become one of my most treasured possessions—a song whose lyrics echoed the sentiment of the letter, written by my father, "Through the Eyes of Joely." The lyrics poignantly impose on my infant eyes the overwhelming responsibility to make the world a better place.

I never got to hear Eddie sing it, but as a gift for our twentieth wedding anniversary, my husband coerced our daughter to record a version for me. When I heard Skylar sing my father's words I was moved by her incredible gift, the addition to the lineage, and I envisioned Eddie's signature final high note with a finger pointed to the sky for emphasis.

So, yeah, it starts with Eddie.

OP LEFT: Lost in the role of Sally Bowles—moment captured by Christopher Duddy. Villiam Ivey Long's stunning costume design TOP RIGHT: Camping it up at Broadway ares with Alan Cumming and Bruce Vilanch MIDDLE LEFT: Lounging between shows n the dressing room at Studio 54 MIDDLE RIGHT: In my dressing room at the O'Neill, reparing my makeup as I'd watched Connie do all my life BOTTOM LEFT: Rizzo on the oad BOTTOM RIGHT: Last curtain call after a run on Broadway as Rizzo in *Grease* at the ugene O'Neill Theatre

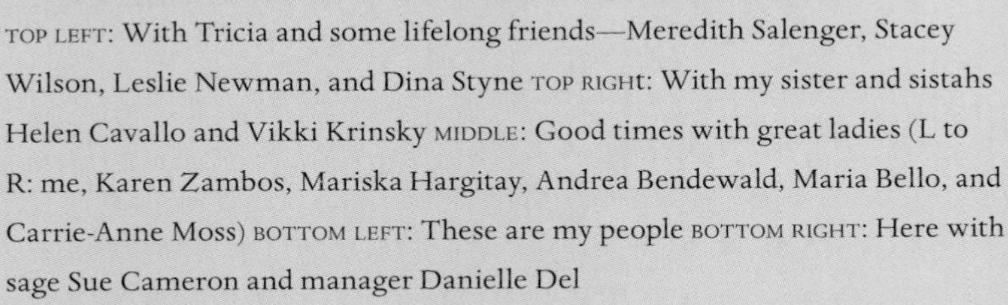

TOP LEFT: With Tricia and some lifelong friends—Meredith Salenger, Stacey Wilson, Leslie Newman, and Dina Styne TOP RIGHT: With my sister and sistahs Helen Cavallo and Vikki Krinsky MIDDLE: Good times with great ladies (L to R: me, Karen Zambos, Mariska Hargitay, Andrea Bendewald, Maria Bello, and Carrie-Anne Moss) BOTTOM LEFT: These are my people BOTTOM RIGHT: Here with sage Sue Cameron and manager Danielle Del

TOP LEFT: Young Hollywood future stars—cast of the Allan Carr–produced musical production number for the 1989 Oscars TOP RIGHT: With Mike Ovitz, then president of Disney ABC, at the opening of the Buy the Book bookstore at Disney's Epcot Center, Florida MIDDLE LEFT: Ruta Lee and Debbie's Thalians honor Connie and the girls, along with Marc Cherry (*© Stephen Shugerman / Getty Images*) MIDDLE RIGHT: With dear friend and director Bob Saget on the set of *Jitters*, Vancouver BOTTOM RIGHT: With my dear friend, the incomparable Jackie Collins BOTTOM LEFT: With Tricia and Connie at the Beverly Hilton with owner Merv Griffin

TOP LEFT: With Connie and my *Baby Bob* TV mom, Holland Taylor TOP RIGHT: With the iconic Norman Lear BOTTOM LEFT: With Tricia and Jenna Elfman at the Jackson Hole Celebrity Extravaganza Gunslinger Shootout MIDDLE RIGHT: With Jenny McCarthy, unbridled laughter between friends BOTTOM RIGHT: The rare enjoying of a stogie with "Uncle Miltie," Milton Berle

TOP LEFT: With actress, activist, and dearest friend, Mariska Hargitay TOP RIGHT: With *Titanic*'s Gloria Stuart MIDDLE: Opening night of *Cabaret* in San Francisco, Sharon Stone shares her secrets BOTTOM: With Priscilla Presley, Connie, and Sheryl Crow in support of Dream Foundation, an organization dedicated to granting the final wishes of terminally ill adults

TOP LEFT: With *Ellen*'s Jeremy Piven, Caesars Palace, Las Vegas TOP FAR RIGHT: With Jennifer Garner and Maika Monroe on the set of *The Tribes of Palos Verdes* TOP RIGHT: The girls in a poignant stand for equality at the Millenium March on Washington MIDDLE RIGHT: With Michelle Monaghan at a shoot for the PROTECT campaign for the International Fund for Animal Welfare, which I produced and directed BOTTOM RIGHT: See Jane march . . . with Jane Fonda at the Los Angeles Women's March

TOP: Post celebrity fashion show supermodel slumber party—hair was braided, pillow fights were had, no food was consumed MIDDLE LEFT: Backstage at the What a Pair! breast cancer benefit, a night of duets by some of my favorite women MIDDLE RIGHT AND BOTTOM RIGHT: Obligatory Obama selfies, White House holiday party

TOP: Love at first glimpse. Christopher Duddy in his element behind the lens MIDDLE LEFT: Chris formally asks Mr. Fisher for his daughter's hand in marriage MIDDLE RIGHT: Connie also said yes to Chris BOTTOM LEFT: Pure bliss—wedding night, just after ringing in the new year

TOP LEFT: An epic trip down the aisle . . . Eddie walked halfway, Connie gave the bride away TOP RIGHT: With Ellen DeGeneres, who introduced me to Chris and still insists she "got" me a husband MIDDLE LEFT: Father-daughter dance MIDDLE RIGHT: With the bridal party on the well-tread staircase at Delfern BOTTOM LEFT: Big Sister "supports" the bride, Billie fulfills her flower girl duties

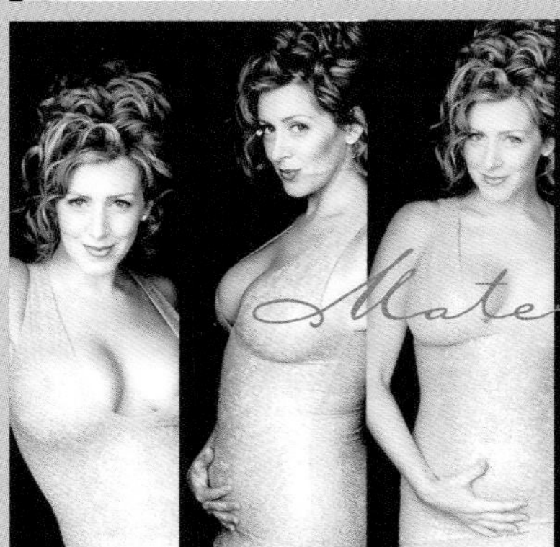
The L.A. Gay & Lesbian Center's
Renberg Theatre Presents
Joely Fisher…
From Here To
Maternity
Musical Direction, Ron Abel
Brilliant and brazen! Sensational and sexy! Thrilling and tawdry!
– CBC Radio

Facing Page TOP LEFT: Newlyweds on the Bridge of Sighs in Venice TOP RIGHT: New Year's Eve 2007, the Mexican Love Jam MIDDLE: My one-woman show, L.A.'s Gay and Lesbian Center BOTTOM LEFT: Pregnant with Skylar BOTTOM RIGHT: Pregnant with True

TOP: Christopher makes me a stepmom. In Canada with Collin and Cameron LEFT: Deckside with the Fisher-Duddys, all hands on hips RIGHT: It's official! The powerful moment Olivia Luna became our daughter

TOP: The family waiting to welcome grandbaby Kitt in Hidden Hills, California LEFT: Nana and her girls and most of their brood BOTTOM: Mama and the girls in the Hole at Moonbather Ridge

TOP LEFT: Beautiful spring wedding with the family in Connie's garden TOP RIGHT: Stepmother of the groom and Fisher-Duddy flower girls in Jackson Hole MIDDLE LEFT: With Skylar and True at the Los Angeles Women's March MIDDLE RIGHT: Post–TED Talk birthday celebration BOTTOM LEFT: The Fisher-Duddy tribe, Father's Day 2017

TOP: Strike a pose . . . Decades apart, Joely channels her inner '70s goddess. You have to be carefully taught *(© Jean Baptiste Lacroix / Getty Images)*

BOTTOM: As Carabosse in the catsuit and Maleficent horns, sent in transatlantic text to big sister Carrie for her amusement and approval. At Laguna Playhouse, *Sleeping Beauty and Her Winter Knight*

TOP LEFT: Behind the scenes for the *Us* magazine swimsuit edition with photographer Davis Factor TOP RIGHT: Morgane Le Fay Jedi jacket, given to me by big sister Carrie MIDDLE: The "Tails for Whales" campaign, lobbying on the Hill for IFAW, Washington, D.C. BOTTOM: An incredible night performing for APLA, Pacific Amphitheatre, Los Angeles

TOP LEFT: Hanging out, girls locker room TOP RIGHT: On the carpet, HBO Golden Glob party, 2016. Unbeknownst to me, my mother was suffering a stroke *(© Frederick M. Brown / Get Images)* MIDDLE LEFT: Me and the twins onstag at the Pantages BOTTOM LEFT: Wonder Wom pose, Mexico BOTTOM RIGHT: At the White House, the Obamas' last holiday party

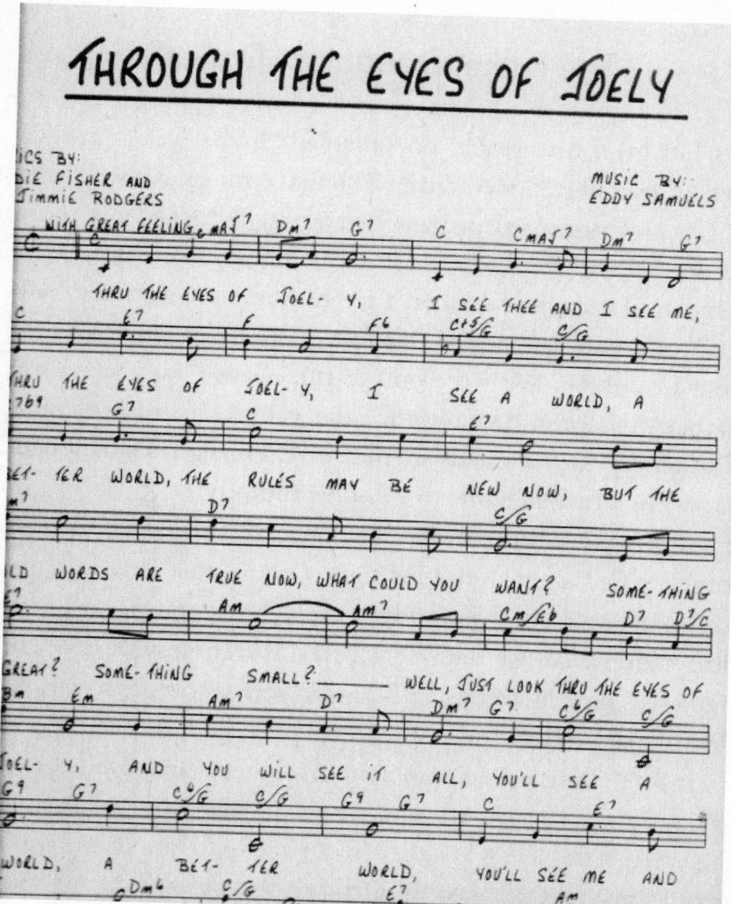

But, throughout my life, I've witnessed actual substance abuse, and its resulting behavior, in most of my family members. Not just my dad. I've seen—and experienced—how it can become this closed circle—the substance, and then the guilt. It's an escape, and then a provocation.

A treat, then a habit.

A one-off, then the need.

The Father-Daughter "Dance"

As has been historically documented, Eddie wasn't around when his children were little. The first time he came to take Tricia and me on an unsupervised outing, it turned into more of an "adventure." He arrived in a white Cadillac. It was the seventies, so he had donned a bright floral silk shirt and bell-bottoms. Our destination: Dodger Stadium (because we sure loved baseball). We were on the 101, headed east, when my father proceeded to plow into the vehicle in front of him. Daughters don't let dads drive drunk. Or high. Plans foiled, we were returned home to Connie promptly.

When we were old enough, on rare occasions, Connie orchestrated a much-needed visit with Eddie. This was uncharted territory. Everybody around him seemed to know him better than we did. Here I was, traveling with my "I'm famous," now infamous, father, who was a stranger to me. At least I had Tricia.

In 1975, in true Eddie fashion, my father married yet again. This time to a twenty-one-year-old former Miss Louisiana, Terry Richard. She was closer to our age than his. Years later, I would realize they wed on October 29, my birthday. (Eddie oblivious.) When we went to visit my father and his new bride, my sister and I were left to our own devices (and this was before there were devices . . . oh, but there were vices). Unbeknownst to Connie, we traveled in a private puddle-jumper plane piloted by Eddie's plastic surgeon, now bestie, possibly dealer?, Rudi Unterthiner, in a dangerous flight to Eddie's Palmdale ranch. Once there, I got an eyeful: there was a round bed with satin sheets, and the adults enjoyed their cocaine. It wasn't like I ever *saw* them do it, but the paraphernalia was everywhere, and I was definitely a kid who knew what it was and why it was there. Thank God for Tricia, who was by my side through all of this.

Mother's Little Helper

The Stones didn't write a song called "Mother's Little Helper" for nothing; they weren't referring to the housekeeper. Eddie wasn't the only one who sought refuge and recreation in substances. My mother didn't have the luxury of indulging with the same sheer commitment as Eddie, since she was a full-time single mom. Of course, it might be more accurate to describe her as a full-time *showbiz* mom, and that comes with a whole different set of ground rules.

My father became addicted in the first place when he had to go on one night and he didn't have a voice, and someone suggested he see Dr. Max Jacobson (aka Dr. Feelgood), who shot him up with amphetamines, plus the kitchen sink. A who's who of other celebrities, including Marilyn Monroe, Judy Garland, and JFK, were also regular disciples of "Miracle Max." Eddie had the best show of his career and quickly came to rely on these drugs. Already predisposed to be an addict, he was soon using all the time. When my mother cried in her trailer because the studio wanted her to wear jeans, and she was afraid of what she'd look like on camera in them, someone suggested *she* try Black Beauties. And what provided her with an appetite suppressant also gave her a boost when she was "dragging" and a feeling of euphoria. Now, there's a recipe for success. And so I bore witness to my mom's reliance on a pharmacopeia of beauties throughout her life.

Forty years later, not long after she had a stroke in early 2016, Connie said to Tricia and me:

"I would kill for a diet pill right now."

Tricia and I looked at each other.

"Why? They haven't worked in years," we both chimed in, trying to lighten the mood and segue the conversation to a place where we all pretended she was kidding.

We all knew she wasn't kidding.

Same shit. But you don't get addicted to something just because you're exposed to it. My father was predisposed to be an addict, clearly; so was my mother; so were we all. I think the reason you drink, smoke, eat, shop—whatever it was for each of us—is that you've got a hole you're trying to fill, or an inner voice you're trying to quiet, or that inner critic, that feeling of worthlessness, or lack, or inadequacy . . . But I digress . . .

When I was a kid, we were around my mom under all kinds of NC-17 circumstances, when we were like *seven,* so we got exposed to *a lot*.

Partly, it was just the lifestyle and the times. As a teenager, it didn't seem out of the ordinary for me to go to a nightclub with my mom and stay there until nine o'clock in the morning. I looked older than my age, and I was rarely asked for my ID. Then again, I was with Connie, so that's what VIP treatment will get you, I guess. It was a definite after-hours club. There were definite shenanigans going on in there. It's not like the other guests were sitting around braiding each other's hair.

Other than the fact that I was a little young to be there (although I had purchased a fake ID at a novelty shop in Times Square, just in case), usually everything went swimmingly. But one fateful morning, in came the battalion with their billy clubs at the ready. It was like a scene in a movie. I watched as my mom was lifted up off her feet, flanked by two of New York's finest, and carried toward the rear door of the establishment.

"Wait! My daughter," she called over her shoulder.

We were taken out the back and put into a squad car and *not* arrested like everybody else, who got shuffled into the waiting paddy wagon. I know what you're all thinking. That's not good parenting. But my mom never saw any danger in it. She wanted the party to continue, and I was her favorite plus-one. That's how we rolled.

Maybe it was the same mentality as when Tricia and I would fight for the "special seat," which was the driver's armrest of my mom's 450 SLC. The winner perched next her, my mom reached across to shield our bodies when coming to a sudden stop (because clearly that would help). We barreled through life the way we barreled through the streets of L.A.: without a seat belt.

The Gateway Drug

I'm a quick study and a keen observer. I watched my mom. I learned how to expertly roll a joint, so of course she enlisted me to add to her stockpile. Tricia and I would sit on Mom's bed with her, and I'd roll spliff after spliff. Fold. Fill. Roll. Lick. Seal.

We didn't smoke it. (Until we were at the age . . . when we did.) It feels very strange to let that particular family tidbit out of the dime bag. But I'm sure there were other kids who rolled joints for their moms, right? I knew other kids whose parents had a canister on the coffee table designated for guests to help themselves. We also had a little silver cigarette box with Connie's initials, on the bar, for people who wanted to indulge in a cigarette. I can remember my favorite comedienne, Lucille Ball, behind her giant glasses, sitting at the bar at Delfern with a Jack and Coke and a cigarette from that container.

By Relative Standards

Here's the part in the book where I bring up the fact that my sister Carrie was also a drug addict . . . recovered, recovering . . . do we ever fully recover? Perhaps we just cover . . . sweep under . . . we are actresses, after all, trained in the art of pretend. Now, you've probably all seen *Postcards from the Edge,* a thinly veiled autobiographical film about an actress who's the daughter of a movie star (who enjoyed her wine) and who does a stint in rehab. Or you've read the book it was based on. Carrie's novel caused a decade-long rift between mother and daughter. For being truthful. So it's not as if I'm telling tales out of school.

In the years leading up to *Postcards from the Edge,* I was just getting to know Carrie. One highly anticipated visit from my big sister happened in 1980. She came to Malibu to spend time with her mother and popped over next door to say hi to her ex-stepmother and two little sisters. She came with John Belushi and her then-fiancé, Dan Aykroyd, and she sat on our couch, flanked by Blues Brothers. I was a teenage girl. It was an odd dynamic, these three very famous, very silent people, with their sunglasses on in my house.

I didn't know what drugs they were using, but it was clear to me that they had indulged in something. Like the infant's-eye view I'd had with Eddie, now what came into focus for my hazels was an ability to recognize off-kilter when I saw it. From that point in my life, I was no longer naïve about what would turn out to be a family trait. My story is full of moments that I now look back on with greater understanding. I've learned to reexamine and reevaluate and get the full picture. What's emerging for me is that we're all alike, we've all got stuff, and as Fishers, the force hasn't always been with us. Everyone is just doing the best they can.

Beverly Hills, 90210

Now, with my training wheels off, I was ready to let loose. Looking for the right fit, we had tried out every other school. It's not like I got kicked out. I just had trouble finding the right educational experience to fit in between stints in Vegas and Atlantic City. Beverly Hills is one of the most coveted school districts in the city of Los Angeles. But we were back at Delfern, which isn't 90210. So in order for us to attend Beverly Hills High for my last two years, my mom rented an apartment directly across the street from the school. We didn't live there. "Fisherman's Wharf" became the party pad and a refuge for, okay, I'll say it, cutting class. This was where my brat pack shacked up. But I was also in the musical theater department, "the muffins." So I was straddling both worlds, not really sure if I fit perfectly in either one. A longtime family friend, Jule Styne's grandson David, was enlisted to help. He was my first husband, whom I'd wed at six years old on the beaches of Hawaii (but not the one Tricia and I had momentarily fought over on a later trip), so of course he would show me the high school ropes.

Not unlike the people who came before me—father, mother, sister Carrie—I had issues that led me to turn to addictive behavior as a coping mechanism. And I may have started to use my access to things, and my sexuality, and my ability to throw parties in the pursuit of what everyone wants: to make friends. Like you, like all of us, I was looking for acceptance. I was still trying to shed some weight . . . and trying to shed the weight of having been bullied in earlier years. At that age, I didn't have the confidence to think people might actually like Joely. So if I put out, or picked up the check, or provided the party favors, I thus established a place for myself in the Beverly High annals . . . at least in my own mind. Whatever gets you through. To a certain extent, it worked.

The crown jewel of my social experiment happened in eleventh grade, when Connie was out of town. I threw a still-legendary party with David Styne and Darren Weinstock and charged admission. I rode the social coattails of these boys—who were a year older than me—and got the response I'd hoped for. The seas parted for notorious promoter Paul Fegen, who showed up in his silver-and-purple Excalibur. There were fights aplenty. The green surface of the tennis court was completely obscured, swallowed up by the sea of drunken high school teens that had come from Taft, Birmingham, Malibu, Uni High, Hami, private schools. The din of anxious, feral,

THE BEACH PARTY
(NOT AT THE BEACH)
12 noon — 12 midnight
Saturday, June 12
243 Delfern Drive, Holmby Hills
given by: JOELY FISHER
ST. REGIS
GREAT NEW BAND!
come and go as you please!
good and drink!
Piña Coladas
SWIMMING!
DANCING!
ADMISSION: $3

hormonal teens was deafening. This was a party that was advertised L.A.-wide, and the damage was extensive. Sprinkler systems destroyed. Vomit everywhere. Super sexy. I felt like one of the popular kids for a moment. And being that I was able to maintain my position as the straight-A student, with the lead in the school play, there weren't any negative consequences for me. It was fun.

It wasn't difficult to find drugs at Beverly Hills High in the eighties. Naturally, someone's dad was a high-profile dentist, with liquid cocaine in his office, which his son snatched and sniffed—and we all got to try it. On another occasion, my friends joined me in a line of cocaine in Mr. Michalisko's advanced trigonometry class—*while class was in session.* Just trying to push the envelope, we tested the limits to see what we could get away with. (And I got an A in trig.)

On prom night, I shared a limo with two of my best girlfriends and we each had an eight ball in our purse. That's *three and a half grams of cocaine,* each, on all of us, at the prom at the Beverly Hilton hotel, home of the Golden Globes. I think about it every time I enter that ballroom. We stayed up all night. And ended up in Palm Springs. Very *Less Than Zero*—but not Robert Downey Jr. *Less Than Zero*; more Jami Gertz *Less Than Zero.* Needless to say, no one ate the post-prom brunch. Oh, c'mon, you remember high school? Now as a mother I keep a very wide open line of communication with my children about the impact of drugs and the dangers of abuse—about addictive behavior in general, from eating to spending. It's a different time. We talk about things in a different way. They hear about things on the news and ask questions. There's social media and other communication tools that didn't exist back then. There are marijuana dispensaries on every corner. My children also know about Big Auntie and her story. And now they know that most of us in the family have been challenged.

So all of you who are friends of Bill may call me on my shit, but although things have gotten out of hand on occasion, I've always managed to bring it back under control. Perhaps it was that I had to regularly return to the role of mother (both to my little sister and Connie) before I actually became one. As a young woman, I would resume my position at the mic, singing backgrounds behind Connie, and my position as the matriarch.

We were doing a gig in Chicago. The Italians always poured out to see my mom, everywhere we went. One night after a show, the owners of a local Italian eatery invited Connie and the whole band to stop by. They were going to keep the kitchen open and have a great Italian meal waiting for the gang. When the curtain came down, it was ten thirty. Everybody piled into a couple of vans. There was the normal electricity of having done a great show, a kind of a buzz. What a treat. There wasn't always a big meal after a show, and everybody was excited. We arrived at the restaurant, mirrored bar to my left, and to my right, the typical row of red leather booths, one obscured from view.

My mother and I were ushered to this "VIP" booth, just as our host was opening up a bindle—a newspaper that had been folded like an envelope, this one the size of the *National Enquirer*—and revealed a giant pile of disco dust. *Abbondanza!!!*

Meanwhile out came a parade of traditional Italian fare. It's unusual they'd provided dessert first—because everyone knows you don't eat when you do cocaine.

Panicked, I looked at my mom. I looked at my surroundings, these strangers, and this mountain of food and drugs.

We have to get out of here. This doesn't feel right to me. No shit!!!

I turned to Connie.

"We have to go," I said.

"Why?" she said, a childlike response.

"Mom, you can't be in this restaurant," I said. "I can't be in this restaurant right now."

"Oh, Joely," she said. "They went to a lot of trouble. We'll just have a little bite, and then we'll go." I convinced her not to take a bite of anything . . . do not inhale!

I went to use the restroom as Connie went to make our apologies to the restaurant's owners. I was in their tiny bathroom, with my tights around my ankles. This girl kicked in the door and got in my face.

"You little bitch," she said.

"What? What?" I stuttered, fumbling to cover myself.

Everything after that was kind of a blur. It was a rant about how they had stayed open late and cooked all this food, but what I do know is it started with "you little bitch."

"Get out," I said, trying to close the door.

I pulled everything together, went and grabbed Connie, and we headed for the door. I was the mother. I was the protector. Not that I hadn't tried cocaine by then, but it was clear that the entire situation was dangerous, not to mention illegal and inappropriate. Realizing the audacity of the night before, the restaurant owners attended the show the next night and brought peace offerings in the form of baked ziti and cannoli.

IN MY OBSERVATION, people who use—particularly the ones I've been closest to, even more particularly the ones I'm linked to by DNA—have let drugs and alcohol take away their power. When we partake in these behaviors, we lose a lot of time, we lose our good judgment, we lose ourselves. In my father's case, losing his power meant losing everything—his family, his fortune, and then his voice, and for any singer this means devastation. In my mother's case, her denial took the form of thinking she could get away with not taking care of herself, leaving her high blood pressure unchecked, not going to a doctor, save for the one who never checked her vitals and always gave her what she wanted—not in pill bottles, but in little manila envelopes—all of which I believe eventually caused her stroke. So for this self-proclaimed Italian street fighter who ate black and blue prime rib ("rare, rare,

rare" . . . she'd order) and drank cosmos, and added salt to everything, as well as that need for speed, it finally caught up to her. Carrie, the queen of getting clean, who was more open about and noted for her hospital stays and rehab stints than anyone else in the family, turned her sickness into a story and became the intergalactic savior of lost souls. But there was a cost for her, too. It's hard enough to deal with these demons as an individual, let alone when your every move is recorded and reported. And there's that infuriating phenomenon whereby people build you up to the impossible height where you can't do anything but fall.

I always felt like I was strong enough to put the shit down. Although I like to think that I've been the successful one at quelling these predilections, it hasn't always been the case. My most vulnerable times happened when I wasn't busy with work or in a happy relationship, and of course, prior to having my children. The past few years have been a meteor storm . . . hurdles doesn't even describe it, we're talking curveballs of steel, and yes, they've taken me off my course—which may have led me back to old destructive behaviors. I've indulged myself in my self-pity, and the licking of my wounds, sometimes the licking of other things, a bottle of Caymus and a pack of Marlboro Light 72s, but still get myself up at six fifteen to make three separate lunches for three different daughters, 'cause True doesn't like peanut butter, and Luna likes spicy mustard like Mommy. Skylar has braces and needs the apples cut into small bits. Carrie came to me in a dream recently and said, "I was a good mother. I didn't make the sandwiches, but I was a good mom." And I believe that. I cut the crusts . . . with a hangover!!!

As much as I've had an amazing life, and amazing career highlights, there were so many times when I reached a point that "this job is gonna change my life." And it just missed. In no way am I owed a career, or anything else, but I've worked hard and tried to be a good person and I think a talented one. It just hasn't added up to where I thought I would be. And rather than going to the gym, or going back to acting class, I dealt with that feeling by going home and having a bottle of wine. There are other people whose disappointment motivates them, and in my case, rejection and loss motivates me to the bar.

Who You Gonna Call?

In 2004, I flew into New York for the weekend for a friend's birthday. I had a three-year-old, who was safe at home with her father, and this was a much-needed girl getaway. With two best girlfriends in tow, we took more than a bite of the Big Apple. Or I did. It was a two-night bender. I was alone in my monofocus.

Not for the first time, I called Carrie from New York at three . . . four in the morning, because I knew I could.

"Carrie . . . I think I'm in trouble."

She talked me down off the ledge. Take a shower, drink a beer. She was the only one I could talk to who wouldn't judge me, who knew the experience I was having. One junkie to another.

"Don't worry, you're a periodic," Carrie said, using a rather dull and clinical AA term. "When you get back, I'll take you to a meeting."

I knew what she meant by the word "periodic." If I went for

it, I went for it. But if I didn't, it wasn't part of my daily life. It wasn't like that for me. Your period comes monthly, right?!

When I got home, she upheld her promise. She took me to a meeting. It wasn't the first time. And as on those previous occasions, I did take a few necessary "steps" to attaining sobriety. It wasn't like one meeting could fix me, but I owed that to her, to actually honor my commitment and go to the meeting with her. And it did create a bond between us, an understanding.

If I'm being super, super honest, which, why not? We are here and we're lit. I think she had a small amount of delight in the fact that she wasn't the only one. I remember her saying, on occasion: "At least you're not bipolar. Eddie's bipolar. I'm bipolar."

It was a symbolic leveling of the playing field, one we drew comfort from. And I drew comfort from having her as a sponsor, I mean sister. When I said she was my hero and my mirror, she was. But, as I've said, when you look into that reflective glass, you don't always like what you see. As funny as she could make everything, some of her life story was definitely not hilarious. But as Carrie often said, and it is one of my favorite lines: "If it's not funny, it's just the truth, and that is completely unacceptable."

And as much as she had in abundance—smarts and humor and talent, fame and light-up knickknacks—there are also ways in which I don't envy her. Never did. She got to be Princess Leia, but I am also a superhero when it comes to the way I dealt with my demons. And I feel like she saw that, too. Even though she was older than me, I always got the sense that she thought I was handling it well. "It" meaning . . . well, all of *it*.

So I can only and will only be responsible for the filling

of my own holes . . . the silencing of the wheels in my own hamster cage of a head and the steps I've taken to quiet them. I had issues with addiction my whole life, but I also, for some reason, never succumbed to it . . . meaning, I am still alive. A personal victory of the most epic proportions. In an extremely poetic turn of fate, I met up with Ralph (my mother's ex) in Las Vegas in the late nineties. I hooked him up with tickets to see the Rolling Stones at the Hard Rock Hotel . . . front row. He had been sober for many, many years . . . that night he plummeted off the wagon. He continued the "party" in a motel and OD'd. This loss was profound. And the coroner's report on Carrie was its own testament to the lifelong struggle addiction entails. It's a battle, truly.

Years of therapy, different doctors, various poses on various "couches" led me to understand why I turned to the drink to cope. Now, it never got in the way of my work or my parenting. This is what I told myself on my super secret smoking patio, far from the madding crowd of toddlers. What I tell myself, now, as I wring out a bottle of Cabernet while I binge-watch Netflix and "pill." I indulge in the grape, or the "laughing brachen," because "it's legal," and don't do the other shit, not because it isn't, but because a long time ago, I found a sobering solution . . . just say no. I still continue to eat, or not eat in a weird, compulsive way. I spend money the way an addict does (a lot or not at all). I know the first step is admitting you are powerless, but I am not powerless. I am powerful. The apple doesn't fall apart very far from the tree.

Chapter 12

Leading Lady Plays House

TRULY THE QUESTION IS NOT how to grow up at this altitude, it's how to parent, how to grow someone else up. In the climate of ego, narcissism, financial uncertainty, and creative chaos . . . how dare we keep procreating? Why would we bring more humans into this already overpopulated atmosphere? (This town, this family, the world.)

Parenting is the most difficult job on the planet. There, I said it. With that being said, I do love my children. I had an intense conversation with Carrie a few years ago about how we were narcissistically parented—by egotistical, career-driven women who knew they could do this *better* than anyone else (on their own), something to control that actually worked out. We four children of Eddie are independent, freethinking, driven, talented, accepting, inclusive, trustworthy, loving, fabulously flawed. Knowing we were just like them, we laughed. Carrie and I agreed . . . we could do better. And Tricia Leigh is one of the best mothers I know.

Actually, how does it happen that we all turned out the way we did? LOVE. We were wanted—wanted to change things, to keep him, to show off, to carry on the line, and . . . babies! C'mon, the smell, the wonder, the promise. I love babies. (Can you tell?) I don't even mind the sleepless nights; I never sleep anyway.

Carrie was, obviously, the first of us to offer up her sampling of the DNA platter. Billie came to her, to us, as the great white hope—proof that there was light in the darkness of celebrity mishaps and mismarriages, misadventures. I would have to wait another decade to "auntie" any children of Tricia's. And almost that long for children of my own. Children have given us all another chance—a chance at accomplishment, a chance at tradition, at family. I include our parents in that, too. These people all became better parents, better humans as grandparents—Popsie, Nana, Billie's Abadaba. And I do believe becoming a mother myself showed me what it was like to hold down the fort, work, and give your offspring full attention.

I couldn't wait to be a mother. I knew I would be great at it. I started mothering at such a young age . . . a nurturer—truthfully, a bit bossy—creative, ready, prepped by raising Tricia, and for all intents and purposes . . . Connie, a few godchildren, and some immature friends (ha!). And finally, on the brink of marriage to Christopher, I was to become a stepmother. I met and connected with his children from his first marriage. The first installment of our *Modern Family.* Chris and his first wife were very young when they married, and she is a good mother, just made interesting choices that affected her children. Cameron and Collin became my "sons" at eight and ten years old. I'm sure I made an impression on them, and I did my best to include them in our lives as much as I could.

Their mother had remarried and was to have another son. She moved our boys away to Northern California, to follow her new husband's work. This was heartbreaking for Chris, as there would no longer be those every-other-Wednesday-night dinners, weekends, holidays, sports, and real quality time. There's no way this didn't take a toll on the father-son relationships. As the boys grew, as boys do, they also wanted to spend more time with friends and activities that would keep them from air travel—understandable. Busy as our lives were, we got up there as much as we could. Having been unfathered myself, I made the effort so that, inasmuch as it was in our control, my husband could be there for his sons. And as soon as the boys graduated from school, they beelined for L.A. and we had room for them! Just as Connie had done for me—you can always go home.

In those years, we all developed a fantastic rapport. Cameron and Collin, half Chris Duddy, half Greek, and a teensy bit Fisher, are loyal friends and creative souls. They are both funny—quite surely I have something to do with that. And now they find themselves with success in the family business. They both chose their mates wisely, each woman brings out the best in her man, and I emotionally witnessed them each pledge their love at their beautiful, uniquely them weddings. Satisfying moments for all of us from broken homes. And I can't believe I'm saying this, but each couple has now given us . . . that's right . . . grandchildren. I'm Glamma! Chris has assumed Eddie's title: Popsie. I'll let that settle in . . .

Love at First Born

Skylar, Skylar Grace, my graceful Sky, my firstborn child. I dare not put in your tiny sweet soul the pressure to change the world, to improve the atmosphere, to . . . who am I kidding? My aim, like those before me: do better.

The circumstances unto which you were born were ideal. A husband and wife who adored each other and had taken a full four and a half years to do just that. We had traveled, and partied, and achieved some wonderful career milestones. And this desire for a family was now what drove us. It was time. I remember announcing to my touring company of *Cabaret* that I was gonna go back to a cushy television job—and start a family—the sitcom life allows you to be home for dinner.

I returned home to Los Angeles, to do a show that had been picked up, *Grosse Pointe,* a spoof of *Beverly Hills, 90210* by its creator, Darren Star, on which I played . . . the female Darren Star. And then I got offered a role opposite John Goodman in the short-lived comedy, not without drama, *Normal, Ohio.* This couldn't fail: John Goodman playing my big, gay brother. Remember that?! That's what I thought—six of you. A few episodes in, feeling the show had found a bit of a groove, Chris and I took advantage of a hiatus week (ya know, I told you about that three-weeks-on, one-week-off, get-into-trouble schedule). We planned a trip to the isle of Lanai, Hawaii . . . and parenthood. The Hawaiian island chain has always been a spiritual location for the family—not only did Connie's career really get started there, but in 1992 (a few years before we met) Chris was involved in a dramatic, near-fatal helicopter crash in the Pu'u 'O'o vent of the Kilauea volcano, on the big island of Hawaii. Three men, three separate rescues, but after two days, my man stuck his hands into the side of a cliff and climbed out—he says, in order to meet me.

We would return to the scene of that climb. This time armed with hope and an ovulation kit. I was ready. I knew my window. Pee on the stick, legs in the air, and voilà! My belief for any of us is that the moment you conceive, roles change. Three weeks later, on the set of *Normal,* I peed on a stick again, and it would confirm my wildest dreams come true. We were pregnant!

We would shoot thirteen episodes, and in one, at almost four months pregnant, my character, Pamela, would attempt to earn extra money as a stripper (go to YouTube and see "Joely Fisher Strips"). They (producers Marcy Carsey and Tom Werner, writers Bonnie and Terry Turner) would have shot the episode in such a way to cover a growing belly. But we were canceled before it came to that. In the course of a career, this happens all the time—schedules change, network and personal. It had been an amazing experience—that cast, John Goodman, whom I adore, and who had struggled with great demons of his own—I got him. The very funny Anita Gillette, Orson Bean, and Mo Gaffney, plus guests like Dan Aykroyd (who at one time might have come close to being my brother-in-law). Maybe people just weren't ready for John Goodman as a gay man. So, there we were, canceled . . . heart-breaking, also because—how was I going to have a child *now*?

They were making a pilot of the "commercially" successful talking baby from commercials. Baby Bob—normal parents give birth to a baby who begins talking like a wisecracking Chicago businessman. Funny . . . once. I was cast, with my eight-month fetus inside, which we would conceal. When we got picked up, I would have delivered.

I was also, during this time, curating a live show, *From Here to Maternity,* my one-woman show at Hollywood's Gay and Lesbian Center—fourteen songs, and stories of my life. Marriage in full swing, and my first child on the way! Performing live, and a television show—working with Adam Arkin, Elliott Gould, and Holland Taylor—promising, if it weren't for the damn talking baby!

But the delivery of Skylar unto me was spectacular. I went

into labor, by induction, with Dr. Paul Crane, at Cedars-Sinai Medical Center—visits from friends and family all day long, and into the night—my progress slow moving until about 10 P.M.—then it all kicked into high gear. She would definitely be born before midnight—I had been in labor all day, with a doula and a midwife by my side. I was positive I could make it without an epidural.

I really wanted to do this naturally (and you know I'm not mad at a drug). But I just couldn't do it.

I had only reached two centimeters and the pain—I couldn't endure it. I had an epidural, and Dr. Crane told Connie and Tricia to go home. It was gonna be a long night. They left reluctantly. Twenty minutes later, I was at ten centimeters and pushed three times—and Skylar Grace Fisher-Duddy was born. Tiny and beautiful. Six pounds, thirteen ounces, with blue eyes (as if I crushed the skies and poured them into her eyes) and no hair. She was perfect. She would be adored by everyone—Connie's first grandchild, and my firstborn.

While CBS and its chief, Les Moonves, deliberated about the fate of *Baby Bob,* they put me to work opposite Daniel Stern in the short-lived show *Danny.* With a newborn Skylar at my breast, I experienced—along with the world—the shock of 9/11. Before heading off to the set that fateful morning, I was nursing Skylar in bed while talking to my mom, who was at our New York apartment. We tried to make sense of the unfathomable, heinous acts of terrorism . . . and the hit to her hometown, which in some ways, she would never quite recover from. It would not be the last time I would find myself struggling to balance the promise of a newborn child with the fragility of life and the evils that exist in the world. Our faith was again tested the following year, when Tricia gave birth to her first child, Holden. After being at the hospital all night,

I left to get a little rest before going to the set of *Baby Bob*. My mother called and told me Holden had been born with transposition of the major arteries and he would require open-heart surgery. I immediately called my dear friend, dreamy Robby Benson, who was directing *Baby Bob*. He'd had four open-heart surgeries, and he not only told me the doctor to call, but also waited with our family at the hospital during the nine-and-a-half-hour ordeal five days later. We got the best of the best, and Holden is now a healthy, happy teenage boy.

Baby Bob was, of course, canceled—'cause, ya know, a talking baby. Not before amazing guest stars Kristin Chenoweth, Richard Lewis, and Barry Bostwick, though. And Skylar, in diapers, taking her first steps on the set.

With Mommy getting a show every season. I was next cast in *Wild Card* for Lifetime—a great part for me. A former blackjack dealer is forced to raise her dead sister's three children, following an accident. Caveat was—we were to shoot in Canada. We packed up Connie's motor home (yup!) and set off. We made our way across the country, stopping in iconic destinations to have one of the most spectacular little family vacations. We saw America through the eyes of a brave, sweet, funny toddler who was born out of such love.

Toronto, Eh?

The next two years were fraught with all sorts of shenanigans. I was really at the top of my game in terms of my work. The role of Zoe Busiek was tailor-made for me, and I loved it. I was first in the chair (hair and makeup) and the last to leave. Fridays turned into Fraturdays, as we pulled all kinds of hours. My costar, Chris Potter, and I had tremendous chemistry, and the storylines, however far-fetched, led me to some plum comedic situations—undercover as a cruise-ship lounge singer, Russian mail-order bride, and reality-show contestant. Loretta Devine joined the cast in season 2, and guest stars were plentiful—Wendie Malick, Christine Ebersole, Jenny McCarthy, Connie Stevens, and Tricia Leigh. We had acclaimed directors and high ratings. Sklyar was thriving being raised on a set. Chris was able to travel back and forth. We were riding high, as a show and as a family.

A regime change at the network caused the show's cancellation, and we found ourselves packing up our little family and heading back to L.A. This was gut-wrenching for me. I loved that show. And what would I do next?

ele

Desperate . . . Housewife?

With Skylar now old enough to be in school a few hours a day, and us being able to afford help, I would be able to stretch out a little bit and play. I now had the leeway to look for another great job. But before that would happen, Chris and I really began to enjoy being home in L.A., loose and fast. We became known for our wild parties and risqué trips, which created an atmosphere for bad habits and really good times. Sorry, not sorry . . . we enjoyed freedom, and the world of fantasy.

We found ourselves pregnant again. I know the moment this one happened, too: ironically, I have a cycle like the

Farmers' Almanac . . . We attended a party for Betty DeGeneres's birthday, and the after-party continued at our home. True Harlowe Fisher-Duddy was conceived.

Meanwhile . . .

Just before I found out I was to be a mother . . . again, I got a call. They want you to audition for *Desperate Housewives*. A guest star, possible recurring. I hadn't auditioned for a guest star role in a hundred years, but with my tail between my legs and a tiny, not-yet-known bun in the oven . . . I did. The show was hot, and I love to work. I got the job.

I played Felicity Huffman's character Lynette's boss, Nina, who was a real ball-breaker. Whenever Lynette was late or unprepared, Nina knew just who to blame . . . Lynette's kids. It was a great, icy part . . . the perfect foil for Felicity Huffman's role, for which she would win a Golden Globe and an Emmy. My role of Nina was set to recur throughout the season sporadically. There was just one problem: Nina downright detests children. Eventually I would have to break it to my boss, Marc Cherry: I was with child.

They assured me they could write it in. My solution: While sexually harassing—i.e., fucking—her young, dumb intern, she gets knocked up. Now she is saddled with blah blah blah—great character development, great drama, great fix. And funny.

Or so I thought. On my way to work on my fifth episode . . . now very pregnant, cruising down Beverly Glen, I got a call from Marc Cherry's office.

"Hi, Joely, we have Marc Cherry for you."

"Great," I said, my baby now joined by butterflies.

"Hey, Joely, have you read the yellows for today?" Marc asked, referring to today's rewrites.

"Nope, I haven't," I said.

"Well, didn't want to surprise you, but we couldn't make it work," he said.

The butterflies became barracudas.

So no, this short and fat drive to Universal would be the surprise he'd try to spare me from . . . and the sad faces in hair and makeup would be . . . what? Condolences?

It's desperate, all right—a desperate attempt to save face. People come and go all the time on this show. Consolation prize . . . we will want you to fuck the intern on your desk in today's scene! So seven or eight months pregnant, spread eagle in bra and panties, cute day player pounding away, and shortly after, I am unemployed. A desperate metaphor.

I Had a Baby on My Bed

My pregnancies were different . . . with Skylar I glowed as I grew. And as first pregnancies go, everything was documented and new. With True, I was sick every day. I just knew she would be a boy . . . and then . . . she wasn't. With no job, I could focus on the task at hand . . . slaying this whole pregnancy and birth thing . . . again. I did absolutely love being pregnant, for a few months, each time.

This time I would choose to bring in this new human, this addition to the brood, at home. Everyone asks, was that planned? Indeed it was . . . all that yoga and meditation . . . the preparation to have a home birth. Again Dr. Paul Crane would deliver, along with my midwife, Debbie Frank, and doula, Joanne. Chris, my mother, Tricia . . . my dearest friends in the world: Helen, Leslie, Lisa . . . the butcher, the baker, the candlestick maker, and *Entertainment Tonight* (that's a joke . . . they were alerted shortly after).

Both girls came into the world with a soundtrack . . . beautiful and spiritual. Everything from classical to contemporary. True Harlowe was born in about six hours, from top to bottom. From a membrane sweep (quite possibly the most painful thing ever) to a short stay in the bathtub, to again, three pushes, and a tiny angel burst onto the scene. She entered this life with her wings still attached. She was silent and direct, as if she was expecting me to make the first move. Skylar opted out of cord cutting but watched her baby sister cross through the ring of fire and land safely in our arms. Thy name is True . . . from this child comes the truth. Faith restored. Again, I've given a baby such responsibility. When she was conceived there was electricity and eccentricity in the air and in my "bed." We were enjoying life and playfulness that would rarely, if ever, return.

My daughters Skylar and True have my face . . . my face at sixteen, my face at eleven, my face at five. It is primal and primordial. I've heard urban legend say the first child looks like the father so all those horny cavemen could recognize and claim babies as theirs. Makes sense. Not in my house. These girls are mine! The same way that all my life, growing up, I heard how much I looked like Connie.

ele

Birth of *'Til Death*

Just after having True, our family felt complete. I'd had this spiritual home birth experience, and everyone was thriving.

True was six weeks old when I got a script delivered on the weekend from casting director and longtime friend Tammara Billik (the casting director for *Ellen*). Was I ready to work?

She knew I would kill in the role of Joy Stark and set up a Saturday appointment for me to chemistry-read with the show's star, Brad Garrett. I was a fan and the script was funny (I thought I was a little young to play someone married twenty years—turns out I wasn't). After an amazing read-through, I tested at Fox the following day and it was undeniable. I remember the feeling as I exited the room—another of those life-changing moments. This one caught between nursing a newborn . . . milk stains and all.

The pilot was shot in front of a live audience, as multi-camera shows always are—there was a line in the show with the word "cumin" (the spice) in it. We argued about its pronunciation, and one of our cameramen (a veteran) remarked that the same argument was made on the pilot of *Mad About You*. We were sure to be a hit!

So once again I was #blessed and grateful to have a great job on a show I loved. Brad played my husband, Eddie. We had an intense chemistry and a similar, sick sense of humor. It was like a real marriage without the sex . . . wait . . . that is a real marriage, right? After a few seasons, it was fraught with the changing of writing teams and questions of where did it fit in the schedule. We bounced around in the ratings. But for a moment I thought this could go on forever. What we were doing in every episode, Brad and me, it was solid and really funny.

He'd say, "Which one of the seven nannies is coming today?" And he could say that because there weren't seven nannies.

Brad knows I'm tattooed. He always used to make fun of me, like I'm not going to be buried in a Jewish cemetery . . . Thank God I'm not Jewish, then. I have Chinese characters down my spine, and if the timing is right, you can see them. On one occasion he took me and slammed me down on the table and went behind me and announced, "I'll have the moo goo gai pan and the dim sum." As if he was reading off the Chinese menu. Everyone on set rapt and laughing, he continued, "What is this one? Is this number thirty-two? Do you get egg rolls with that?" Bawdy and brilliant.

In one episode, we decided we were going to have separate beds—twin beds, like Ricky and Lucy. Brad's character, Eddie, says, "Because you like it like the jungle, and I want my snacks, and the lamps need to be this way, and I don't want scented candles." Like a man and wife. (I sound like my mother . . . husband and wife.)

So then, in the last scene, we decided we missed each other. He emerged through the jungle of plants to my side of the room, to climb into my bed. My gentle giant. The hair and makeup department had given me this big furry . . . it's called a merkin, fake pubic hair. I had a bodysuit on, because I was supposed to be naked. I put this big thing where, ya know, it was anatomically appropriate. I surprised him, flashed him . . . four cameras rolling, the audience was all there, it was spectacularly funny, and we kept it in. It made the episode. People still come up to me and tell me how much they can relate to this show, often only having found it in syndication.

ele

Adoption Blessed Option

When I was in my early twenties, I saw the image of babies lined in trays on the nightly news. Untouched—no nursing, no cuddling, no holding. No bonding. The image reminded me of loaves of bread stacked up, awaiting baking—they were babies, tiny humans, left there. The fallout from a war I didn't know anything about. Where were the mothers of these children? Where was my mother? Onstage, on the road.

If I were a mother, I would . . . if I were *my* mother: "We should just take them all." The mere idea that she would "take them all." Where? On the road? To Disneyland? To the doctors' appointments? The zoo? To school? It came from an authentic, loving place, but it was absurd, ludicrous, that she would think she could, or that it was okay. What that actually would entail: Travel to a foreign country. "Select" your favorites (oh, wait, I forgot—she's gonna take them *all*). So now they all need visas, passports, shots, medical records—just to leave. No babies from Romania would cross our threshold, sadly. In the late nineties many people around me were adopting babies from China . . . girls!!!! The state of things there left unwanted female children without homes, and for a time, it was fairly easy to adopt these babies, even as single parents or same-sex couples. In the midst of all this, I thought: *Could this be a possibility for me?* I had not yet married or had a child of my own . . . I gave it some real consideration.

Not Out of Africa

In early August 2008, I got a humbling and awesome call to travel to Mozambique, Africa, to join the efforts of Save the Children. They hadn't done a fund-soliciting program for decades. So I was going to be the new Sally Struthers. Infuse the program with new blood. You remember them. The vintage ask, "If you give $28, a child in Africa will get to eat and have access to water, perhaps even an education." A resounding "Yes" to that. My children were old enough to be without me for a short while and I explained to them, just as Connie had to me, that we are so fortunate, and I wanted it to always be okay to share me with the world, if it meant giving back. And Daddy would hold down the fort while I was gone.

Save the Children graciously agreed to let me bring along a plus-one. I couldn't think of anyone better than Tricia Leigh. Knowing we could stand on that soil together and give each other a little pinch to say, "Look where we are." The journey was life changing. I met and spent time with incredible children, who just purely deserve a chance. I used the lens of my camera to document the trip, and eventually I curated an exhibition, with all proceeds going back to Save the Children.

Meanwhile, back at the ranch, everyone thought I was, for sure, going to bring home a baby, because that's what celebrities do, right?!

From the moment we touched down, I realized that the women of Africa don't want you to have their babies. They want you to enlighten, educate, empower—you know, all the *E*'s—and, yes, feed them. Help them assimilate back into society and raise their children, even though a whole generation of mothers has been devastated by loss from HIV/AIDS. Aunts and grandmothers, and sometimes even other children, are raising these children. The *Eyes of Hope* film completed, as well as the powerful journey with my sister and our friend Jane Berliner, talent manager and former CAA agent, I headed back to my family and to work, now locked and loaded in the fight against world poverty. I couldn't even have imagined the next few years and what they would bring.

So, no, I did not return home with a baby. Not long after I returned, however, a friend (my stand-in on *'Til Death*) brought her two boys to the set. Brain trust that I am, I knew these two beautiful ethnic boys weren't the biological children of my beautiful, redheaded, pale-skinned friend. We began a dialogue about adoption.

"Have you ever thought about it?" she said.

I said, "Yes, but I already have four children."

In a fantasy world that number would continue to grow.

"Well, if you ever do . . . the lady who I used as a facilitator is amazing. She gets calls from hospitals about babies either coming soon or born to mothers with no prenatal care who give up their children just after delivery."

My wheels started to turn . . . could this be something we would do? Can we afford it? Do we have the capacity to love a child who was born to someone else? Of course there are so many factors . . . Moments later, I got on the phone and called Nikki Biers of Best Gift Adoptions. We exchanged pleasantries and I got right to it: "Are there any babies right now?" Simmer down, Joely.

The next step was to create a letter to a potential birth mother . . . stating the case for us to be the selected family for their child. What a heady experience. You're not only putting down images of what your family looks like without their baby in it, but also you're auditioning your values and how you would choose to raise their baby. And you're proposing to shape a human being, which is a big, giant offer. You're asking them to judge the success of what you've already done—in our case, the children and the life we already had—so they'll feel comfortable letting us become everything to their child. Having given birth twice, I cannot imagine the pain of this decision, but I do find it a courageous option for someone who is not equipped to parent in that moment.

We were selected, only a week later, by a young woman of sixteen, an athlete, and her boyfriend, who were in love but too young and not ready. The baby, a boy, was due on October 29, my birthday . . . it was fate. Ultimately, a grandparent decided to raise the child, and we were given a moment to stop and think about what all this would really mean. It made us pause and reconsider everything. It was a weeklong flurry of questions and feelings: *Did we have the capacity to have our hearts broken again? Did we have the capacity to actually go forward and love someone else's child? Did we feel like this was a blessing? What would the ramifications be for our biological children? Were we really ready?* Okay . . . breathe . . .

Then, a call on Labor Day . . . ah the irony . . . and me without having to labor. Nikki said, "Can you get to South Central L.A. right now? There's a baby, a girl . . . teenage birth mom . . . go . . . I've already shown her your letter."

We were skeptical, but Chris stayed with the girls and I headed there. I arrived at the hospital and found my way to the Labor and Delivery floor. I had stopped briefly along the way to pick up a little gift, an offering. I don't even know what possessed me . . . she was a teenage girl. I brought magazines, gum, chocolate, I think even a candle. I was nervous. Did I imagine that any of this would make the relinquishing of a child she had carried for months any easier?

When I arrived at the room, the lights were down and the television was on . . . cartoons. In the bed sat a beautiful young black girl, sad and spent from the previous night's event. I handed over the goodies, and I reached out for her, one-cheeking it on the edge of the hospital bed. I held her for what seemed like a few minutes and rubbed her back . . . she cried a little. It dawned on me that I was older than her mother; that I was soothing her where her own mother wasn't. I was a surrogate comfort. I wanted to be everything for her, and yet I wanted to run from there, because the emotions in the room were so thick.

She recognized my face, kind of, not sure from what. After a brief time together, I asked if I could go to the nursery to see the baby.

"That's what you're here for, right?" she asked.

I promised to return. I found the nursery, downstairs and through security. They had been told of my arrival. I walked into a bright, pleasant room, and just ahead of me were two rows of plastic bassinets . . . probably fourteen or fifteen babies . . . noisy babies of all colors, except white. Then I spotted her . . . my little chocolate love drop, swaddled so tight she was unable to utter a sound. My little burrito.

I suited up in a gown, mask, and gloves, and cradled her in my arms. Besides the on-duty nurse, I was the first one to hold her. Mama had refused the bonding moment. We found each other. The nurse snapped a few cell phone pics, and I sent them to Chris. "What do you think? Should we do this?"

He said: "Come home, let's talk about it."

I knew that part of him was skeptical and not sure that he could be enough for her. But I was already in love. *It's not a car, or a puppy. It's a human being. She's beautiful and she needs us.*

I quickly tried to advance the home movies and see her in our lives.

Before venturing home, I stopped back in to see Mama . . .

She told me: "I want you to take her."

I knew she was mine.

She asked how she was. I told her beautiful.

She asked if I had taken a photo. I told her I had.

She asked to see her. I asked if that was really what she wanted.

She looked at my phone, as tears brimmed up in her eyes, and she said, "She looks like my other one."

In a nightlong deliberation, Chris and I made the only choice we could. We knew she was ours. We promised each other to love this child like our own and made the commitment to each other, and to her.

The following day, in a made-for-L.A. moment, I was scheduled to appear on *The Chelsea Handler Show*. I was still in full hair and makeup from the set. Chris and I raced to pick up our bundle. When we arrived at the hospital, standing out and getting stares, we headed to Mama's room first, for her to meet Chris . . . she was gone. She had discharged herself, so as not to incur the grief of having to say good-bye. We collected our daughter and left the hospital in shock, ready to do this baby thing all over again, brimming with excitement about introducing her to the rest of the family.

She didn't have a name for a couple of days . . . Everyone scrambled to help restock our house with newborn accoutrements . . . we needed everything . . . again. Carrie dusted off Billie's crib and a red double-decker bunk bed for big sisters. A new car seat was purchased. We invited everyone over to see the new addition to the tribe, as we were still wrapping our minds around a fifth child. My body seemed to know what to do. Even though I had not given birth to her, I received the golden nectar of the gods . . . colostrum. She was clearly ours. We would call her Olivia Luna. And ten months later, we would make our commitment official—and legal—before the court, and family and friends.

As fate would have it, in an incredible twist of the plot, *'Til*

Death, which had been picked up to the tune of an additional two seasons, was abruptly canceled and pulled from the Fox schedule.

Historically, this would have meant a bit of downtime . . . and think of all that great parenting I would be doing. But now we had five children, a rogue business manager, and multiple mortgages.

This period of time, I'm not even sure "blue" describes. Blue is one of my favorite colors. It was dark. I was bruised, injured. Black and blue. Right about now, I was wishing Lexapro came in a patch, so it could be time-released and constantly distributed into my bloodstream. In lieu of that I did my best *Walking Dead* impression, backwards, in high heels—I am an actress, after all—got the children to school, waving to the skinny mommies in big Escalades from behind my sunglasses and fake smile; numbly handed off my infant daughter to her baby nurse, Joanne. (Thank God she was there.) And climbed back into my bed, in a darkened room, for a midmorning sulk. Then pulled it all together long enough to receive my girls back into my arms, masking my pain of grief and loss and existential crisis. My commitment to being there, present, around a dinner table with them was absolute, so I Stepford Wifed it, trying to take in the day's events, delivered to me by their joyful faces. Thankfully they were young and I could shield them, making sure they knew this would never be their burden. Mom was going to get her shit together and we would be okay. And I did. And we are. But it would take me years to climb out and repair.

I was told by a wise woman, Gurmukh, a yogi and inspiration to a lot of celebrity mamas and other women in L.A., babies come with their "baskets," meaning a child comes to you with gifts. Sometimes they aren't a picnic.

I absolutely adore my children—they are everything. The best of times and the worst of times. They are all so different. Different sections of my heart, running around outside my body. I am now acutely aware, having children of my own, how Debbie and Connie became like lionesses with their cubs and did whatever necessary, by whatever means possible, to provide and "surthrive."

I am still learning, however. And shielding them from the pain has been of utmost consideration. How can you explain to a child that Mommy doesn't have a job? Or when someone has stolen everything? You can't. You don't. You put on a brave show, as our mothers did, and press through the darkness every day.

My children came to me at various stages in my life. During ebbs and flows of a marriage. And peaks and valleys of a career. I have tried to be a constant, while constantly challenged to be a person, an artist, a wife. Again, my career is evolving, and I am taking on the role of director and picking up the pieces from a tragic few years. I want my wildly enthusiastic, imaginative girls to evolve into soulful women who find passion and purpose inside themselves. I want them to love with abandon—first loving themselves. I want them to dream in a world that is inclusive, to pick up Mommy's passion for activism and Big Auntie's light saber. I love that they love *Hamilton* and *Dear Evan Hansen,* and ask Alexa to play the soundtracks while we cook and sing at the top of our lungs (the melodies and lyrics move them).

I want them to giggle at inappropriate times and to champion the underdog. I want them to be confident enough to carry a little weight, but not the weight of the world, that's my job. I got this. I got you. I want my daughters to know I will always be cheering wildly from the wings . . . if they choose the stage or a desk. I want them to linger at dinner tables. Put down their phones. Treat family like friends and friends like family. I want them to party and dance and be silly. To make excellent choices, and to keep secrets and promises, always.

Connie asks me: "Do they love their nana?"

Do you love your nana?

Does anyone love me?

Why doesn't anyone love me?

Can anyone love me?

Will anyone remember me when I'm gone?

So many questions—demanding so much of my little girls.

This is the legacy of this family—these women who came before us, and this job I have chosen for myself. I want my girls to find their own way to be a part of this legacy. I want them to be enamored of their grandmothers and aunties but not to be without their own opinions about what is good and what makes them feel good. I want my children to be seekers, explorers, and to have the same thirst for righteousness and truth that I was given. I want them to sing harmony with me.

Chapter 13

Blind Trust

BLIND TRUST. C'MON, YOU ALL know what that is, because it's been thrown out on the daily since the election of the misogynistic, racist, narcissistic disaster of titanic proportions that is Trump. Sure, this is something above most of our pay grade. I didn't know what the words "blind trust" meant, either, until recently. I mean in legal, banking terms, anyway.

I always just trusted blindly—that's a family trait, too.

I come from a long line of gamblers. We like blackjack, gin, backgammon, the ponies, and unmitigated risk when it comes to flying by the seat of our Calvin Kleins. It's a conundrum when you think about where my fancy parental types were from originally—the streets of South Philly and Brooklyn, and the wilds of Texas. The very idea that these humans, coming from next to nothing, would make and lose fortunes time and again boggles the mind. Someone must have stepped in dinosaur shit lifetimes ago, paying the karmic price that created the atmosphere for these talented souls to prosper.

And prosper they have, which has afforded them to set themselves up for some fairly phenomenal fails. That's how I ended up here, in this back room, adjacent to the Crate & Barrel, with cameras everywhere. I know a guy . . . he knows a guy . . . actually it's not really that shady. Lots of women in the Hills of Beverly do it. Everyone is doing it. That's not entirely true. Sometimes it's because they are bored with their baubles. "Bored with my baubles"—that has a *ring* to it. These bored ladies are the lucky ones, who get to play princess pawnshop. On the other hand, sometimes there's trouble: right here we got trouble, with a capital *T* that rhymes with *P*, that stands for Poor.

In our case, we had to raise the monies, *this week,* to cover the seventy-four thousand dollars in mortgages—for Delfern, Cherokee, the Robertson Building, and the properties in Jackson Hole and Puerto Vallarta—that were due. And so, with my mom's permission, I loaded up all the "good stuff"—the emeralds, the sapphires, the rubies, the diamonds—the rocks—all the stuff my mother had absolutely adored and absolutely overpaid for. And there I sat, with my big satchel filled with the beautiful leather boxes housing her exquisite jewelry.

My mom and Tricia were out of town, doing a play. Last month, when we'd had to cover the seventy-four thousand dollars in mortgage payments, we'd borrowed the money from five dear friends. Most of us can't say, "Can I borrow seventy-four thousand dollars?" We were lucky enough to be able to say, "Can I borrow ten thousand dollars? And I'll have it back to you within two to four weeks." Once again, thank God for our angels.

It was embarrassing, and humbling, but the payments had to be made. It hadn't always been like this—when she'd first taken on these mortgages, she'd been more than flush, thanks to her Forever Spring money. But then, for the past couple years, there just wasn't the same money coming in. We'd sold the New York apartment first—more than tripling the money she'd paid for it; a smart investment by Connie—which had kept us financially afloat. But it had also given my mom the illusion she was back in the chips again, and that she could spend. And that she did! When I'd been working, I'd sometimes covered the mortgages until my mom could give me the money back—how could I say no to someone who had given me so much? And so we'd hobbled along, until now, with my syndication money drying up, we were fucked. And the reality is, you're not allowed to have all that stuff if you can't pay for it—that's how Tricia and I felt about it, anyhow. It sucked. But we'd lived to tell the tale. Now, the bills were coming due again, and I was the only one in town to deal with it. So I'd taken some of my mom's jewelry to the guy in Beverly Hills.

The way it works is he will either pay you for your "goods," or you will take out a very high-interest loan and leave your stuff, like a fancy pawnshop, in hopes that one day you can go retrieve your gems. They clearly knew who I was. They knew whose fucking jewelry this was I was looking to hock. That just added to the feeling of vulnerability—now the whispering would begin: Connie's in trouble.

If the sparkly pile would have fetched enough money, I might have sold it, but as the guy pulled out his jeweler's loupe and presented me with his lowball offer, I balked. I quickly shoved it all back in my goody bag—and, with my tennis bracelet between my legs, ran out the door. An alternate solution had to be found, and it would have to be just in the nick of time.

I was happy to help my mom out. We'd always kind of pooled our resources in that way (mostly her resources). If I couldn't pay, I always knew my mom would help me out. And that wasn't a manipulation of her generosity. It was the way she thought about money. My mom always said, "You're never going to want for anything." And she always made sure that if my sister and I didn't work much in a year, in this topsy-turvy industry, she would help us. I always knew I could count on her. In fact, I *still* know if I need anything, she'll be there. My mom handed me a hundred-dollar bill yesterday.

"If I have it, you have it," she always says.

For her survival, and her psyche, and her sense of herself, she has to be the person who pays for everything, that person who has that control. It's almost like there's this need to spend, to not look at price tags, to say, "I need some beautiful things to wear." Never mind the rooms and rooms full of beautiful things she'd "needed" in the past, and then never wore. It's almost like it's really more about a need to spend money, to fill holes (much in the same way that members of my family have filled holes with work, with drinking, with drugs). Most people don't have that luxury, and so they find another way to feel good. Some people even put money in the bank and save it for a rainy day (can you imagine?!)—but we were raised to think that if you were working and you got your paycheck, it was time for "shopping." (Sung in the soprano range.) Sometimes Mom even pulled Tricia and me out of school for the day to go shopping with her. Everybody gets an Easter basket. Everybody gets pajamas on Valentine's Day. Every holiday is celebrated with special goodies and treats. It's a tradition. In this family, we have the tendency to treat our money like this, until the time when we can't afford to do so anymore. And then what?

Forever Spring

There comes a time when you have to reinvent yourself in our business. By the 1980s, Mom had gone a little bit out of vogue and wasn't getting the same number of gigs as she had before, and a friend of hers brought her a skin-care line.

"We want to put your name on these products," the friend said.

"Well, if I'm going to put my name on products, they have to be products I use," Connie said. "I want to be involved completely. Let's start from scratch."

Whatever you can do, she can do better. She does like control, not just in her finances—in all areas of her life. But also, she cared about her integrity. She felt like, if you have great skin, and you're talking about skin products, you want to honestly be able to say that you use the products, and you believe in the products, and they work for you.

So she started to experiment with of-the-moment ingredients. We went with her to visit the labs and choose the smells.

"How much ground apricot pit should be in this? Is there enough emollience in the Super Rich Cream? Should the Baby Soft Facial Clay be baby blue or pale green?"

We tested out how the products felt and how they worked (we were the guinea pigs—no animals were used for testing this line). And then we were enlisted to help come up with clever names. Evoking the idea of eternal youth, the line was called Forever Spring (which for twenty-five years inspired my naughty sense of humor—I felt it evoked a perpetual douche, like Summer's Eve, always—but Forever Spring it was). It became not only Connie's livelihood but also her focus. She was still doing guest star television spots and her nightclub act, from here to Atlantic City, but not as frequently, and her career—and her passion—transitioned to this company.

Connie made a lucrative deal at the Home Shopping Network, under the advisement of her manager at the time, Norton Styne, son of legendary composer Jule Styne, and father of my friend and first husband, David Styne (we were six), and George Simone, an ex-lover of hers, who's still huge in the skin-care business at the HSN. This would later create problems, when these two men *claimed* they were full partners in the venture and that my mom had promised them that they would participate as full partners in this company, in perpetuity. She hadn't.

But for a time, it was fantastic. They traveled to Tampa, Florida, once a month, to the Home Shopping Network, and Mom would go on the air and sell the shit out of Forever Spring. The cornerstone of the line was the Time Machine, which worked with negative-positive ions to exercise the muscle underneath the skin. It looks like a vibrator, I swear to God. (This device is NEVER to be used anywhere but the face.) But no one has ever seemed to mind. Connie owns the patent.

Up until now there was a stigma attached to celebrities hawking anything. It meant you weren't working and had to resort to selling your wares. Only a few had been successful at it. This was the beginning of celebrities embracing the Home Shopping Network craze. As far as I can remember, it was Cher, Joan Rivers, Suzanne Somers, Jane Fonda, and my mom. That was it. And my mom was so great at it. Here she was, this natural, radiant beauty, promising viewers that her skin-care line could give them the same results. And she really made them believe. Her ability to connect, and to sell, was miraculous.

On occasion, I went with her to Tampa. Or when we stayed behind at home, we'd watch her on TV, and it was incredible to follow along with the ticker that blared with how many of each item she'd sold. She had the gift. She really did. She looked gorgeous but relatable. She talked to the women who were her customers as though they were her girlfriends.

"You know, when you go to bed with your man, you don't

want to have all those heavy creams on your face," she'd say. "I've selected the finest ingredients. It's all very light and clean smelling. Girls, you're going to love it!"

That's the thing about television that's different from film: there's a way to lean in toward the viewers at home and make them feel close to you. I think that's why she connected, and why so many of those ladies still buy her products today. Many are now living on a fixed income, but they're still her fans, and they're still loyal customers. And the products *are* great.

So she mobilized her fan base across America, and soon enough, the line consisted of many more products. She loved the feeling of success and of being a *Forbes* 500 woman. I think it even said on the cover of some business publication that she was up there with these major CEOs, and she was very proud of that. She loved buying real estate and feeling like a mover and a shaker. The company's profits afforded us the luxury of purchasing our homes in Jackson Hole and Mexico, and a beautiful Manhattan apartment. And for her to be generous to everybody in our extended family. During her best years, she was the top-earning woman in that business.

Not that her new career wasn't without its bumps. She resented that it wasn't show business. I heard her say on more than one occasion, "I'm not going to die *the cream lady.*" At the same time, she had this feeling that it wasn't ever going to stop. And that made her arrogant about her success. She received a big offer from Revlon to buy her out while staying on as the CEO and figurehead. They were going to put her products in every department store, and in Sephora.

"Well, if Revlon can do it, I'll do it myself," Connie said.

She parted ways with the Home Shopping Network, and her "partners"—all the people who had been involved from the start—as they were demanding unsubstantiated percentages, in perpetuity. She retooled the line, bought a building on Robertson, and created a spa, the Garden Sanctuary, where the products could be used and sold.

From there, the empire started to crumble. My mom still wanted to direct films and remain vital in her original industry. She should have let someone else take over Forever Spring, so she could return to her creative pursuits. Instead, she used her own money to get back into showbiz, eventually financing a movie inspired by events from her own life, which she directed. Her attention was divided. Business began to suffer. I knew we weren't going to be able to sustain all this real estate and extravagance. And it frightened me, bringing me back to that same little girl I'd been, who came home in her Catholic school uniform and heard the word "foreclosure."

Eddie Jack

When Harry met Sally—wait, I mean when Connie met Eddie, she met her match (at least in how they viewed their moola). They played gin together for hours, owing each other money, back and forth. And let's face it—their line of work often took them to palaces of temptation. Eddie couldn't pass a green felt table without slamming down some chips. On one occasion, he forfeited his entire paycheck for his week's stint at the Sands. He was up, he was down, in the end he lost in one sitting $750,000. But you can't win if you don't play. The addict always has a line to spin in his defense—you either play the line or do a line. For years, Eddie did both.

Connie was the only one of Eddie's ex-wives who didn't trash-talk him. She never really talked much about him at all, but there were a few stories that regularly appeared in her repertoire. She often, with the same incredulous tone, told the tale of the time she and Eddie were getting out of a cab in New York City, and he was wearing a pair of expensive diamond-and-sapphire cuff links she'd given him. A fan admired them, and Eddie gave them away to his fan, on the spot. My mom couldn't believe it (well, she could *believe* it, she just couldn't get over it)—how frivolous and hurtful Eddie could be, or maybe she saw herself in the gesture. Because that was so him (so them, really): the generosity, the impulsiveness, and the easy-come, easy-go approach to life.

Eddie did love to shower his women with presents. He gave great jewelry. He prided himself on his hundreds of handmade silk suits. (He couldn't eat just one.) He liked to collect wives (an expensive habit, but I would venture to guess he never paid any of his exes alimony—or child support). Like my mom, he loved to give me hundred-dollar bills. They both sure loved their hundies.

He behaved this way when he was at the height of his success, and as I saw firsthand, he exhibited just the same largesse even when decades of addiction and the irresponsible, hedonistic behavior it encouraged had left him without gigs or, literally, a voice. He just couldn't anticipate—or imagine—not being a star, not being the top-earning nightclub act in Vegas, not working at all. Neither could Connie. They had that in common, too.

Do as I Say, Not as I Do

It doesn't take much rumination on the building of fortunes, and the spending habits, and the lack of financial discipline of the generation that came before me, to see *now* that a trail had been blazed for my own financial misadventures. But back in 2008, before the lessons had been completely doled out, it seemed like nothing could go wrong. The show on which I starred opposite Brad Garrett, *'Til Death*, had just been picked up for two seasons, in order to go into syndication—that rarefied situation all actors hope for. After which, the idea is, you're set. In other words, things were going incredibly well in my career.

And then I found the house of our dreams—one that was closer to my mother and sisters, and large enough to accommodate our family, which now included my stepsons, who had decided to live with us. Following in Connie's family tradition of everyone always being welcome, and wanting my amazing blended family to have an influence on each other, I took the plunge. I bought the new house without selling our first home, as we just knew its sale was imminent. And because *'Til Death* had been renewed for two seasons, I was sure it would continue, which supported the idea of taking this risk.

Life was running at full throttle. Five kids, two houses, and suddenly, when *'Til Death* was canceled in the middle of a season—no job. Because I'd been committed to a show already, I'd missed the opportunity to go out on any auditions during pilot season. But I wasn't worried. Historically, my reps had always said: "Joely is without a job for like six and a half minutes." So I felt sure the next thing would come along, and soon.

Well, it didn't.

Around this time, I was entering my forties, and as so many actresses have publicly discussed, I found the abundance of roles was no longer there for me. So I took the work I could get. I'd had regular TV work for the past seven years, so we'd be all right. Well, except for the fact that I paid two mortgages for two years—that killed me.

Like most people in my family (and Hollywood), I had a business manager. The same woman had been handling my accounting for the past twenty-five years. Because I never saw my bills firsthand, but I saw money go in and out of my accounts, I assumed everything was getting paid. And then, I came home one day and found a notice on my door, saying my gas was getting turned off. *What do you mean my fucking gas is being turned off?! Why is the gas bill not paid?!* When I called my business manager and told her, she had a ready reply: "Oh, I paid that."

When I called to tell her that six more bottles of Arrowhead water had arrived on our doorstep, when we'd told her not to have it delivered anymore, she was adamant:

"Oh, we canceled that. Didn't we? I'll look into it."

"Yeah, well, it's gone to collections," I said. "What's going on here?"

"What do you mean, what's going on?" she said. "I'll fix it."

For someone who had communicated with me often and well, she started to seem surprisingly distant. When we would ask for copies of statements, our calls went unreturned. But after so many years of loyal service, she had earned my trust, and I dismissed any misgivings.

Blind . . . trust?

Great news. I was going to be in every movie theater, during the previews, in an ad for Fandango, and I was due a nice-size payment for that work. At a time when the work wasn't really flowing, I would need this money to cover my major bills. Payment was being held up, and I had to get to the bottom of why. My business manager, whom I'd trusted for decades to guide me and to help me to navigate my financial life (and my family's financial life), continued to deny anything was amiss.

And yet:

"Hey, that commercial is wanting to pay you," my agent said. "But your corporation's been suspended."

"What does that mean?" I asked.

"I guess it has something to do with your taxes."

"That's weird, let me check on that."

Anxiety sets in.

So, once again, I called my business manager. And once again, I was met with avoidance, lies, and enough bullshit to make me really start to worry.

Then my husband, Chris, had reason for concern as well.

"My wages are being garnished," he told her. "Why is that?"

"Oh, I'll look into that," she said.

Yes, please do look into it—everything is at stake.

Months prior, she had given me the financial go-ahead to lease an expensive car. So I assumed we were in the money, as we had been during my past decade of regular, high-paying, leading roles on network TV shows.

Then I fielded a call on my cell phone that would have normally gone to my business manager.

"You're in default on your mortgage," the man said.

What?!

"Let me get you a payment right away," I said, obviously concerned.

He sort of laughed.

"You owe five payments," he said.

What the FUCK?!

As happened so often during the mortgage crisis, our loan had been bought up as part of a bundle by a private banking entity in Boston. The head of this entity didn't have any other properties in California, so I got to know him, and for a moment, he was sympathetic to my situation. But that didn't change the fact that we owed him a shit ton of money . . . which we shouldn't have.

Understandably, I was *freaking out*. Two friends, who happened to be a business manager and a banker, gave me an idea of how to catch my current business manager in a lie. The private banker had offered to sell us the mortgage at a reduced rate, but we had to provide him with our past five years of tax documents.

So I became a forensic accountant. G.I. Joely, I called myself. And why not?

What I found gobsmacked me.

But first . . . Why didn't I know any better? Why didn't I learn?

Like I said, my family had a long history of business managers—and their duplicity. Forty years earlier, when I was a young girl and my mom was grieving the loss of her father, she started receiving bills that made no sense to her. Her business manager had invested Connie's money in an athletic clothing line and had also charged her other clients' bills to my mother. It would take her years to recover as well.

It has also been recorded publicly that something similar had happened to Debbie, although in her case, her husband was the culprit (no, not Eddie—he just left her heartbroken; it was her second husband, Harry Karl, who left her three million dollars in debt). I can't say I personally watched it happen; I can only comment on what was documented in the news.

But, certainly, I had grown up with the knowledge that even those people we trust the most—especially those people we trust the most—can do us grave harm, if we're not careful. So why hadn't I been more careful?

Sure, my business manager had been recommended to Tricia by the record label she signed with in her twenties. So it seemed like she was a reputable accountant. By the time of her betrayal, she hadn't managed Tricia's money in years. But she had been managing mine for twenty-five years—and, as I now realized, doing so poorly, one might even say recklessly. Most recently, she'd told me, yes, I could buy that dream house, even before our first house sold. She had given us the go-ahead to fly 150 friends and family members to Mexico to celebrate our tenth wedding anniversary. And, well, yeah, there was the Maserati. She had become closer to me, perhaps, than an employee should. But who can say? In this business, in any business I'm in, really, I prefer to work with people who I value as if they were family members. That's how I always saw it done, growing up. There's just that little matter of the blind trust I also give them . . . gave them . . . believe me, this is not a mistake I'm going to make again.

Get ready, here's the kicker—there's more . . . I asked her for the five years of statements I needed to refinance my house. And I kept asking . . . and they kept not arriving. By this point, it was clear that she was double-talking, and backpedaling, and all the stuff you absolutely don't want to find your business manager doing to you. And obviously we were starting to catch her in a web of lies.

"So the bank said they need the physical copies of the tax returns," I told her.

"Oh, okay. Let me get those together for you," she said.

I went to see her and pick them up, and she handed me an envelope.

"Here," she said. "Do you want me to walk these in?"

"What do you mean . . . walk them in?"

"Do you want me to file these?"

"Are they filed or are they not filed?"

"No . . . they're filed," she said. "I'm just saying I can send them in."

Now she was totally caught.

"No," I said. I grabbed them out of her hand, and I took them with me to give to the people I'd hired to help me excavate my finances.

It got worse.

She hadn't filed my taxes in five years—not just not *paid* them, but not filed them.

She was at the very least a shitty business manager, and at the very worst a liar, who stole from me and abused my trust. It was a violation of epic proportions. It was like having things taken from my children—not just *like,* actually—she *had* taken things from my children. For the past twenty-plus years, I had worked hard and made a very good living, and assumed the whole time that money was being saved—that my family was provided for. And now, in an instant, that security was taken from me. Sure, I was frustrated that I had been blindsided so completely. But this mammoth betrayal was about so much more than money—I'd always been the observer, the one who could read others so well, and I'd been fooled. It would lead me to an existential crisis of the greatest magnitude—I'd heard so many of these types of stories over the years, and never believed this woman would do that to me. And yet, she had. How had this happened?

I'd been raised in a family where no one ever looked at price tags. I didn't think twice about ordering lavish meals, and treating people to dinner. I gave generously to anyone who asked. I was sheltered. My mom had had her financial issues over the years but had always seemed to rebound from them. The same with Debbie. The same with Carrie. The same with all the women in the family.

It was a dramatic lesson for me. I went from somebody who'd never had a problem with money, other than loving to spend it on everyone, to suddenly having nothing, and worrying about how I was going to put gas in my car. And Connie, who'd always told me if she had it, I had it, didn't have it right now. So I couldn't go to her. I did my best to keep up appearances—it always "appeared" as though we were flush during this crisis, but we just weren't. We struggled for seven years, and we still, to a degree, are struggling. Rebuilding all of that credit. Trying to figure out how we're going to pay everything off all the time. Then there's the emotional aspect of it, which carries through to today. It's like getting out of a bad relationship and knowing I'm never going to let anyone do that to me again. But also fearing, somewhere deep inside, that there's something within me that allowed it to happen, and worrying . . . well, *could* it happen again? *No* . . . but even so, how to rebuild?

ele

The People Who Don't Look at Price Tags

In the aftermath of financial devastation, I had to take certain steps to start getting myself back on my feet. We sold our dream home in Sherman Oaks for what we'd paid for it. And before we moved out, we had an estate sale. I purposely didn't go over to the house on the day of the sale.

Imagine people walking through your home, pawing through your precious belongings (and, well, yes, you did invite them to do so, but that knowledge doesn't really make it feel any better), picking up stuff, examining it with a disinterested air.

"I'd pay ten bucks for that," they say.

You can't go: "Well, I paid three thousand for it."

'Cause you're stupid if you paid three thousand dollars for it.

But you did. And now . . . okay, I'll take the ten dollars.

That's how my mom's always been with regard to her own belongings.

"Do you know what I paid for that?" she asked.

"Yep, I do. A lot. Too much."

It was then that I realized that I was more like my mother than I cared to admit—we were the people who never looked at price tags. Well, it took forty-nine years, but I look at every price tag now. I comparison shop. I've couponed. I'm not asking for a medal for that (saving a buck is saving a buck, and my kids always had a blast when we'd sit around watching *Extreme Couponing* and clipping our own). But I know the reality of losing your health insurance, and doing a financial negotiation between what's on the grocery list and paying the utility bills. Again, not saying I should be sainted for this.

ele

Celebrity Lap Dance

Leave it to Carrie to find the funny in all this. Yes, like a true Fisher, she also purchased a lot of *stuff*—I went into a store the other day, and they still had items on hold for her. And she probably wasn't that responsible with her money (I'm really in no position to say—I just observed what she showed us, as we all did). She was hilariously, movingly frank about what she called her "celebrity lap dances"—the many fan conventions she attended to sign autographs in exchange for money she really needed. But she grew to thrive on this, and came to love the one-on-one with her fans, and was the last one to leave the auditorium at each one.

I've been there. It starts off as a need for cash. As I've said, in this business, we never know when our next job is. That's how we find ourselves at the autograph shows, the conventions, the "celebrity lap dances." Sure, it could feel a little shameful. Standing behind a table of glossy photos from the various roles we inhabited over the years. Or in Carrie's case, a role she inhabited for *decades*. Grappling with the fact that our signature on said photo is worth enough to the person standing across from us, that they've actually gotten in their car and driven down here, or even flown here, and plunked down their hard-earned cash in exchange for this "honor." The ultimate autograph show is one called Chiller in New Jersey—people travel from all over the country to attend. I've never been.

However they may feel at first, these cash-yielding fans, these conventions, become like a drug. You are meeting, touching, and selfie-ing with the *people*—the people who watch and admire you, who crush on you, who, these days, google you. And tweet you . . . if you're lucky. "Likes" have become currency. There used to be a stigma—you only did them when you couldn't get a job—I mean you were in between jobs—wink wink. But now, they're the new normal. Why wouldn't you do them if you can? It does remind you that you meant something to someone, made them laugh, moved them, so they'll pay money to meet you, which is a pretty fucking great thing on a day when you're maybe questioning your value.

ee

Hologram Butterflies

We Fisher gals love us a tchotchke. If it sparkles, or lights up, or is adorned with a badass catchphrase—all the better. Carrie was in a position to indulge her tastes, and she did. I can remember her coveting these super-expensive hologram butterflies for the wall of her house.

Apparently, she wrote an article for *Esquire,* and she had a direct, immediate instinct.

"I'm getting the butterflies now," she said.

And she did.

They all did that. *We* all did that. Like my parents before me, when I was doing a long-running series, I assumed it would go on forever. That's what the evidence suggested. Every time one ended, I'd get another show. So I spent money—on the splurgey stuff. Much as I'd seen Connie do. As I'd seen Carrie do. I couldn't buy a fabulous Gucci purse without getting one for Connie, and Tricia, too. I once had a manager say: "You'd better keep working, because you're the kind of girl who likes to drop three hundred dollars in one lap around a candle store."

Yes, and two-thirds of those candles went to Connie and Tricia.

That's how I was raised.

With my mom passing the credit card to her boyfriend under the table, so it could look like he was the great provider, the man who picked up the check for everyone. While she was always picking up the check. As I enjoyed doing during the years I could. Like when Chris and I treated our families and friends to that luxury trip to Mexico, the "Mexican Love Jam," to celebrate our tenth wedding anniversary and the renewal of our vows. Because we could.

But, honestly, most of the money did get spent on stuff—lots of which was given away. Carrie did this. Eddie did this. From his brownstone on Seventy-Fourth Street to his beautiful San Francisco apartment with a view of Alcatraz, he was always handing you stuff.

"Here, you have to have this," he'd say as he handed me a green jade horse sculpture. "I want you to take these," he'd say as he insisted I take his vinyl records.

The urge was very recognizable in Carrie, because she had so many beautiful objets d'art. She did the same thing, padding around her house, handing out her stuff.

"You'll love this!" she'd say, handing over a sexy Princess Leia collectible.

I walked into her house a year ago and found Carrie on her elliptical. She got off, lit a cigarette, got her Diet Coke, went straight to her closet. Then she gave me this gorgeous Morgane Le Fay top.

She made up a little song and dance as she wrapped me in it: "If you're not gonna wear it, give it back, 'cause it was expensive."

But I knew she didn't really want it back. She wanted to *give*. And I wanted it . . . I wear it.

After that same visit, my daughter Luna showed me this little ceramic dog.

"Big Auntie gave this to me," she said.

Maybe people do this in place of giving you their actual attention or time. Not that gifts aren't appreciated. But it's a strange dichotomy, for the people in this family, how they value things the way they do, and fill up their spaces, and their souls, with material things. And yet, there are very few things they wouldn't give away. It's almost like an obsessive-compulsive generosity—OCG. Look, I've diagnosed it. Maybe if they give it away, they can get more. Get back to the feeling of getting. Me, I'm just trying to get back to the feeling of being at peace.

"What are you up to now? What's up next for you?" people ask me at the conventions, in interviews, at the grocery store.

Well, I don't know, Oprah . . . or average Joe . . . I'm just trying to keep my shit together and survive another day. I'm just trying to get a job. And I will. Because I'm talented. And we are resilient. We costume up for our children, so they can take dance classes. Go to Disneyland. Eat dinner. Our DNA makes us resilient. We may be black belt in rock bottom, but we are hall of fame in second acts, as the femme fatales in this family have proven—we even outdo our previous success with our reinventions. Just as my mom pivoted from actress and singer to skin-care maven to director; and Carrie remade herself again and again—Princess Leia to bestselling author and back again; I have successfully launched a new career as a director. Even better, I've got the advantage of all the lessons that have come before me—and been forced on me—and I now enter into all of my ventures with 20/20 vision, and only give my trust where it's earned. And now, hopefully, I can protect my children from the shrapnel, while imparting to them the wisdom that was gained from losing—about the value of a dollar, about the power of reinvention, about what really matters in life.

So, I've done the hokey pokey. I've turned myself around. And I've got a great pitch—a show called *Celebrity Hoarders*. Dr. Drew and I can come in and help you to simplify your life—you don't need all those self-help books you've never read, or those ceramic owls you got on sale. I know, I know, one man's trash is another man's treasure, but really, it's time to take out the trash. And let me tell you, it will feel good. Believe me. I've had enough estate sales and slashed my own price tags enough times that I can tell you this: the people in my life mean more to me than my pineapple collection.

Chapter 14

Come Fly with Me

THE AIR IS DIFFERENT UP here. There are no calories. You can fart without hesitation. The flight attendants are always sweet—the gay male ones particularly appreciate my work and offer me champagne and coloring books, and on occasion I'm brought up to the cockpit. There is a low vibrating hum—the sound of the silver bird barreling through the sky, high above the earth's surface—this frightens me. How does this giant, heavy metal cocoon stay in the air? Carrying families, lovers, businessmen, showbiz folks, and on occasion, a terrorist. No matter, I step on with my right foot, consume the complimentary beverage and a courage pill, chat up my neighbor in 2C, and pray. I do a little creative visualization . . . I envision myself at my destination. Am I on the beach? Am I on a set? Have I returned home? Whatever the case, I picture the location, the temperature, the reason, the people around me—creative, right? Whatever gets you there.

My fear of flying started at a very young age—ironically, given that my only ever in-flight emergency was on descent, it is takeoff that sends me into full-blown panic. A friend, actress Vicki Lewis, once told me to count to thirteen—her father was an air traffic controller. Not that nothing bad happens at fourteen . . . but it gets me to ten thousand feet, where I let down my hair and my guard.

At eight years old, I was shaken to my core, and so began my ritual of in-flight fear and panic. It was flight 83 from New

Orleans to LAX—the airline TWA, remember them?! We were en route home from one of Mom's gigs—band in the back! Imagine—it was on initial descent that the flight crew discovered the faulty landing gear—the cabin bustling with flight attendants—"stewardesses" at the time—all females in tight-fitting, short skirts and a smile. The smiles had faded as they approached my mother and tagged her personal belongings. *Why, you ask?* To prepare for a crash landing.

It was the seventies. Connie was at the height of her popularity. The captain sent the ladies back again to Ms. Connie and asked if she would like Tricia and me to be seated with two able-bodied men, in anticipation of impact. *Holy shit.*

"Well, yes," she said. "If that's what he suggests."

We were seated with two large men as we circled LAX. A new plan was devised. We would fly straight up in the air and try to force the landing gear down. We did this—still nothing. The last resort—they would foam runway niner, and we would slide in on the belly of the aircraft. It *almost* sounded fun. When this was decided, the now not-at-all-smiling young lady who had thought this job would be glamorous came back with grave news: "Miss Stevens, the captain would like your daughters to be seated with you. For . . . identification purposes." FOR IDENTIFICATION PURPOSES. Now you understand why I self-medicate, even though we made a safe 'n' soft landing that time.

YOU CAN'T ALWAYS get *where* you want—but if you board sometimes . . . So, over the years, we (the witches of the Fisher-Stevens coven) have listened to our instincts about air travel. I imagine the Princess shuffling through immigration, modern-day security checks that sometimes allow for the infamous to cut the lines and hold on to their computers and their shoes. The TSA acknowledgment of a shared love of all things *Star Wars* or *Ellen* or *Oprah* or whatever, and you are herded to a less-populated line, or a private pat-down if you're feeling frisky. Security cleared—check. Now Duty Free is screaming the Fisher name. We are beckoned by the glitter and smells of the brightly lit pedestals on which lifesaving fragrances are displayed "freely." Is it not our "duty" to liberate them from this hostile environment and shove yet another gift for our girls into the already-stuffed carry-on that will not fit into the allotted space overhead or at our feet?

Remember a time when air travel was sexy? When travel attire was planned and perhaps you connected with 16B . . . You shared your innermost thoughts and fears . . . you laughed, you cried . . . you had too many Bloody Marys and then tried the merlot with a Dave from Des Moines. The youthful exuberance of the soccer team traveling to compete in nationals, and the single mother traveling with a colicky baby for the first time . . . none of this really bothered you because a summer abroad awaited a nubile young collegian with dreams and an American Express card from Mommy.

His name was Danny B. . . . he worked at the Pan Am counter at LAX. I would sidle up to the gate and hand him my boarding pass for that prepurchased coach seat on the red-eye. And he'd slyly pass off a first-class seat, if the "load" was light. On a transpacific flight. After competing for the affections of one David K. on the shores of Kaanapali, we holiday vacationers crammed thirteen people, including Lawrence and Gregory, the Zarian twins, into a tiny aircraft lavatory in order to break the record, much to the dismay of stewardesses dressed in island garb yearning for the safety of touchdown on the mainland. The humorous attempts at going mile high with lovers and other famous strangers. A nine-hour layover in the Johannesburg airport, hours circling Singapore, ten hours on the tarmac, forever-lost Louis Vuitton luggage on the way to embark on my freshman year of college, harrowing private flights to Jackson Hole with Don Felder of the Eagles and a suckling newborn, hilarious misadventures on the Fox jet to the Super Bowl with Jennifer Morrison, ending with a heated game of five-card stud for gum wrappers with James L. Brooks and dear friend Missy Halperin . . . Julio Iglesias cross-country adventures in the private G5 jet . . . a wing struck by lightning and frightening turbulence ripping the door off the puddle jumper. . . that time I was mistaken for a drug mule and strip-searched in Toronto . . . a midair refueling of the Bob Hope C141 plane over the Indian Ocean . . . buzzing the tower just like in *Top Gun* . . . landing in the most exotic locales . . . standing in the upper deck of Virgin's upper class with none other than Tom Jones, dishing satirically that what goes up must come down . . . that year Mariska and Stephanie T. and I were flown in on Donald Trump's jet as eye candy for his fiftieth birthday in Atlantic City . . . caught by those around me as my daughter asked for her airplane medicine . . . and the reminder from the captain of United flight 67 that he had escorted me around an aircraft carrier in the Persian Gulf . . . the familiar smell of jet fuel . . . vodka and tomato juice . . . the little glass box room in which we used to suck on cigarettes prior to boarding . . . landing after red-eyes with dead eyes . . . first-class lounges that provided an atmosphere for Wi-Fi and wife swapping. Detained in Nanjing Airport, stripped of our passports and any means of communication for an uncomfortable amount of time, because Bangkok Airport had failed to issue us boarding passes. Overweight baggage and bloated bodies. Welcome to the friendly skies.

All of this before 9/11 . . . before the skies were filled with real terror . . . before life as we knew it changed forever, before . . . when we would bust through the clouds, no matter the weather, and were greeted by the ball of fire that rises and sets no matter your coordinates on the globe.

I was asked recently if I was frightened to fly . . . now. I hadn't thought about it like that. That the very method of getting from point A to point B would bring my sister Carrie to her untimely end. That like any transient, any tourist, any weary traveler, she boarded an early transatlantic flight not knowing it would be her last. That a call for final boarding would never ring more true.

Chapter 15

#CarrieOn

TIME FLIES WHEN YOU'RE ALIVE . . . life is short . . . the show must go on . . . clichés all, but truer words have never been spoken. Time passes . . . I'd like to say the pain lessens . . . but I'd be lying. And by now, you know I never do that. I have flashes of her—her tiny frame, with added and subtracted pounds, depending on the season or the sequel. Her pursed lips, as if always posing for an unending selfie. The eyes, pools of chocolate brown, slightly hidden by progressive violet lenses and candy-colored frames. Only our vision of her eyes was slightly obscured, while her vision of us was amplified and enhanced by genius.

There it is, another mention of the Force, and the fact that her force is no longer with us. The cover of *Vanity Fair* appears in my feed today . . . Carrie as General Leia, cloaked in traditional Jedi garb . . . a dark cape, a shroud, but her gaze is omniscient and direct and powerful. She is looking directly at each and every one of us, as if with a foreshadowing of the tragedy, even many months ago, when Annie Leibovitz locked her in her sights.

It was never clearer how deeply my departed sister affected people than when we lost her . . . expressed in the immediate, raw upwelling of grief was the truth of how much she was genuinely and fiercely loved.

You Never Know

So what is the lesson here? Hold your loved ones fast and hard because you never know when your turns around the sun will screech to a halt. No shoulda, coulda, woulda. If I only had more time . . . You never know whether this day will be your last.

In vintage Carrie style, Debbie gave her daughter a farewell to her fifties party in November 2016. She had turned sixty on October 21. Carrie's birthday parties were legendary—they celebrated having survived to another one; inclusion; the fact that as we grow older, we get so busy and caught up in our own shit that we need a milestone as an excuse to get together. For decades, "the party" was a doubleheader with Penny Marshall, and the invite list was always off the charts. On occasion, her little sister (me) got thrown into the mix, since we're both October babies, which was always thrilling for me. It was a way for all of us to gather around her and hold court.

Over the years, the invite list became streamlined, and no matter how rarefied some of the personalities might have been, they were her true friends. But the menu was always the same, cooked by her longtime staff, her other mothers, Mary, Gloria, and Freddie—fried chicken, black-eyed peas, mac 'n' cheese—real soul food. The ones who came for more than the chicken—the inner circle—always ended up closing out the night in her boudoir, which eventually will be a museum at the Debbie Reynolds Dance Studio so you can visit it, too.

Once again, Carrie's sixtieth birthday was a great party. I was so glad to get to see my sister and Debbie, whom I sat with, wrapped in a beautiful cashmere blanket holding court.

As we disbanded at evening's end with casual pleasantries and well wishes, I couldn't have imagined never getting to see Carrie again.

I've always hated text messaging. My feeling about text messaging is that you never really express the emotion of what you're saying, and oftentimes you misconstrue the way something is being expressed to you. But if it was the only way to stay in touch with my sister when she was working across the ocean, I'd take it, and, in this case, sisters never misunderstood anything.

In December, I was doing the play *Sleeping Beauty and Her Winter Knight* in Laguna Beach. I hadn't done a musical in sixteen years . . . and I was exhausted, frankly. Just kidding. I was having a ball playing the Maleficent-inspired evil queen Carabosse, rocking a catsuit, complete with horns. I knew Carrie was portraying a witch in a film in Italy about this time, and I thought why not compare notes—or looks?

She texted back right away. She was in London. I was so happy I'd caught her. We texted at length, as we did from time to time. And on this occasion, for some reason we went deep—career, aging, family. We talked about our moms. I wrote: "I'm going to be married 20 years."

Her response was pure Carrie and not fit for prime time.

We covered a little politics, which we were so in line about. (Wouldn't you love to hear the political satire of Carrie Fisher right now? #goldenshowers—pee pee on the Russian hookers—was a gift from the beyond from Carrie. She would surely be leading the impeachment parade.)

Her phone died midconversation, but when I woke up in the morning, she had picked up where we'd left off with the time difference what it was. We promised to see each other for Christmas, a promise I would uphold, just not in the way

I'd imagined. I didn't know at the time how important this communication would forever be to me.

Not long after that came the shock. As I was getting ready to leave for my matinee performance, mysteriously, I kept receiving calls from the same unknown number. Normally calls didn't come through here. The cell phone service was absurdly bad in this area. Feeling that someone must be desperate to get hold of me, I finally answered. It was Harvey Levin at TMZ, asking for confirmation that Carrie had suffered a massive heart attack on the descent of her flight from London. *What?! And how did Harvey Levin get my cell phone number?*

Needless to say, I couldn't deny or confirm, as I hadn't heard the news yet. As I drove down the hill and into better cell phone reception, my phone blew up with texts: "So sorry." "So sorry." "Oh my god."

So, naturally, I texted Carrie: "Is everything okay?"

No reply.

Fear set in.

I called Tricia, who had no idea what I was talking about, but she jumped into action and raced to the hospital.

With an impending matinee and no understudy, I had no choice but to suit up and get ready to take the stage. Just before my first entrance, Tricia called me.

"I'm here at UCLA, with Billie," she said. "Do your show, and then come."

With that, I struggled through a matinee.

Just off the stage, I raced up the 405 toward UCLA with Tricia on the other end of the line. Although there really wasn't any news, having her updates made me feel not so alone. Carrie was in a coma. She had indeed gone into cardiac arrest aboard her flight home to L.A. She was being treated in the

ICU—as a way to protect her privacy and limit access, had been given the code name Trauma Villa. It was a non sequitur with the dark humor Carrie would have so loved.

The family and a few close friends gathered around. It was surreal. As we digested medical terms and updates about her vitals, we couldn't believe this was happening. Billie was there; so were her father, Carrie's ex, Bryan; Tricia and I; Carrie's best friend, Bruce Wagner; Carrie's assistant Corby—she'd been on the plane with Carrie; and Donald, who had taken care of Debbie for years. And, of course, Mama Debs was already there, in a wheelchair. I stopped and talked to her, tried to offer her some comfort, as she did for me. She told me she had talked to Jesus and prayed for more time, for Carrie, for herself, and for Connie. Apparently she had a direct line. Although I hadn't seen Carrie yet, it was starting to get very real.

Todd arrived and came into the tiny little waiting area where we were. He had driven as fast as he could from Vegas to be by his sister's side. He was pulling this wheely black leather bag with a beautiful, elegant black box on top of it.

He opened up the box . . . and he pulled out an Oscar. It was Debbie's honorary Jean Hersholt Humanitarian Award, which, a year earlier, Tricia, Connie, and I were among those who had contributed letters to the Academy to secure. Todd placed it in Debbie's lap.

"I thought, maybe, you'd want to hold this at a time like this," Todd said.

She was frail and had a blanket over her and looked like she didn't quite know what to do with this thing that was in her lap.

"It's so heavy," Debbie said softly.

A VIGIL FOR Carrie was kept by friends and family, at her bedside and worldwide. We sang, we prayed, we fielded texts, e-mails, and calls—messages of love—everyone hoping and assuming that Carrie would be coming back to us, any day now. She'd open up her eyes—and her smart mouth—and start delivering the bawdy bons mots that would pepper her next book: *Trauma Villa*.

Tricia and I had just gone through this with our mother, and the sights and smells brought it all back for us, like Vietnam flashbacks. We couldn't believe it, here we were again, and this time with our sister. After spending Christmas morning with my children, I returned to the hospital and Carrie's side, and again on December 26—Tricia's birthday—still wanting to be there, as if I could will her recovery. I had honored our promise to spend the holidays together, even though it was now under such terrible circumstances. Carrie was being kept alive by a robot doctor and a cacophony of machines, which were horrifying to behold. I tried not to let it reduce me to being terrified so that, along with Tricia et al., we could be there for Billie. We carefully monitored Carrie's machines, celebrating her smallest improvements. There was a reveling in medicine and science and a steep learning curve. Similar to years earlier, standing over my father, I felt her spirit was hovering somewhere over her room and her body. It took everything in my being to leave that night. The only reason I was able to do so was that they convinced us it would take time—there was a tempo at which they brought people out of this deep sleep. Otherwise I wouldn't have left her side.

Reluctantly, I kissed her hand and returned to Laguna late on the twenty-sixth, as I had been dragged back to finish up another day of shows (again, I had no understudy). I brought my daughters back with me to finish the show's run, thinking things would remain unchanged. But the rental property's bad cell service would only keep me from the tragic news for so long.

As I descended the hill the next morning, the devastating truth of what had happened descended upon me. Carrie had succumbed to a cluster of heart attacks. The only consolation was that, thank God, she wouldn't survive only to be kept alive with her heart beating to the drums of medical machinery.

I knew Debbie was not far behind. But it was shocking that the loss was a mere twenty-four hours later. And then it made complete sense. They were best friends. It was mother first, friend later in their lives, but Debbie did live for her daughter. And she died because she couldn't be without her—a hand-in-hand Princess Leia–Kathy Selden walk into the sunset.

As if all of this weren't devastating enough, it brought into stark contrast for Tricia and me how intense our own mother's medical fight was—and what the outcome could be. She'd always been the hero of our story, when she was in her power and in her body, but now she was feeling very trapped by that body that wasn't working anymore. Really, her brain and her heart, both were deteriorating at the same time. And it was heartbreaking for us.

It may have been because my mom had experienced a stroke, which can cause the muting effect of depression, but she didn't grieve as violently as I'd seen her do my whole life. Or maybe it was because she didn't know her place in all this. Because it wasn't her daughter. It wasn't her sister. It was someone she'd shared a husband with . . . kind of, but not really. What really mattered was that, when they'd connected later in their lives, they'd developed a real relationship that was valuable for both of them. Debbie often reached out to Connie, calling on her "real, true friend" in times of loneliness. They reveled in the real and true relationship of the children they had raised.

I think what was hardest for Connie was that she really didn't know how to support Tricia and me. Obviously, as we took on the role of mothering our mother more and more, it made us look at our own mortality. And then I went and manifested my stress in my own high blood pressure. And every day, the dance continues.

#Resistance

My sister was the leader of the resistance, evidenced by how her image was everywhere at women's marches around the world following the inauguration. You can use your fancy Instagram filters to change the hue of the sky, the color of people's skin, hair, and hats . . . but you cannot invent or modify the sheer number of humans—men, women, and children—who took to the streets to shine, march, meander, shuffle, and dance along so many city streets. Or how potent Carrie's presence was. It was a surreal experience for me on the front lines of the L.A. Women's March. When I arrived and walked into the crowd, arm in arm with Jane Fonda, seeing Carrie's image everywhere on posters, my first thought was: *Carrie wouldn't be caught dead in a place like this. (Or maybe only be caught dead here.)* And yet, in death, she embodied, empowered, and lifted that crowd to soaring heights.

Her face, that Princess power, was everywhere. There was the classic, all in white, with iconic buns, clutching herself, as if to say, "Love thyself today and every day." The gun-toting, come-hither, badass Princess, who actually challenges us to #RESIST—I mean, *that* lady was the face of the resistance. Then there was metal-bikini-clad Leia, on her side, beckoning, toying with us all. Mostly, in all of them, it was the eyes that were as deep and dark as the cosmos with all that insight. Even without words, she said to us: you can be stunning, smart, prepared, sexy, comforting, nurturing, chic, gun-carrying—female—and you can rule. A face that launched a thousand ships. A fleet of females that sailed into the city streets on a mission—the rebel forces, on full alert, with their leader at the helm.

The Seven Stages of Grief, Hollywood-Style

The initial shock has worn off, but a loss that's so public is shared in a way, and that makes the grief process an even stranger beast than it normally is. I felt like because people were aware of the loss—as everyone was—it made them feel able to connect with me on that level. That's how I've felt with so many people I've run into around town, and also on social media. Because my loss was leading every conversation, whether I mentioned it or not, it created an immediate communion with others in a similar emotional space. It can be incredibly comforting and make me feel a sense of our shared community. And it can be a heavy responsibility, especially on a day when I've got to do my best to pack up my grief so I can tackle this audition, this school event, this shopping list. And then, it makes me wonder how people perceive who I am right now, and that can send me down the rabbit hole.

It feels awkward. So, when I'm already feeling so exposed, why write a book right now? When I don't know how the movie I'm directing will be received, whether I'm going to get a pilot, whether my finances are going to work out? Because I want to go public with the fact that, as Carrie gave us permission to be, all of this is in process—most of all my grief—and that's okay. The conversation itself can be important and healing, even if the long-term resolution is unclear. There is a part of me that feels like a superhero in the way that I'm coming out of the fetal position and dealing with all these things as they come at me. I want other women to see that in the pages of this book, and to connect with all the ways they're superheroes, too.

What Now?

How do you put on your face in the wake of grief, and in the midst of watching what's happening in politics and health care, and worrying about how it will impact my family, my friends, the entire world? A few months back, I retweeted a video of young, vibrant, passionate, brilliant congressman Joe Kennedy debating the proposed health-care bill and the devastating impact it would have on those in need of mental health treatment. I wrote, "For those of us who have mental health issues in our family, where does that leave us?" A Twitter debate ensued where some people argued that Carrie got help because she was rich and could afford to.

I responded in one hundred and forty characters (or less): "Yes, she was, and she could afford it, but still she struggled chronically, with care, and medication, and a lifetime of mental health issues and addiction."

And she was a crusader for the many, many, many people with problems related to both mental health and addiction, who can't afford, or can't admit, or can't commit to the help they need. And she was open about how, without the treatment they need, people with bipolar disorder often self-medicate (herself included) to quiet the voices, or to come out of their lows and their highs, and to try to be a functioning person in society. And in order to combat this vicious cycle, they need real, medical help. I believe in self-awareness, and meditation, and all of that, but when you have demons that dark, you have to get help outside of yourself. You just have to. And there are many people who can't afford to.

Carrie was very aware of this need, and she helped to lift the stigma of both her illnesses and getting help for them. Carrie notoriously made several trips to rehab including the Betty Ford Center. Betty Ford pioneered changing the face of addiction and mental health. I know many people who, truly, are still alive only because of getting the care that they needed, there and elsewhere.

Antisocial Media

Social media, it's called . . . but it should be called antisocial media. We as a society, this generation, at least, have collectively decided to communicate via texts, posts, blogs, vlogs, snaps, and GIFs. (I know what some of that is.) And I definitely know it is a poor excuse for reading, for speaking, for informing, for relating.

I know, I know, we feel like we *must* be online to stay current!

And yet, what we really must do is to get back to full-blown eye contact. I admit I am guilty of it at times. I watch my children, and their peers, lead with the tops of their heads. The screen generation. What makes them laugh is different. Have we really run out of energy, enthusiasm, for storytelling, for great production value, for contacting and communicating with someone directly across the table from us?

New measures of popularity are getting more influential in the industry as well. The most obvious beneficiaries are the reality TV and Internet stars—the people whose career is made based on likes. One six-second loop, or a YouTube channel broadcasting nonstop unfunny vignettes with banal points of view and poor lighting. Or slick production and no content. My big question is "Why is this what people watch?"

Isn't there more to life than increasing its speed? New media is an art form, after all. Wait, that's a contradiction—but if you can't beat 'em, join 'em. I'm not gonna lie, have I yet? I hired someone, for a time, to help me with social media. There are ways to hashtag your posts, and control the timing of them, and the content, and blah, blah, blah. It was like learning a foreign language.

You know who was doing it well? Carrie. She would make entire posts, in code, just about what she had for breakfast, or where she was headed next. Ironically, all of this from one of the greatest storytellers of modern times. She did confess that she didn't *really* understand—she was learning by doing. But her followers, clinging to her every emoji, every quip, every post, would have begged to differ. Even if it is a fake way to carry on a relationship (or at least feel that you are), why not Carry On with Carrie Fisher?

She responded to many. "Oh, we're friends on Facebook, Instagram, Twitter," she would often say. "You should see who *my* friends are." And if you happened to get a bona fide response, perhaps even a PM (private message) or DM (direct message)—private *and* direct, from someone you love, admire, rely on, even worship? Jackpot.

Maybe it's the musician in me (or just the needy human), but I want the sound of someone's voice on the other end, and to see their eyes when they say they love me, or they're sorry, or whatever. You cannot decode the *message* of a text message, often, without that.

However, there are a handful of people, or a thousand handfuls of people—in my estimation, mostly young women—who have lost their Twitter touchstone with the loss of my sister. She was the poster child for bipolar disorder and addiction—so many turned to her for perspective and acceptance, and how she held together the fabric of the galaxy with her wisdom and her humor. They genuinely relied on her expertise in navigating the world while dealing with depression, bipolar disorder, and problems with addiction.

With her loss, I have gained a following pool of fishies. These were not just her fans, her disciples—they were her friends. Now, Carrie already had the smartest, most famous friends, but these people got to know her in the pages of her books, at conventions and celebrity lap dances—and continuing on social media, they really were her friends, too.

In the days leading up to the loss of Carrie, as the world prayed for her recovery, a phenomenon occurred. Now, it is the new normal. I started developing relationships with people all over the world. Pulling for us, praying for her recovery.

And me supporting them. We were all holding each other up with the embrace of our tweets. We could feel the power of it—though we eventually failed to keep her here, tweets and modern medicine being no match for the willpower of a soul whose time has come.

Since then, in the zeitgeist, and in the Twittersphere, where people everywhere awaited gems and tweets from General Leia, or Momby, her bereft followers have been adopted by JMama and Spissy Dish, as they call us. My space babies are in need of an outlet for their grief and a response to their poetry, their questions, and their flaws.

We console each other. We all need it now and again. There are Kelsey and Katie and Suzanne and Sarah and so many others. They asked of her time and her expertise. And since she is departed I feel not only a responsibility but an undeniable pull toward these women. I would never attempt to replace someone who was so important to so many. I will, however, pick up the light saber. And an autopsy report does not change a fucking thing . . . she was their hero.

The Fisher Foundation

At the memorial for Carrie—the one put together by her daughter, my niece Billie, on hallowed ground, the compound that Carrie and Debbie shared, with her favorite people, among Carrie's peculiar, whimsical, and prized possessions—eating her favorite soul food, Tracey Ullman, Beverly D'Angelo, Jamie Lee Curtis, Tricia Leigh, and I vowed to try to have the same chosen few every year at a #CarrieOn party.

Another inspiration born of that day was the Fisher Foundation, which Tricia Leigh and I have vowed to launch. Our hope is to eventually be an organization that provides a safe haven for those suffering from mental illness and addiction, while also supporting research, education, and recognition of others that are doing work in this area. A place for people who need help, as well as an opportunity to end the stigma that has historically surrounded these afflictions, just at a time when our country may be on the verge of losing funding for these types of very necessary programs.

It's still in its fledgling stage at this point, but I know it can be just as influential and powerful as the philanthropic organizations started by the generation before us—Debbie's Thalians, which she cofounded in 1955 to provide mental health education, and Connie's Windfeather. Historically, I have been inspired and compelled (as taught by Connie, by Debbie, by so many other generous entertainers I grew up around) to believe that we who are fortunate enough to have enjoyed success in this coveted business are obligated—no, privileged—to "give back." Even when we are strapped financially, we have the blessing to be able to donate the gift of our time, and to give back that way—especially something so close to home.

Chapter 16

Home

I AM PACKING AGAIN, LAYERING boxes and bins with shoes, and scarves, and sparkly bags, transporting them to their new resting place. Nesting place. Will they be settled in there? Will I find peace there? I have done this many times in the past few years. Packing and purging. Listening to others' well-meaning advice . . . "This will be good for you." Who's to say what's good for me? Moving through this life-shedding stuff . . . do I need these commemorative mugs, this set of candlesticks, these Barbies, all this craft stuff, the *Star Wars* toys? Wait, yes, I want all of those.

What makes a home? Is it where the commemorative mugs are or, as they say, where the heart is? Whose heart? Collectively, everyone in the family? The leader of the pack? What if the heart is broken? Is that when you deem it a broken home? Maybe it's where you lay your hat? What if you wear many hats . . . and you're forgetful?

And are eyes windows to our souls? What if the windows, the lenses, are in need of a cleaning? What if you can't find anyone who does windows? What if you want someone to see your soul, and when they arrive, you are sleeping—in the heat of summer, can we shutter our souls?

You came into this with your eyes wide open—thank God. Because you might have run into the closed door to which you hadn't yet found a key. An open heart usually requires surgery—and closure, and sutures, maybe even a transplant.

I have fire in my belly—spicy food, or intention, or hot flashes, signaling what some would have me consider the end of my worth.

If these walls could speak . . . we build walls around ourselves to keep monsters out but keep in our own demons. My walls are adorned with pictures. They represent me, my history, my her-story; some of them I have looked at for decades.

I am a recorder, a keeper of time; the walls may change, but what I plaster to them has followed me—with familiar, familial images I am safe. I am home.

This new house, which we will call home, is bright. And the moment I crossed the threshold I felt lighter—the weight of the immediate world, and the wait for a place to find that levity, had ended.

There have been many walls around us—craftsman, Spanish, ranch-style. But now they are traditional—oh the irony—the nontraditional girl making her way toward transformation.

It was in the last home I experienced so much loss—it wasn't Hidden Hills' fault—although they don't call them hidden 'cause they want you in. The house was as dark as the time. Everyone thought it—no one said it.

It was the first time in many years I'd had a landlord, some responsibilities lifted and left to the Lord. My children don't know, nor should they care, if you pay rent or a mortgage. But I did! I knew.

This was the place where I would learn of my mom's life-threatening stroke and from which I would brave the 101 multiple times a day. I remember very vividly spending the day with her, then battling traffic home, finding myself completely boxed in, and receiving the call that her blood pressure had skyrocketed. I was stuck—couldn't move my car, my body heaving with sobs. Is this where I'd be when I lost my mother? I'd only left a half hour earlier. Had I said something sweet as I left Cedars hurriedly, in order to put my children to bed?

She would make a partial recovery—but the light has dimmed, and she will never grace another Vegas stage.

Where would Connie now hang her hat? Delfern had sold, and we had searched for a new home that felt right, not knowing the level of care she might need. One place was lovely and new, but we would need to put in a stairlift, as her mobility would be compromised. That sounds polite. On more than one occasion, she said, "This will be my last house." The sound of those words, echoing through open houses, staged beautifully with random objets d'art—owned by no one. Cold. What would this look like if someone really lived here? Couldn't we just leave everything behind and live this brand-new façade?

Before settling into her new "last" home, she lived with us in the barn. No, really. We had a big red barn that I made into a lovely bedroom. All of her favorite things—photos, her favorite bedding, and all those medications. She would be able to visit with her granddaughters on the daily, and I would be able to play "nurse-daughter."

We found a place after two months. She moved and both of us were content. Neither wanted this to be the new normal, but we'd be forced to admit: it was. I want her to feel self-sufficient, and I already have five children. It is the cycle of life to care for one's parents, I suppose, but my mom isn't ready for the end, nor am I.

She is happy-ish, settled-ish, and we make it our mission to be with her a lot, as much as we can. Tricia and I split the duties, divide and conquer, the loneliness, depression, and spending. It is a unicorn property—smaller but peaceful, and the garden is flourishing—it's wonderful (she always said it would happen). That's her thing. Making things grow. Just look at me.

Her room is quaint and comfortable—the things are familiar—the piano, the Ertés, the dream catcher I made and hung for her—to continue the time-honored familial tradition of trying to ensnare our dreams.

Already it has become like Delfern, in that we celebrate there. We even had our first family garden wedding. There are tall trees, fountains, and she can get from room to room with little effort.

Meanwhile, back at the ranch (literally), we have been given an ultimatum. Buy or move! We have extended our time here since the most recent tragedy struck. I will forever remember in great detail where I was in the house when Donald Trump was elected to lead the country. The cowboy den full of remnants, beautiful souvenirs, of another home lost to financial tragedy—Jackson Hole. I didn't have the heart to get rid of some symbols of the mountain retreat we had called home for two decades. Another loss of epic stature. Connie had impeccably designed and built it, painstakingly chosen fixtures, backsplashes, etched glass doors, stones, and the bone fragments and feathers of fallen animals, as well as art by fallen natives. So here we were in said cowboy den, where I had promised my children that women can do anything, that the world needs mothering, and that the bully doesn't win. And he fucking did! I sobbed, gut-wrenching sobs, among the peace pipes and the antlers, and that room will always contain the condensation of my tears . . . and my fear.

Months later, I would be racked again in despair, running back and forth from my Laguna rental, a special hillside house where I would hear of Carrie's on-arrival heart attack, and eventually, of her departure. Once again, traveling the freeways of Los Angeles in a flood of tears, this time in full evil queen stage makeup, in a torrential downpour.

Lease extended—my lease on life and the ranch—but sooner or later, I would have to move. I couldn't stay in an overinflated multimillion-dollar fixer-upper that was decorated with pain and grief.

So now I sit and write in a beautiful bright room that is mine. We own this. I've packed up my belongings—my books, my memorabilia, my familiar portraits, the piano, and even the feathers and antlers—only here the walls are white, a blank canvas. There are windows that reflect and let the light into my soul. We are bathing in it. I still have way too much stuff. Shelves that have been made into shrines of accomplishment. Homages to people and places that populate my heart. There is a space for it all. It is a lot to unpack, literally and figuratively, but I have found a home to rest my heart, and the walls will have tales to tell very soon. Stay tuned!

Chapter 17

After Thoughts

MEMOIR, FROM THE FRENCH *MÉMOIRE*, the Latin *memoria* . . . meaning memory or reminiscence, is a collection of memories that an individual writes about moments and events both private and public that took place in the subject's life. The assertions made in this work should be understood to be factual . . .

IF MEMORY SERVES . . . mine has served up a bountiful selection of images, lessons, temptations, failures, tragedies, and victories. My mother has taught me many things . . . One important thing she taught me—and up until now, with the burden of stroke, she has practiced what she preached—is to remember. Remember people's names and faces, play little associations—try that game that husband and wife or sisters play when you introduce someone to them by saying, "Oh, you remember so-and-so . . . we met at such-and-such." And your partner says to that person, "I do. What was your first name again?" Saved. I can't stand when people challenge your memory of them and withhold their name till you all struggle with when and where we all met. When you see someone, and you are nearing fifty and you just—ahhhh, who was that?—it's just at the tip of your tongue—Marc Cherry. Oh, I should've said, "Hi." It's always best to just remember . . . until you can't. Remember places—Connie would say click off pictures in your mind. Take in all the amazing sights you've seen, the exotic locales, architecture, the smells, the sounds, traffic noise, protesters' chants, jasmine, snow, incense, garlic, an aura, babies' laughter, a train going through a crossing, good movies, belly laughs. Just remember.

REMEMBER WHEN WE stood at the edge of the Grand Canyon, illegally spewing the crystalline remains of my beloved uncle John. Just before his death, he had embarked on a trip to "bucket list" locations. On a tranquilizing dose of morphine, he revealed he had made it only as far as Flagstaff. Remember standing over the falls at Niagara, or the peak on Hong Kong, or the Hotel du Cap–Eden-Roc at Cap d'Antibes; audiences with presidents from both sides of the political spectrum, those whom I respected, those whom I did not. The masked man who put a gun to my head and demanded of a trio of teenagers the Mercedes and the money. The victory of a surprise celebration of Connie's sixty turns round the sun. Anne Meara, beloved wife of Jerry Stiller, mother of Ben and Amy—then rug rats running the halls of Harrah's in Reno—years later beautifully portraying my mother in the film *Jitters*, under the tutelage of Bob Saget, that ever-so-brief slumber party after the celebrity moms fashion show. Remember singing with Frank Sinatra in the iconic Capitol Records studio. He does one take and drops the mic (and the sheet music, but not before I get him to sign it). Connie would tell us to click a picture in our minds. True would later ask why would we do that, though, Mommy, when you have an iPhone 7? There are maybe seven minutes of my life that are undocumented, and I might just have my new iPhone but—"Well, True, in case one's not handy."—I will still click away.

As the years scream by, I remember, a new lease on life . . .

and the utter despair with which I confront the setting of the sun . . . the consumption of the slumberaid that created the monster/siren named "Amber" who eats and gets it on like a stripper or a trucker . . . like in a good way. There's nothing wrong with Pirate's Booty and a blow job to advance the night and the world, right?

THE ANGER . . . THE separation . . . the divisiveness that I have observed of late in the world has re-created in me a passion and a commitment that I first encountered when Connie Stevens walked out on Eddie Fisher, resolute . . . convinced she could make her family and the world a better place. Perhaps she would rely on her god or her own moxie. She may have a drastically different moral compass, but she was a good teacher.

People surprise me . . . the burden of having to cheer me on is a heavy one. We are, as a species, supposed to love and support each other. In order to survive as people . . . we must procreate and be allowed to create. I am thankful for those (good, bad, or ugly) who have made me who I am—championed me in life, supported and believed in my artistry. I am grateful for each and every opportunity. I am even going to go out on a limb (which, as you know by now, I often do) and count blessings for those who spent immeasurable time trying to break me down—it is they who have helped supply me with my balls of steel and my courage to fail and learn.

THE PAIN . . . YES, to give it any other name would be unjust. The pain of my own personal summer, the tropical effect of aging, albeit gracefully, in the female body. It starts down low, base of the spine, the middle section, as if we are separated into orchestra and balcony, so let's say somewhere in the loge, I start to bake. The color is red. The temperature "island." My Jewish Italian curls become more defined, then almost pubic. My face flushed like a toilet. Naturally, my emotions are heated, like my spinal column.

So my feminine mystique feels as if it's nearing the feminine mistake. I find myself now at an age when my child-bearing abilities have been suddenly stripped. As if I could "afford" another child—another mouth to feed, education, all that future therapy. Not to mention the idea of the construction zone in my womb, the assembly of another human, like a model airplane. The nausea, the swelling, the irritability, the emotions, the idea that I can't possibly go on another moment without a bowel movement, the constant need to urinate, the sleeplessness, lack of sex—wait, I'm describing menopause. Time flies when you're alive. Alive and shuffle ball changing toward fifty. Middle-aged. Is this the middle? Are you fucking kidding? My inner child needs a spanking, to grow up, she's a work in progress.

You know what happens to Aphrodite when her tits start to sag?

Why does aging make me ugly-cry? The stuff that brings stuff up from my gut, pushes toward the surface into the . . .

I'M WATCHING *FEUD*—JESSICA Lange and Susan Sarandon are working it out! "How does it feel to be the most beautiful girl in the world?" "Great, and it was never enough." "And how does it feel to be the most talented?" "Never enough." The reason I sob uncontrollably and then vigorously wipe away the salt liquid—it's not as if I've collected them in a vessel around my neck—but I will reminisce as I move through the saline and yet again relive having slipped through the cracks—throughout my life—not quite pretty enough, not the best for the role—unfocused, unprepared, un-right, under renovation, open for business during construction—the scenes between Bette Davis and Joan Crawford and their daughters expertly portray an era and a relationship I know too well. Is it that these women lived in a time warp, an alternate universe where they needed to inject botulism or silicone into those well-earned crevasses of their faces in an attempt to keep away years, emotion, and an exaggerated expression of anything in order to save them for the screen? Or is it all women, all humans, who want to deny the inevitable—the holding back of the dawn, the down? I want proof of all that laughter, all that anguish . . . I want a road map of the miles my smiles have traveled, of a life well lived. What is devastatingly raw for me is that these women, our mothers, came in during an era when cleavage, walk, and eyelashes were everything—is this who I am destined to become? Is this suddenly who I am? Of course it is.

I CANNOT FATHOM the idea that we don't all meet up somewhere, in some other dimension—that our energy here on this planet doesn't get reconstituted and redistributed. Somehow we will find our loved ones once again. No one can prove this doesn't happen. I know I see shades of people I have known in the vistas, or in melodies. Just in case this is it, we memorialize.

In the pages of this book, in the excavation, in the writing, I have learned more about myself than ever before. Mostly, I have discovered that I am enough, that the circumstances in which I was born do not define my existence. And yet . . .

yes, they do. So fifty being the new whatever it is, or just being fifty . . . older, wiser, more accepting, more tired, more ready . . . just more . . .

In a way I've always been directing—setting the scene, the blocking, the choreography—making sure to protect my actors, my artists—knowing them and myself so well. Anticipating the next scene based on history—listening for preparedness and predilection—settling everyone into my proposed composition—malleable enough for slight changes and mood swings. Adjustments, always gonna be adjustments—and then we roll—the scenes vary from what I call "pipe" or exposition (necessary to progress the story)—then all the delight, the intimacy, the comic turns, the fantasy, the climax and the inevitable lesson.

Everyone must soar and be who they are without critique, but perhaps with suggestions and encouragement. Sit back and watch it play out—the masterpiece that has been created—and CUT!!!

ACKNOWLEDGMENTS

MY FAMILY

Concetta Rosalie Ann Ingolia and Edwin Jack Fisher

Christopher Duddy/Skylar Grace Fisher-Duddy/True Harlowe Fisher-Duddy/Olivia Luna Fisher-Duddy

Cameron and Harper Duddy/Collin and Rome Duddy/Bowie/Kitt/The Duddy Family/Billie Lourd/Bryan Lourd/The Megnas/The Ingolias

Tricia Leigh/Byron Thames/Hudson/Holden/Wylder/Todd and Cat Fisher/Debbie Reynolds/Donald/Dora Sanabria

My HarperCollins family. Lisa Sharkey and Tessa Woodward/Alieza/Greg/Beth/Elle/Bonni

Sarah Tomlinson/Rhona Cleary/Helen Cavallo/Stephanie Thomas/Elizabeth Keener/Sabina Ghebremedhim/Brittany Duddy

Susan Cameron/Danielle Del/John Carrabino/Chuck James/Janet Carol Norton/British Reece/Heidi Schaffer/Harry Gold/Barry Krost/Byron Griffiths/Connie Tavel/Dan Pietregallo/David Altman/Barry Greenfeld/Jusin Kalma/Larry Stine/David Weber/Denéa Buckingham/Nicola P.

Ellen DeGeneres/Brad Garrett/Matthew Broderick/Norbert Leo Butz/John Goodman/Holland Taylor

James L. Brooks/Nora Ephron/Chuck Russell/Jordan Kerner/Marc Cherry/Robb Marshall/Sam Mendes/Frank Darabont/Jimmy Burrows/Jamie Widdoes/Robby Benson/Gil Junger/Rob Schiller/Ron Oliver/Chris Grismer/Nigel L./Rob Lotterstein/Tommy Billik/Bob Saget/Cedering Fox

My Oliver Storm Team. Daemon Hillin/Rachvin and Kulthep Narula/Geneva Wasserman/Tim Marlowe/Kerry Barden

Sandra Seacat/John Ingle/Joel Pressman/Leo Nicole/Nancy Fishman/Julie Ariola/Eric Vetro/Michael Orland/Ron Abel

Bruce W./Bruce R./Bruce C./Bruce T.

Clay/BP/SteveT/Thomas R./Bryant/Guy/Russell/Matt/Jagat Joti and Gene/Jim Brady/JV Mercanti/Benjamin/Todd

Laurent and Fabienne/Carissa/Amberlee/Susan S./Annabelle/Karen Z./Wendy/Lackmeyer/Donna G./Jeffrey F./Judy Brooks/Lisa F.

Keely/Stacey and Tamara/Lester T./Nikka/Mincie/Ashley/Sarah E./Robbie B./Mandy/Camrym M./Ricki L./Spike/Jenny M./Denise R./Sascha/Lisandra/Cheri O./Lynn M./Missy H./Beverly D./Kim L./Jamie Lee/Cindy S./Corby/Vicki L./Vikki K./Elisabeth/Meredith/Shondrella

KD/Jessica/Melora/Stephanie Q./Helga/Annie R./Sheryl A./Tricia S./Anzu/Merle/Utta/David and Dina Styne/Ania

Jill Baron/Stefi Blumberg/Stephanie Schramm/Claire Kellerman Krane/Kathy Wellman/RaeRae Jensen/Jackie T./Laura Dern

Carol Tamburino/Diane Ladd/Renée Taylor/Lainie Kazan/Deanna Lund/Judy Butala/Frances Davis/Diane Feldman/Josie Powell/Margie and Jeannie Kahanowich/Dawn Moore/Helena Heaney/Francesca DeVito/Betty Moran/Nancy Dugan/Elaine R./Nancy Sinatra/Frances Fisher/Jerry Lewis

Sammy Shore/Norm Crosby/Jack and Roxanne/Red Buttons/Milton Berle/Phil Foster/Sid Caesar/Sid Gould/Danny Welkes/Joe Cassini/Michael Peters/Allan Carr/Manya Johnson/Frank Carroll/Lonnie Shorr/Peter and Pauly Shore/Dr. Paul Crane/Beverly Piontak/Stan Ziegler/Dr. David Frisch/Robert Mitchell/James May/Doug Kunin/Jade Mills

CREDITS

All photos courtesy of the author unless otherwise noted.

FIRST INSERT

Page 1 (*top right*) © photo by Paul Kammet; page 7 (*middle left*) courtesy of Russell Brown; page 8 (*bottom right*) courtesy of Dream Foundation; page 15 (*bottom right*) courtesy of Sony Pictures Television

SECOND INSERT

Page 5 (*bottom right*) courtesy of Dream Foundation; page 6 (*middle right*) photo courtesy of IFAW; page 8 (*bottom left*) and page 9 photos © Tom Rafalovich; pages 12 © Lisa Franchot; page 10 (*middle left*) © Lisa Dorn Photo; page 14 (*top left*) © Harry Langdon; page 15 (*middle*) photo by M. Garcia, Washington, D.C.

ABOUT THE AUTHOR

JOELY FISHER is an actress, director, singer, writer, animal rights advocate, butcher, baker, candlestick maker. She is a proud mother, daughter, sister . . . Fisher. The star of numerous TV shows and films, including *Ellen*, *'Til Death*, and *Inspector Gadget*, she has also starred in Broadway productions of *Grease* and *Cabaret* and performed around the world. She lives in Los Angeles, California, with her beloved tribe of family, friends, and animals.